Maths
Mindstretchers
for ages
7–9

CONTENTS

INTRODUCTION

Maths Mindstretchers provides perfect opportunities both for learning number facts and for 'using and applying mathematics'. In tackling each puzzle the children are:

- solving one-step and two-step problems
- identifying patterns and relationships involving numbers
- developing logical strategies to follow their lines of enquiry.

At the same time they are deriving addition and subtraction facts – the repeated calculation practice required to solve each puzzle helps them to learn these facts subconsciously. Many of the puzzles also help pupils to learn appropriate multiplication facts and the corresponding division facts, as well as developing their skills in doubling and halving.

There are various strategies that pupils may begin to employ. For example, how quickly will they realise that the biggest number is always going to be the first number entered in the puzzle at Levels A and B? Those pupils who discover this strategy quickly should be moved on to higher levels. Those who don't discover the strategy should be encouraged to continue working at the early levels, not necessarily to find the strategy but to gain the valuable practice in addition and subtraction.

You may find it useful to have prepared sheets from several levels of **Maths Mindstretchers**. Numerically confident pupils will complete the early levels very quickly and can move on to a point where they find the **Maths Mindstretchers** challenging. Encourage them to enjoy the challenge, perhaps by competing against their own time score for each **Maths Mindstretcher**.

The accompanying CD contains all the **Maths Mindstretchers** which you can print out or display on an interactive whiteboard.

Name **Date**

Look carefully at the puzzle. It has a target number of 8.

You need to write some numbers to make a subtraction with an answer of 8 and an addition with an answer of 8.

Here are the numbers you must use:
2 3 5 10

Here is another puzzle. This one has a target number of 5.

The numbers you must use are:
1 3 4 8

Now try this one. Target number: 9.

Numbers to use:
2 3 6 11

Now try this one. Target number: 12.

Numbers to use:
3 5 7 15

Teacher's notes

Some children will need lots of help with these puzzles and may find a number line useful. Other pupils will find them more straightforward and can be challenged by completing each puzzle 'against the clock'. Those children who are numerically competent and confident can move on very quickly to higher levels.

Name		Date	

Complete each of the puzzles using the numbers provided.

Write these numbers in the correct places to make the target number:

2 2 5 9

Write these numbers in the correct places to make the target number:

1 2 5 8

Write these numbers in the correct places to make the target number:

3 4 5 12

Write these numbers in the correct places to make the target number:

2 4 6 12

Teacher's notes

Some children will need lots of help with these puzzles and may find a number line useful. Other pupils will find them more straightforward and can be challenged by completing each puzzle 'against the clock'. Those children who are numerically competent and confident can move on very quickly to higher levels.

Name

Date

Complete each of the puzzles using the numbers provided.

Write these numbers in the correct places to make the target number:
1 2 6 9

(—) ➡ **7** ⬅ (+)

Write these numbers in the correct places to make the target number:
3 6 7 16

(—) ➡ **10** ⬅ (+)

Write these numbers in the correct places to make the target number:
3 4 6 13

(—) ➡ **9** ⬅ (+)

Write these numbers in the correct places to make the target number:
4 6 8 18

(—) ➡ **12** ⬅ (+)

Teacher's notes

Some children will need lots of help with these puzzles and may find a number line useful. Other pupils will find them more straightforward and can be challenged by completing each puzzle 'against the clock'. Those children who are numerically competent and confident can move on very quickly to higher levels.

Name		Date	

Complete each of the puzzles using the numbers provided.

Write these numbers in the correct places to make the target number:
3 4 7 14

Write these numbers in the correct places to make the target number:
3 4 8 15

Write these numbers in the correct places to make the target number:
3 8 9 20

Write these numbers in the correct places to make the target number:
3 4 12 19

Teacher's notes

Some children will need lots of help with these puzzles and may find a number line useful. Other pupils will find them more straightforward and can be challenged by completing each puzzle 'against the clock'. Those children who are numerically competent and confident can move on very quickly to higher levels.

| Name | | Date | |

Complete each of the puzzles using the numbers provided.

Write these numbers in the correct places to make the target number:
5 5 10 20

Write these numbers in the correct places to make the target number:
3 4 12 19

Write these numbers in the correct places to make the target number:
4 5 9 18

Write these numbers in the correct places to make the target number:
5 7 8 20

Teacher's notes

The puzzles on this page are at a higher level than those at previous levels. Pupils now need to use their knowledge of multiplication facts as well as addition and subtraction facts together with a logical approach to problem solving. Some pupils may advance very quickly and can be set time challenges before moving on to higher levels.

Name _____   **Date** _____

Look carefully at the puzzle. You need to find the target number that goes in the middle and you need to write numbers in the correct places to make a subtraction sentence and an addition sentence.

Here are the numbers you must use:
3 3 6 9 12

Here is another puzzle. You need to find the target number and the numbers to make the subtraction sentence and the addition sentence.

The numbers you must use are:
1 3 6 7 10

Now try this one.

The numbers you must use are:
3 4 5 8 12

Now try this one.

The numbers you must use are:
3 4 6 10 13

Teacher's notes

The puzzles on this page are at a higher level than those at Level A. Pupils need to use their knowledge of addition and subtraction facts and a logical approach to problem solving. Some pupils may advance very quickly and can be set time challenges before moving on to higher levels.

Name _____   **Date** _____

Look carefully at the puzzle. You need to find the target number that goes in the middle and you need to write numbers in the correct places to make a subtraction sentence and an addition sentence.

Here are the numbers
you must use:
2 2 6 8 10

Solve this puzzle.

Here are the numbers
you must use:
2 3 6 9 11

Solve this puzzle.

Here are the numbers
you must use:
2 3 4 7 9

Solve this puzzle.

Here are the numbers
you must use:
2 3 4 6 9

Teacher's notes

The puzzles on this page are at a higher level than those at Level A. Pupils need to use their knowledge of addition and subtraction facts and a logical approach to problem solving. Some pupils may advance very quickly and can be set time challenges before moving on to higher levels.

Name   **Date**

Look carefully at the puzzle. You need to find the target number that goes in the middle and you need to write numbers in the correct places to make a subtraction sentence and an addition sentence.

Here are the numbers you must use:
2 2 3 5 7

Solve this puzzle.

Here are the numbers you must use:
5 5 5 10 15

Solve this puzzle.

Here are the numbers you must use:
2 4 5 7 11

Solve this puzzle.

Here are the numbers you must use:
2 3 7 9 12

Teacher's notes

The puzzles on this page are at a higher level than those at Level A. Pupils need to use their knowledge of addition and subtraction facts and a logical approach to problem solving. Some pupils may advance very quickly and can be set time challenges before moving on to higher levels.

MIND 9
STRETCHER

Name   **Date**

Look carefully at the puzzle. You need to find the target number that goes in the middle and you need to write numbers in the correct places to make a subtraction sentence and an addition sentence.

Here are the numbers you must use:
2   5   6   11   13

Solve this puzzle.

Here are the numbers you must use:
3   6   8   14   17

Solve this puzzle.

Here are the numbers you must use:
2   4   12   16   18

Solve this puzzle.

Here are the numbers you must use:
5   7   8   15   20

Teacher's notes

The puzzles on this page are at a higher level than those at Level A. Pupils need to use their knowledge of addition and subtraction facts and a logical approach to problem solving. Some pupils may advance very quickly and can be set time challenges before moving on to higher levels.

MIND **10**
STRETCHER

Name

Date

Look carefully at the puzzle. You need to find the target number that goes in the middle and you need to write numbers in the correct places to make a subtraction sentence and an addition sentence.

Here are the numbers you must use:
2 8 9 17 19

Solve this puzzle.

Here are the numbers you must use:
5 5 8 13 18

Solve this puzzle.

Here are the numbers you must use:
8 11 12 20 31

Solve this puzzle.

Here are the numbers you must use:
6 11 13 19 30

Teacher's notes

The puzzles on this page are at a higher level than those at Level A. Pupils need to use their knowledge of addition and subtraction facts and a logical approach to problem solving. Some pupils may advance very quickly and can be set time challenges before moving on to higher levels.

Name

Date

Look carefully at the puzzle. It has a target number of 6.

You need to write some numbers to make an addition with an answer of 6 and a multiplication with an answer of 6.

Here are the numbers you must use:
2 2 3 4

Here is another puzzle. This one has a target number of 8.

The numbers you must use are:
2 3 4 5

Now try this one.
Target number: 9.

Numbers to use:
2 3 3 7

Write these numbers in the correct places to make the target number:
2 4 5 6

Teacher's notes

At Level C the puzzles require manipulation of addition and multiplication facts. Once again, those children who are numerically competent and confident can be challenged by completing each puzzle 'against the clock', then move on very quickly to higher levels.

Name   **Date**

Complete each of the puzzles using the numbers provided.

Write these numbers in the correct places to make the target number:
3 4 4 8

Write these numbers in the correct places to make the target number:
2 5 7 9

Write these numbers in the correct places to make the target number:
3 5 7 8

Write these numbers in the correct places to make the target number:
2 7 8 9

Teacher's notes

At Level C the puzzles require manipulation of addition and multiplication facts. Once again, those children who are numerically competent and confident can be challenged by completing each puzzle 'against the clock', then move on very quickly to higher levels.

Name

Date

Complete each of the puzzles using the numbers provided.

Write these numbers in the correct places to make the target number:
3 5 6 13

Write these numbers in the correct places to make the target number:
2 3 6 9

Write these numbers in the correct places to make the target number:
2 6 9 12

Write these numbers in the correct places to make the target number:
3 4 4 13

Teacher's notes

At Level C the puzzles require manipulation of addition and multiplication facts. Once again, those children who are numerically competent and confident can be challenged by completing each puzzle 'against the clock', then move on very quickly to higher levels.

| Name | | Date | |

Complete each of the puzzles using the numbers provided.

Write these numbers in the correct places to make the target number:
2 8 10 12

Write these numbers in the correct places to make the target number:
3 9 12 15

Write these numbers in the correct places to make the target number:
4 6 8 16

Write these numbers in the correct places to make the target number:
4 7 11 17

Teacher's notes

At Level C the puzzles require manipulation of addition and multiplication facts. Once again, those children who are numerically competent and confident can be challenged by completing each puzzle 'against the clock', then move on very quickly to higher levels.

Name   **Date**

Complete each of the puzzles using the numbers provided.

Write these numbers
in the correct places
to make the target
number:
3 7 9 12

Write these numbers
in the correct places
to make the target
number:
5 5 10 15

Write these numbers
in the correct places
to make the target
number:
4 5 9 11

Write these numbers
in the correct places
to make the target
number:
3 8 11 13

Teacher's notes

At Level C the puzzles require manipulation of addition and multiplication facts. Once again, those children who are numerically competent and confident can be challenged by completing each puzzle 'against the clock', then move on very quickly to higher levels.

| Name | | Date | |

Look carefully at the puzzle. You need to find the target number that goes in the middle and you need to write numbers in the correct places to make an addition sentence and a multiplication sentence.

Here are the numbers you must use:
3 4 5 7 12

Here is another puzzle. You need to find the target number and the numbers to make the addition sentence and the multiplication sentence.

The numbers you must use are:
2 6 7 8 14

Now try this one.

The numbers you must use are:
4 4 8 8 16

Now try this one.

The numbers you must use are:
3 5 6 9 15

Teacher's notes

The puzzles on this page are at a higher level than those at Level C. Pupils need to use their knowledge of addition and multiplication facts and a logical approach to problem solving. Some pupils may advance very quickly and can be set time challenges before moving on to higher levels.

Name _____   **Date** _____

Look carefully at the puzzle. You need to find the target number that goes in the middle and you need to write numbers in the correct places to make an addition sentence and a multiplication sentence.

Here are the numbers you must use:
5 12 2 7 6

Solve this puzzle.

Here are the numbers you must use:
18 10 30 3 12

Solve this puzzle.

Here are the numbers you must use:
15 2 5 20 10

Solve this puzzle.

Here are the numbers you must use:
3 18 9 6 9

Teacher's notes

The puzzles on this page are at a higher level than those at Level C. Pupils need to use their knowledge of addition and multiplication facts and a logical approach to problem solving. Note that the numbers provided for each puzzle are not written in order of size on this sheet. Some pupils may advance very quickly and can be set time challenges before moving on to higher levels.

     Andrew Brodie: Maths Mindstretchers 7–9 © A&C Black 2009

Name   **Date**

Look carefully at the puzzle. You need to find the target number that goes in the middle and you need to write numbers in the correct places to make an addition sentence and a multiplication sentence.

Here are the numbers you must use:
16 4 8 12 2

Solve this puzzle.

Here are the numbers you must use:
4 20 7 13 5

Solve this puzzle.

Here are the numbers you must use:
8 15 9 3 24

Solve this puzzle.

Here are the numbers you must use:
7 11 28 4 17

Teacher's notes

The puzzles on this page are at a higher level than those at Level C. Pupils need to use their knowledge of addition and multiplication facts and a logical approach to problem solving. Note that the numbers provided for each puzzle are not written in order of size on this sheet. Some pupils may advance very quickly and can be set time challenges before moving on to higher levels.

Name

Date

Look carefully at the puzzle. You need to find the target number that goes in the middle and you need to write numbers in the correct places to make an addition sentence and a multiplication sentence.

Here are the numbers you must use:
31 40 5 9 8

Solve this puzzle.

Here are the numbers you must use:
5 35 9 7 26

Solve this puzzle.

Here are the numbers you must use:
8 7 4 25 32

Solve this puzzle.

Here are the numbers you must use:
6 29 36 6 7

Teacher's notes

The puzzles on this page are at a higher level than those at Level C. Pupils need to use their knowledge of addition and multiplication facts and a logical approach to problem solving. Note that the numbers provided for each puzzle are not written in order of size on this sheet. Some pupils may advance very quickly and can be set time challenges before moving on to higher levels.

Look carefully at the puzzle. You need to find the target number that goes in the middle and you need to write numbers in the correct places to make an addition sentence and a multiplication sentence.

Here are the numbers you must use:
8 5 45 37 9

Solve this puzzle.

Here are the numbers you must use:
7 5 23 6 30

Solve this puzzle.

Here are the numbers you must use:
28 36 4 8 9

Solve this puzzle.

Here are the numbers you must use:
8 39 6 9 48

Teacher's notes

The puzzles on this page are at a higher level than those at Level C. Pupils need to use their knowledge of addition and multiplication facts and a logical approach to problem solving. Note that the numbers provided for each puzzle are not written in order of size on this sheet. Some pupils may advance very quickly and can be set time challenges before moving on to higher levels.

Name

Date

Look carefully at the puzzle. It has a target number of 8.

You need to write some numbers to make a subtraction with an answer of 8, a multiplication with an answer of 8 and an addition with an answer of 8.

Here are the numbers you must use:
2 2 3 4 6 11

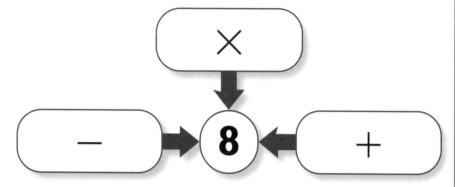

Here is another puzzle. This one has a target number of 9.

The numbers you must use are:
3 3 3 3 6 12

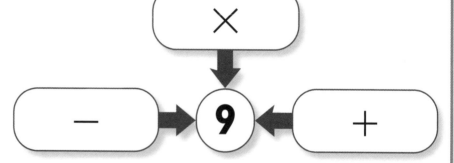

Now try this one.
Target number: 12.

Numbers to use:
2 3 4 5 10 17

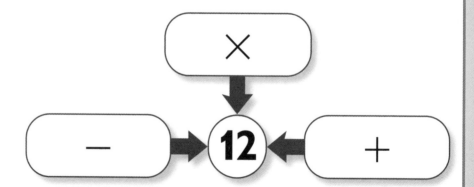

Teacher's notes

The puzzles on this page are at a higher level than those at previous levels. Pupils now need to use their knowledge of multiplication facts as well as addition and subtraction facts together with a logical approach to problem solving. Some pupils may advance very quickly and can be set time challenges before moving on to higher levels.

Name		Date	

Complete each of the puzzles using the numbers provided.

Write these numbers in the correct places to make the target number:
2 4 6 7 8 18

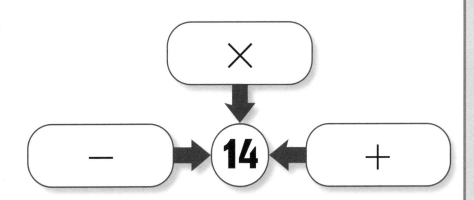

Write these numbers in the correct places to make the target number:
3 4 5 7 8 19

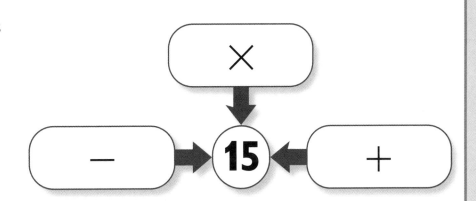

Write these numbers in the correct places to make the target number:
2 3 4 6 14 20

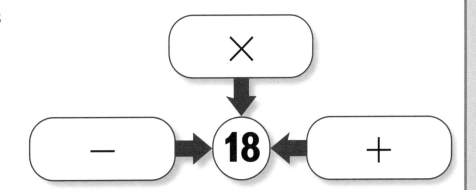

Teacher's notes

The puzzles on this page are at a higher level than those at previous levels. Pupils now need to use their knowledge of multiplication facts as well as addition and subtraction facts together with a logical approach to problem solving. Some pupils may advance very quickly and can be set time challenges before moving on to higher levels.

Name		Date	

Complete each of the puzzles using the numbers provided.

Write these numbers in the correct places to make the target number:
3 4 4 4 12 19

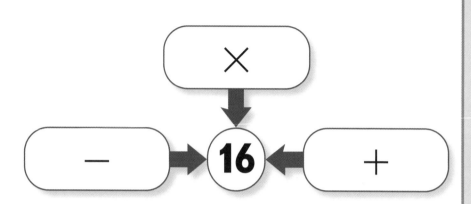

Write these numbers in the correct places to make the target number:
1 2 8 9 10 19

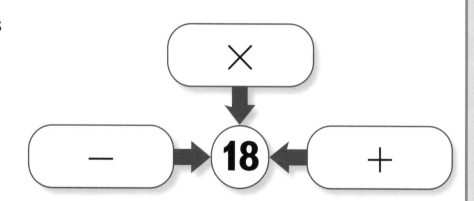

Write these numbers in the correct places to make the target number:
2 3 4 5 7 14

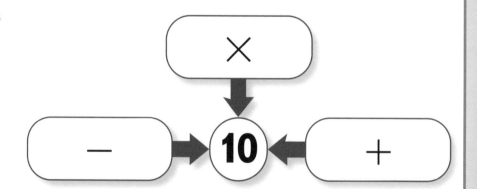

Teacher's notes

The puzzles on this page are at a higher level than those at previous levels. Pupils now need to use their knowledge of multiplication facts as well as addition and subtraction facts together with a logical approach to problem solving. Some pupils may advance very quickly and can be set time challenges before moving on to higher levels.

Name		Date	

Complete each of the puzzles using the numbers provided.

Write these numbers in the correct places to make the target number:

2 3 6 8 9 20

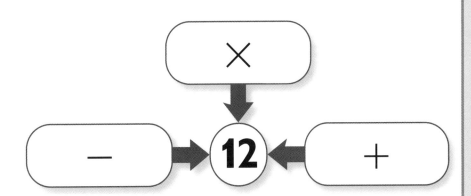

Write these numbers in the correct places to make the target number:

3 7 9 10 11 30

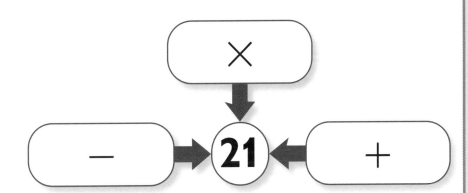

Write these numbers in the correct places to make the target number:

3 4 5 6 14 23

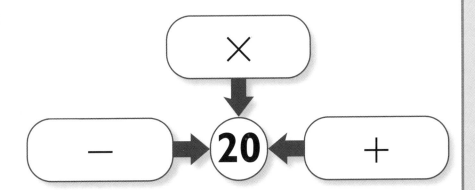

Teacher's notes

The puzzles on this page are at a higher level than those at previous levels. Pupils now need to use their knowledge of multiplication facts as well as addition and subtraction facts together with a logical approach to problem solving. Some pupils may advance very quickly and can be set time challenges before moving on to higher levels.

Name _____ **Date** _____

Complete each of the puzzles using the numbers provided.

Write these numbers in the correct places to make the target number:
2 4 5 10 15 24

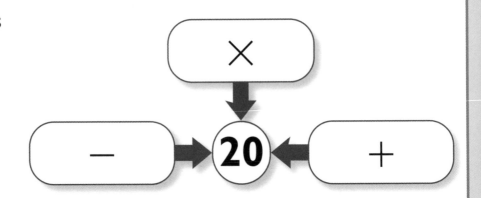

Write these numbers in the correct places to make the target number:
5 5 5 5 20 30

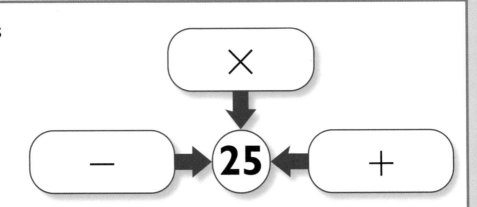

Write these numbers in the correct places to make the target number:
3 5 6 8 19 30

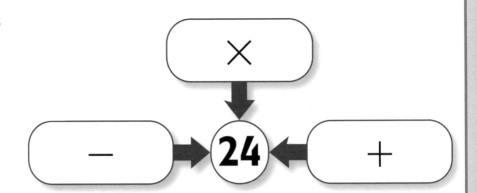

Teacher's notes

The puzzles on this page are at a higher level than those at previous levels. Pupils now need to use their knowledge of multiplication facts as well as addition and subtraction facts together with a logical approach to problem solving. Some pupils may advance very quickly and can be set time challenges before moving on to higher levels.

Name

Date

Look carefully at the puzzle. You need to find the target number that goes in the middle and you need to write numbers in the correct places to make a subtraction sentence, a multiplication sentence and an addition sentence.

Here are the numbers you must use:
2 2 2 3 4 6 8

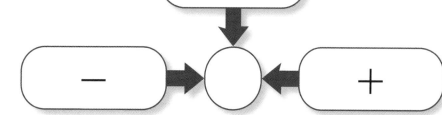

Here is another puzzle. You need to find the target number and the numbers to make the subtraction sentence, the multiplication sentence and the addition sentence.

The numbers you must use are:
2 4 5 8 11 16 20

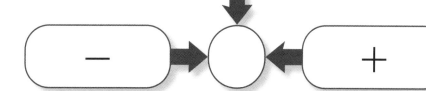

Solve this puzzle.

Here are the numbers you must use:
3 4 4 6 20 24 27

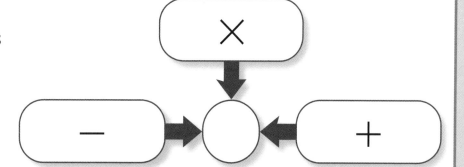

Teacher's notes

The puzzles on this page are at a higher level than those at previous levels. Pupils now need to use their knowledge of addition, subtraction and multiplication facts to create the number sentences and to find the target number. Some pupils may advance very quickly and can be set time challenges before moving on to higher levels.

Name

Date

Look carefully at the puzzle. You need to find the target number that goes in the middle and you need to write numbers in the correct places to make a subtraction sentence, a multiplication sentence and an addition sentence.

Here are the numbers you must use:
2 3 4 4 5 8 12

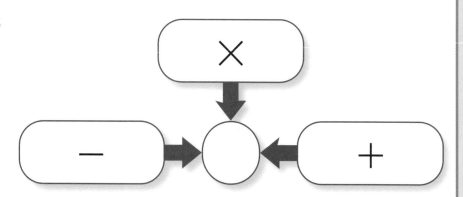

Solve this puzzle.

Here are the numbers you must use:
2 2 4 5 8 10 14

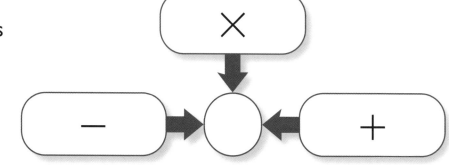

Solve this puzzle.

Here are the numbers you must use:
3 3 3 3 6 9 12

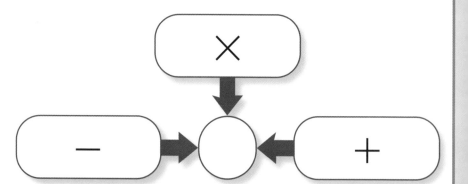

Teacher's notes

The puzzles on this page are at a higher level than those at previous levels. Pupils now need to use their knowledge of addition, subtraction and multiplication facts to create the number sentences and to find the target number. Some pupils may advance very quickly and can be set time challenges before moving on to higher levels.

Name		Date	

Look carefully at the puzzle. You need to find the target number that goes in the middle and you need to write numbers in the correct places to make a subtraction sentence, a multiplication sentence and an addition sentence.

Here are the numbers you must use:
3 4 5 7 7 12 19

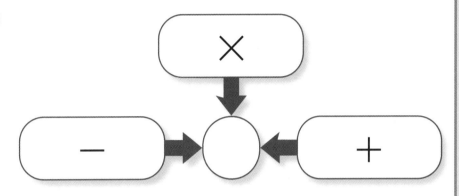

Solve this puzzle.

Here are the numbers you must use:
3 3 5 6 9 15 18

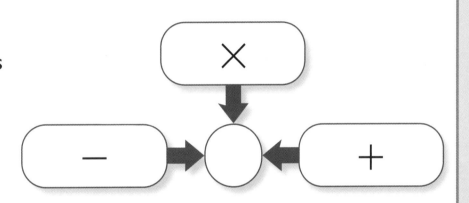

Solve this puzzle.

Here are the numbers you must use:
2 9 9 9 9 18 27

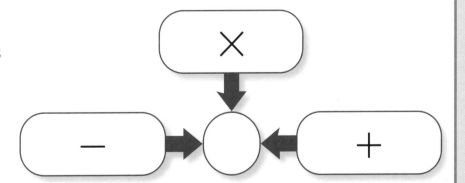

Teacher's notes

The puzzles on this page are at a higher level than those at previous levels. Pupils now need to use their knowledge of addition, subtraction and multiplication facts to create the number sentences and to find the target number. Some pupils may advance very quickly and can be set time challenges before moving on to higher levels.

| Name | | Date | |

Look carefully at the puzzle. You need to find the target number that goes in the middle and you need to write numbers in the correct places to make a subtraction sentence, a multiplication sentence and an addition sentence.

Here are the numbers you must use:
3 6 8 12 12 24 30

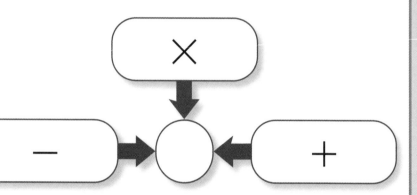

Solve this puzzle.

Here are the numbers you must use:
5 5 7 11 14 25 32

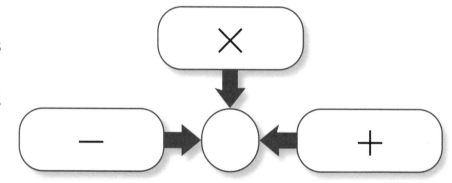

Solve this puzzle.

Here are the numbers you must use:
2 4 4 8 12 16 20

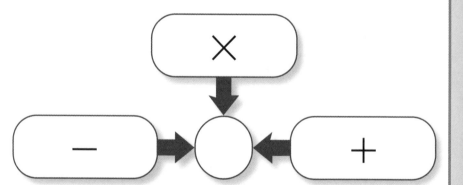

Teacher's notes

The puzzles on this page are at a higher level than those at previous levels. Pupils now need to use their knowledge of addition, subtraction and multiplication facts to create the number sentences and to find the target number. Some pupils may advance very quickly and can be set time challenges before moving on to higher levels.

Name

Date

Look carefully at the puzzle. You need to find the target number that goes in the middle and you need to write numbers in the correct places to make a subtraction sentence, a multiplication sentence and an addition sentence.

Here are the numbers you must use:
4 5 5 7 13 20 25

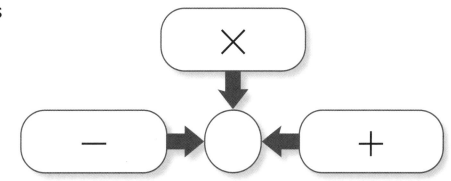

Solve this puzzle.

Here are the numbers you must use:
4 7 8 10 18 28 36

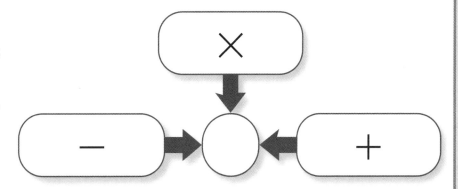

Solve this puzzle.

Here are the numbers you must use:
3 7 9 9 12 21 30

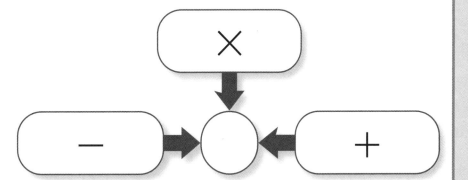

Teacher's notes

The puzzles on this page are at a higher level than those at previous levels. Pupils now need to use their knowledge of addition, subtraction and multiplication facts to create the number sentences and to find the target number. Some pupils may advance very quickly and can be set time challenges before moving on to higher levels.

Name   **Date**

Look carefully at the puzzle. It has a target number of 9.

You need to write some numbers to make a multiplication with an answer of 9 and a division with an answer of 9.

Here are the numbers you must use:
2 3 3 18

Here is another puzzle. This one has a target number of 8.

The numbers you must use are:
2 2 4 16

Now try this one. Target number: 6.

Numbers to use:
2 2 3 12

Write these numbers in the correct places to make the target number:
2 2 5 20

Teacher's notes

At Level G the puzzles require manipulation of multiplication and division facts. Once again, those children who are numerically competent and confident can be challenged by completing each puzzle 'against the clock', then move on very quickly to higher levels.

Andrew Brodie: Maths Mindstretchers 7–9 © A&C Black 2009

Name

Date

Complete each of the puzzles using the numbers provided.

Write these numbers in the correct places to make the target number:

2 2 6 24

Write these numbers in the correct places to make the target number:

2 3 4 24

Write these numbers in the correct places to make the target number:

2 3 3 18

Write these numbers in the correct places to make the target number:

3 3 3 27

Teacher's notes

At Level G the puzzles require manipulation of multiplication and division facts. Once again, those children who are numerically competent and confident can be challenged by completing each puzzle 'against the clock', then move on very quickly to higher levels.

Name

Date

Complete each of the puzzles using the numbers provided.

Write these numbers in the correct places to make the target number:
2 4 5 40

Write these numbers in the correct places to make the target number:
2 32 4 4

Write these numbers in the correct places to make the target number:
24 2 3 4

Write these numbers in the correct places to make the target number:
2 40 4 5

Teacher's notes

At Level G the puzzles require manipulation of multiplication and division facts. Once again, those children who are numerically competent and confident can be challenged by completing each puzzle 'against the clock', then move on very quickly to higher levels.

Name   **Date**

Complete each of the puzzles using the numbers provided.

Write these numbers in the correct places to make the target number:
3 30 2 5

Write these numbers in the correct places to make the target number:
45 3 5 3

Write these numbers in the correct places to make the target number:
5 5 2 50

Write these numbers in the correct places to make the target number:
2 4 24 3

Teacher's notes

At Level G the puzzles require manipulation of multiplication and division facts. Once again, those children who are numerically competent and confident can be challenged by completing each puzzle 'against the clock', then move on very quickly to higher levels.

| Name | | Date | |

Complete each of the puzzles using the numbers provided.

Write these numbers in the correct places to make the target number:
1 3 7 21

Write these numbers in the correct places to make the target number:
2 6 3 36

Write these numbers in the correct places to make the target number:
5 4 40 2

Write these numbers in the correct places to make the target number:
80 2 8 5

Teacher's notes

At Level G the puzzles require manipulation of multiplication and division facts. Once again, those children who are numerically competent and confident can be challenged by completing each puzzle 'against the clock', then move on very quickly to higher levels.

Name　　　　　　　　　　　**Date**

Look carefully at the puzzle. You need to find the target number that goes in the middle and you need to write numbers in the correct places to make a division sentence and a multiplication sentence.

Here are the numbers you must use:
2 24 8 4 3

Here is another puzzle. You need to find the target number and the numbers to make the division sentence and the multiplication sentence.

The numbers you must use are:
2 24 6 2 12

Now try this one.

The numbers you must use are:
2 2 7 14 28

Now try this one.

The numbers you must use are:
2 3 5 15 30

Teacher's notes

The puzzles on this page are at a higher level than those at Level G. Pupils need to use their knowledge of multiplication and division facts and a logical approach to problem solving. With some of the puzzles the children will need to use their skills in doubling and/or halving. Some pupils may advance very quickly and can be set time challenges before moving on to higher levels.

Name

Date

Look carefully at the puzzle. You need to find the target number that goes in the middle and you need to write numbers in the correct places to make a division sentence and a multiplication sentence.

Here are the numbers you must use:
2 3 5 6 30

Solve this puzzle.

Here are the numbers you must use:
3 3 3 9 27

Solve this puzzle.

Here are the numbers you must use:
2 2 8 16 32

Solve this puzzle.

Here are the numbers you must use:
2 4 5 8 40

Teacher's notes

The puzzles on this page are at a higher level than those at Level G. Pupils need to use their knowledge of multiplication and division facts and a logical approach to problem solving. With some of the puzzles the children will need to use their skills in doubling and/or halving. Some pupils may advance very quickly and can be set time challenges before moving on to higher levels.

| Name | | Date | |

Look carefully at the puzzle. You need to find the target number that goes in the middle and you need to write numbers in the correct places to make a division sentence and a multiplication sentence.

Here are the numbers you must use:
2 3 6 18 36

Solve this puzzle.

Here are the numbers you must use:
2 2 12 24 48

Solve this puzzle.

Here are the numbers you must use:
1 2 13 13 26

Solve this puzzle.

Here are the numbers you must use:
2 2 7 14 28

Teacher's notes

The puzzles on this page are at a higher level than those at Level G. Pupils need to use their knowledge of multiplication and division facts and a logical approach to problem solving. With some of the puzzles the children will need to use their skills in doubling and/or halving. Some pupils may advance very quickly and can be set time challenges before moving on to higher levels.

Name

Date

Look carefully at the puzzle. You need to find the target number that goes in the middle and you need to write numbers in the correct places to make a division sentence and a multiplication sentence.

Here are the numbers you must use:
24 4 12 3 2

Solve this puzzle.

Here are the numbers you must use:
4 16 2 4 32

Solve this puzzle.

Here are the numbers you must use:
22 11 2 2 44

Solve this puzzle.

Here are the numbers you must use:
15 30 2 2 60

Teacher's notes

The puzzles on this page are at a higher level than those at Level G. Pupils need to use their knowledge of multiplication and division facts and a logical approach to problem solving. With some of the puzzles the children will need to use their skills in doubling and/or halving. Some pupils may advance very quickly and can be set time challenges before moving on to higher levels.

Name

Date

Look carefully at the puzzle. You need to find the target number that goes in the middle and you need to write numbers in the correct places to make a division sentence and a multiplication sentence.

Here are the numbers you must use:
2 26 13 52 2

Solve this puzzle.

Here are the numbers you must use:
10 40 20 2 2

Solve this puzzle.

Here are the numbers you must use:
2 18 9 2 36

Solve this puzzle.

Here are the numbers you must use:
3 48 8 2 24

Teacher's notes

The puzzles on this page are at a higher level than those at Level G. Pupils need to use their knowledge of multiplication and division facts and a logical approach to problem solving. With some of the puzzles the children will need to use their skills in doubling and/or halving. Some pupils may advance very quickly and can be set time challenges before moving on to higher levels.

Name		Date	

Look carefully at the puzzle. It has a target number of 7.

You need to write some numbers to make a subtraction with an answer of 7, a division with an answer of 7 and an addition with an answer of 7.

Here are the numbers you must use:
3 4 4 5 12 28

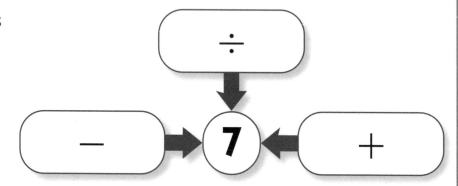

Here is another puzzle. This one has a target number of 8.

The numbers you must use are:
2 3 4 6 12 24

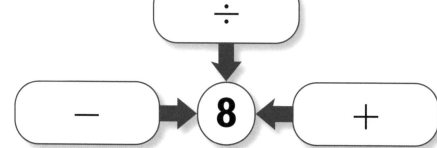

Now try this one. Target number: 12.

Numbers to use:
2 3 4 8 15 24

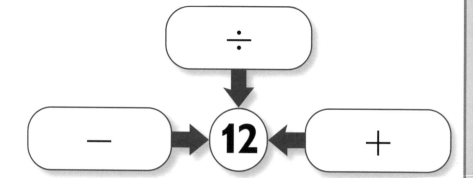

Teacher's notes

The puzzles on this page are at a higher level than those at previous levels. Pupils now need to use their knowledge of division facts as well as addition and subtraction facts together with a logical approach to problem solving. Some pupils may advance very quickly and can be set time challenges before moving on to higher levels.

| Name | | Date | |

Complete each of the puzzles using the numbers provided.

Write these numbers in the correct places to make the target number:
30 2 8 5 4 2

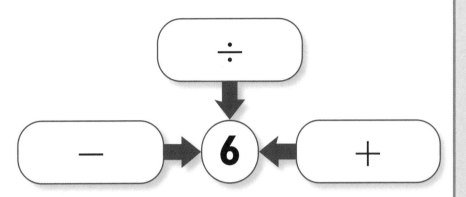

Write these numbers in the correct places to make the target number:
18 2 5 3 16 10

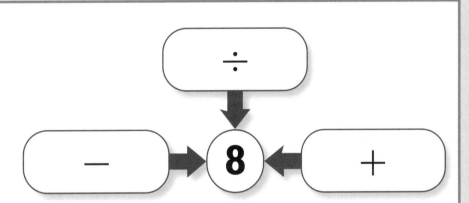

Write these numbers in the correct places to make the target number:
6 5 13 35 2 5

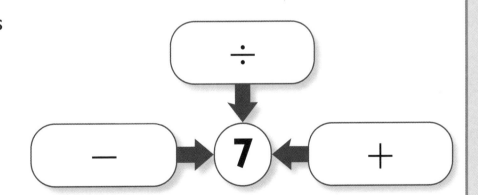

Teacher's notes

The puzzles on this page are at a higher level than those at previous levels. Pupils now need to use their knowledge of division facts as well as addition and subtraction facts together with a logical approach to problem solving. Some pupils may advance very quickly and can be set time challenges before moving on to higher levels.

Name _____ Date _____

Complete each of the puzzles using the numbers provided.

Write these numbers in the correct places to make the target number:
7 3 45 12 5 2

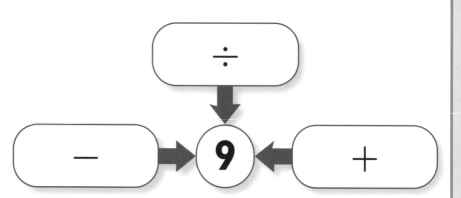

Write these numbers in the correct places to make the target number:
14 40 7 6 5 1

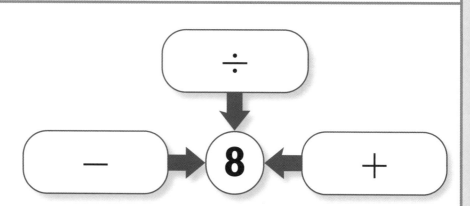

Write these numbers in the correct places to make the target number:
6 3 4 11 21 1

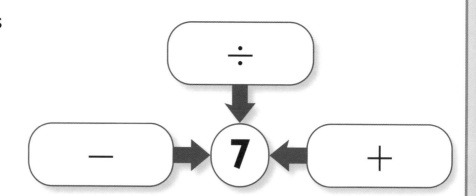

Teacher's notes

The puzzles on this page are at a higher level than those at previous levels. Pupils now need to use their knowledge of division facts as well as addition and subtraction facts together with a logical approach to problem solving. Some pupils may advance very quickly and can be set time challenges before moving on to higher levels.

| Name | | Date | |

Complete each of the puzzles using the numbers provided.

Write these numbers in the correct places to make the target number:
4 32 4 2 20 12

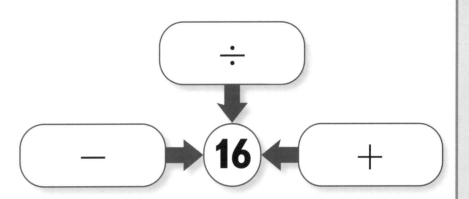

Write these numbers in the correct places to make the target number:
14 0   10 7 3 2

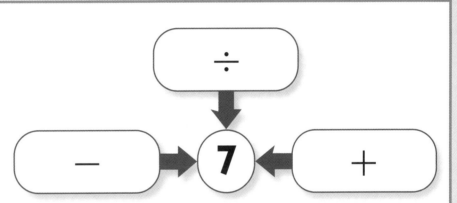

Write these numbers in the correct places to make the target number:
2 6 28 6 8 20

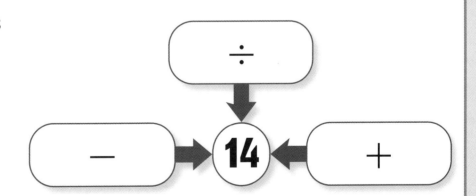

Teacher's notes

The puzzles on this page are at a higher level than those at previous levels. Pupils now need to use their knowledge of division facts as well as addition and subtraction facts together with a logical approach to problem solving. Some pupils may advance very quickly and can be set time challenges before moving on to higher levels.

Name

Date

Complete each of the puzzles using the numbers provided.

Write these numbers
in the correct places
to make the target
number:
4 2 36 20 2 14

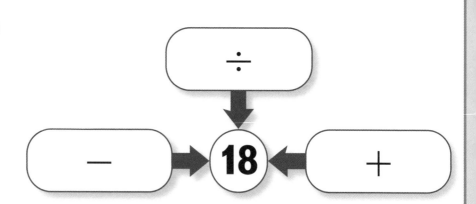

Write these numbers
in the correct places
to make the target
number:
4 7 4 4 15 32

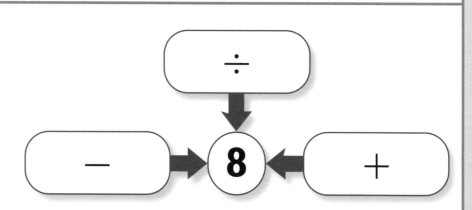

Write these numbers
in the correct places
to make the target
number:
18 30 48 6 2 6

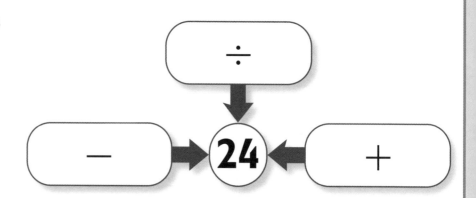

Teacher's notes

The puzzles on this page are at a higher level than those at previous levels. Pupils now need to use their knowledge of division facts as well as addition and subtraction facts together with a logical approach to problem solving. Some pupils may advance very quickly and can be set time challenges before moving on to higher levels.

Name   **Date**

Look carefully at the puzzle. You need to find the target number that goes in the middle and you need to write numbers in the correct places to make a subtraction sentence, a division sentence and an addition sentence.

Here are the numbers you must use:
1 2 3 4 6 8 32

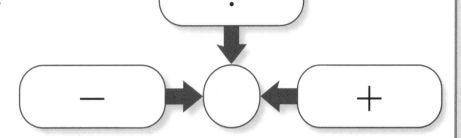

Here is another puzzle. You need to find the target number and the numbers to make the subtraction sentence, the division sentence and the addition sentence.

The numbers you must use are:
2 4 5 6 7 11 42

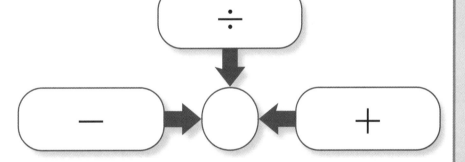

Solve this puzzle.

Here are the numbers you must use:
2 5 6 8 10 15 60

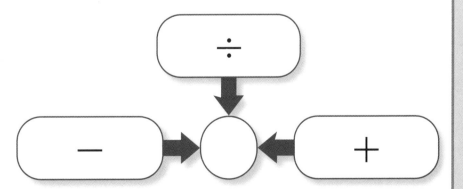

Teacher's notes

The puzzles on this page are at a higher level than those at previous levels. Pupils now need to use their knowledge of addition, subtraction and division facts to create the number sentences and to find the target number. Some pupils may advance very quickly and can be set time challenges before moving on to higher levels.

Name   **Date**

Look carefully at the puzzle. You need to find the target number that goes in the middle and you need to write numbers in the correct places to make a subtraction sentence, a division sentence and an addition sentence.

Here are the numbers you must use:
2 3 4 6 7 9 42

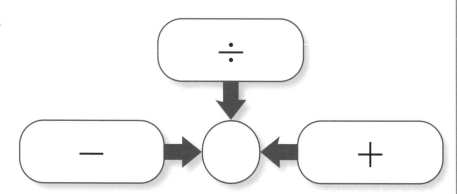

Solve this puzzle.

Here are the numbers you must use:
2 6 6 6 8 14 48

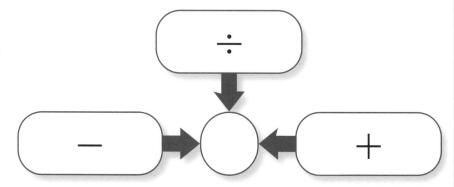

Solve this puzzle.

Here are the numbers you must use:
2 3 7 7 9 12 63

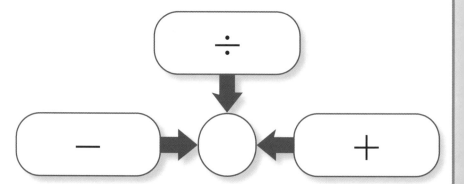

Teacher's notes

The puzzles on this page are at a higher level than those at previous levels. Pupils now need to use their knowledge of addition, subtraction and division facts to create the number sentences and to find the target number. Some pupils may advance very quickly and can be set time challenges before moving on to higher levels.

Andrew Brodie: Maths Mindstretchers 7–9 © A&C Black 2009

MIND
STRETCHER **48**

Name

Date

Look carefully at the puzzle. You need to find the target number that goes in the middle and you need to write numbers in the correct places to make a subtraction sentence, a division sentence and an addition sentence.

Here are the numbers you must use:
2   5   7   8   13   20   26

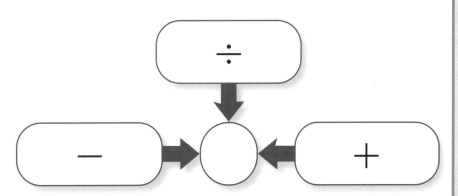

Solve this puzzle.

Here are the numbers you must use:
2   6   6   8   14   20   28

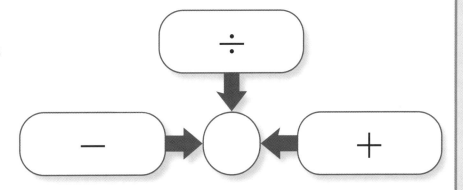

Solve this puzzle.

Here are the numbers you must use:
2   2   2   15   17   19   34

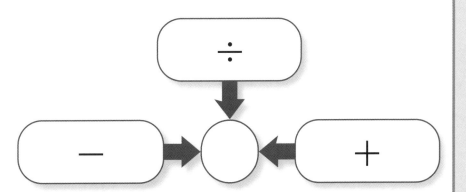

Teacher's notes

The puzzles on this page are at a higher level than those at previous levels. Pupils now need to use their knowledge of addition, subtraction and division facts to create the number sentences and to find the target number. Some pupils may advance very quickly and can be set time challenges before moving on to higher levels.

MIND STRETCHER **49**

Look carefully at the puzzle. You need to find the target number that goes in the middle and you need to write numbers in the correct places to make a subtraction sentence, a division sentence and an addition sentence.

Here are the numbers you must use:
2 4 6 7 9 15 36

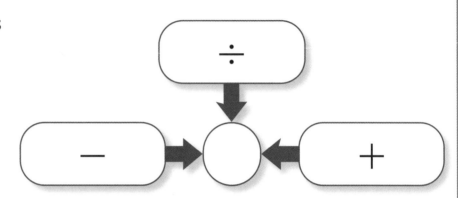

Solve this puzzle.

Here are the numbers you must use:
2 5 6 9 11 20 22

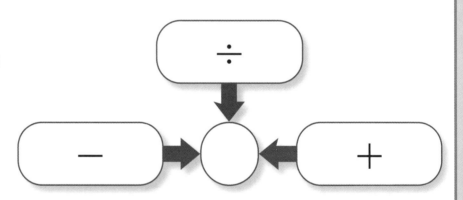

Solve this puzzle.

Here are the numbers you must use:
2 3 3 5 5 8 25

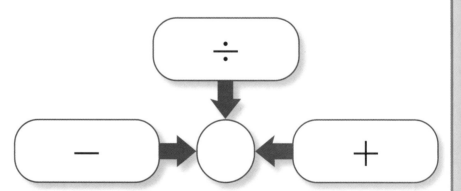

Teacher's notes

The puzzles on this page are at a higher level than those at previous levels. Pupils now need to use their knowledge of addition, subtraction and division facts to create the number sentences and to find the target number. Some pupils may advance very quickly and can be set time challenges before moving on to higher levels.

Name

Date

Look carefully at the puzzle. You need to find the target number that goes in the middle and you need to write numbers in the correct places to make a subtraction sentence, a division sentence and an addition sentence.

Here are the numbers you must use:
2 6 6 9 15 21 30

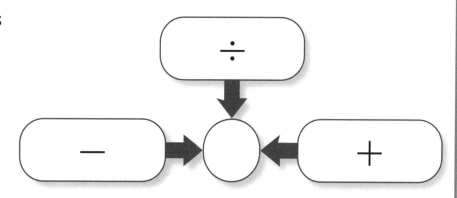

Solve this puzzle.

Here are the numbers you must use:
2 5 5 7 12 17 24

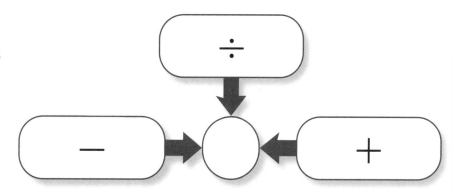

Solve this puzzle.

Here are the numbers you must use:
2 4 8 8 16 20 32

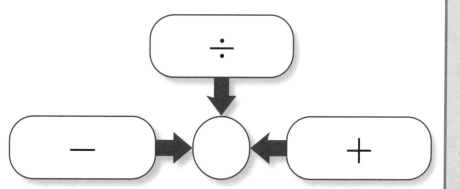

Teacher's notes

The puzzles on this page are at a higher level than those at previous levels. Pupils now need to use their knowledge of addition, subtraction and division facts to create the number sentences and to find the target number. Some pupils may advance very quickly and can be set time challenges before moving on to higher levels.

Name

Date

Look carefully at the puzzle. It has a target number of 6.

You need to write some numbers to make a division with an answer of 6, a subtraction with an answer of 6, an addition with an answer of 6 and a multiplication with an answer of 6.

Here are the numbers you must use: 2 2 3 3 4 7 13 18

Write them in the correct places on the puzzle.

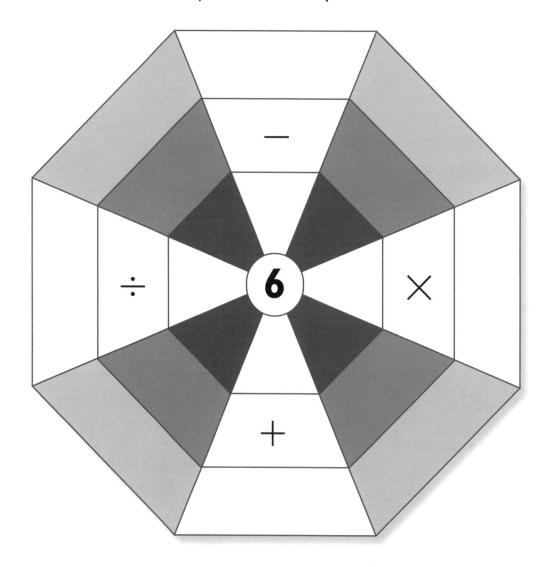

Teacher's notes

This puzzle requires pupils to use their knowledge of addition, subtraction, multiplication and division facts to create the number sentences to make the target number. Ensure that the pupils understand where to enter the numbers on the puzzle – in the white boxes, leaving the shaded boxes blank. Note that the numbers may be entered in one of two ways in each of the addition and multiplication sections. Some pupils may advance very quickly and can be set time challenges before moving on to higher levels.

Name

Date

Look carefully at the puzzle. It has a target number of 8.

You need to write some numbers to make a division with an answer of 8, a subtraction with an answer of 8, an addition with an answer of 8 and a multiplication with an answer of 8.

Here are the numbers you must use: 2 3 3 4 5 6 14 24

Write them in the correct places on the puzzle.

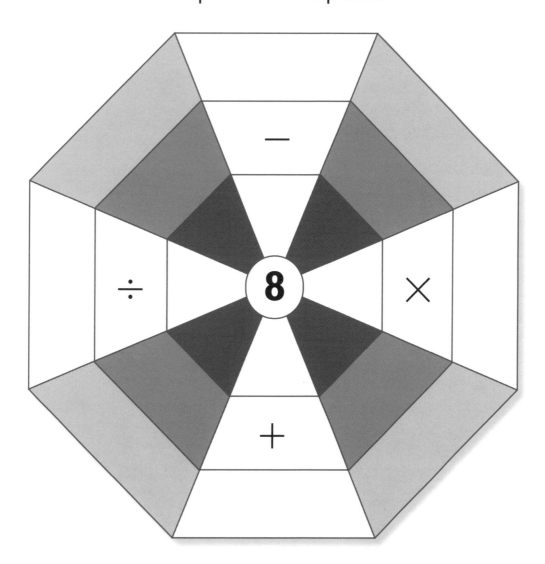

Teacher's notes

This puzzle requires pupils to use their knowledge of addition, subtraction, multiplication and division facts to create the number sentences to make the target number. Ensure that the pupils understand where to enter the numbers on the puzzle – in the white boxes, leaving the shaded boxes blank. Note that the numbers may be entered in one of two ways in each of the addition and multiplication sections. Some pupils may advance very quickly and can be set time challenges before moving on to higher levels.

Name

Date

Look carefully at the puzzle. It has a target number of 5.

You need to write some numbers to make a division with an answer of 5, a subtraction with an answer of 5, an addition with an answer of 5 and a multiplication with an answer of 5.

Here are the numbers you must use: 1 1 4 4 5 6 11 20

Write them in the correct places on the puzzle.

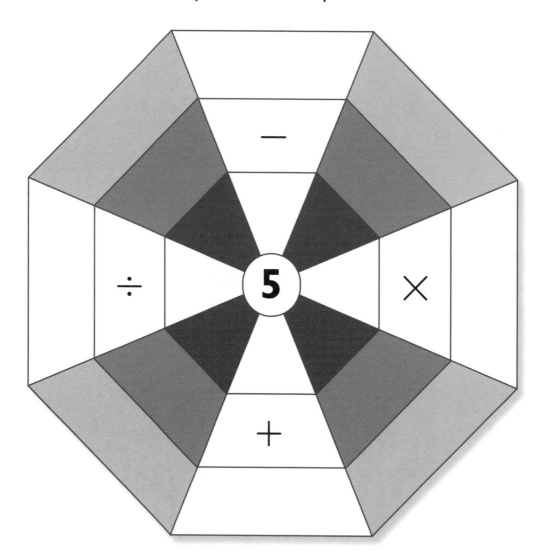

Teacher's notes

This puzzle requires pupils to use their knowledge of addition, subtraction, multiplication and division facts to create the number sentences to make the target number. Ensure that the pupils understand where to enter the numbers on the puzzle – in the white boxes, leaving the shaded boxes blank. Note that the numbers may be entered in one of two ways in each of the addition and multiplication sections. Some pupils may advance very quickly and can be set time challenges before moving on to higher levels.

MIND
STRETCHER 54

Name

Date

Look carefully at the puzzle. It has a target number of 4.

You need to write some numbers to make a division with an answer of 4, a subtraction with an answer of 4, an addition with an answer of 4 and a multiplication with an answer of 4.

Here are the numbers you must use: 1 2 2 3 5 6 10 20

Write them in the correct places on the puzzle.

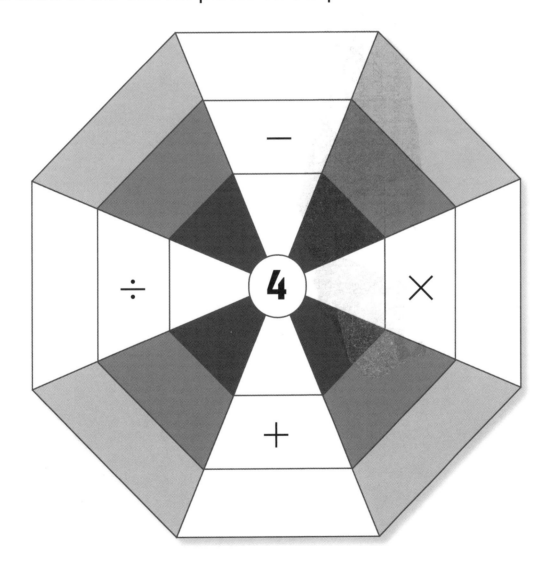

Teacher's notes

This puzzle requires pupils to use their knowledge of addition, subtraction, multiplication and division facts to create the number sentences to make the target number. Ensure that the pupils understand where to enter the numbers on the puzzle – in the white boxes, leaving the shaded boxes blank. Note that the numbers may be entered in one of two ways in each of the addition and multiplication sections. Some pupils may advance very quickly and can be set time challenges before moving on to higher levels.

Name

Date

Look carefully at the puzzle. It has a target number of 9.

You need to write some numbers to make a division with an answer of 9, a subtraction with an answer of 9, an addition with an answer of 9 and a multiplication with an answer of 9.

Here are the numbers you must use: 3   3   4   5   5   7   16   45

Write them in the correct places on the puzzle.

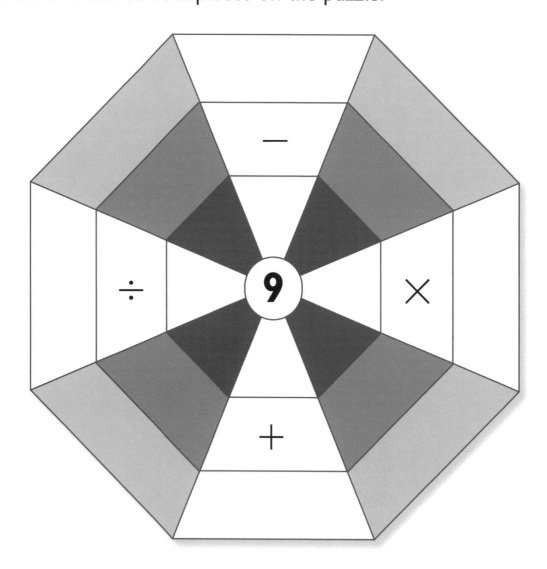

Andrew Brodie: Maths Mindstretchers 7–9 © A&C Black 2009

Name

Date

Look carefully at the puzzle. It has a target number of 10.

You need to write some numbers to make a division with an answer of 10, a subtraction with an answer of 10, an addition with an answer of 10 and a multiplication with an answer of 10.

Here are the numbers you must use: 2 3 4 5 7 8 18 40

Write them in the correct places on the puzzle.

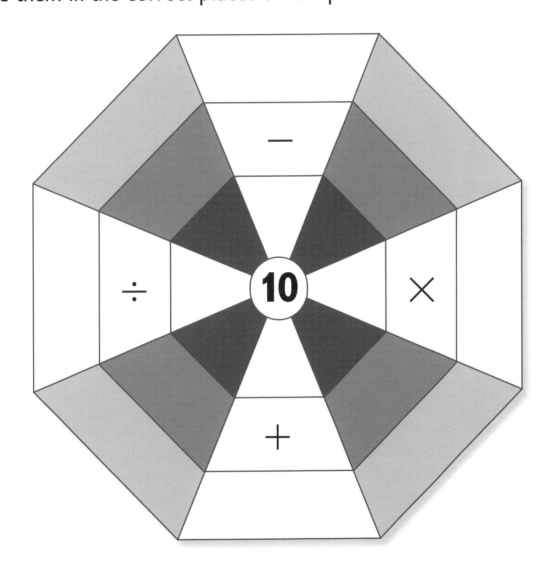

Teacher's notes

This puzzle requires pupils to use their knowledge of addition, subtraction, multiplication and division facts to create the number sentences to make the target number. Ensure that the pupils understand where to enter the numbers on the puzzle – in the white boxes, leaving the shaded boxes blank. Note that the numbers may be entered in one of two ways in each of the addition and multiplication sections. Some pupils may advance very quickly and can be set time challenges before moving on to higher levels.

Name   **Date**

Look carefully at the puzzle. It has a target number of 12.

You need to write some numbers to make a division with an answer of 12, a subtraction with an answer of 12, an addition with an answer of 12 and a multiplication with an answer of 12.

Here are the numbers you must use: 2   3   4   5   7   8   20   24

Write them in the correct places on the puzzle.

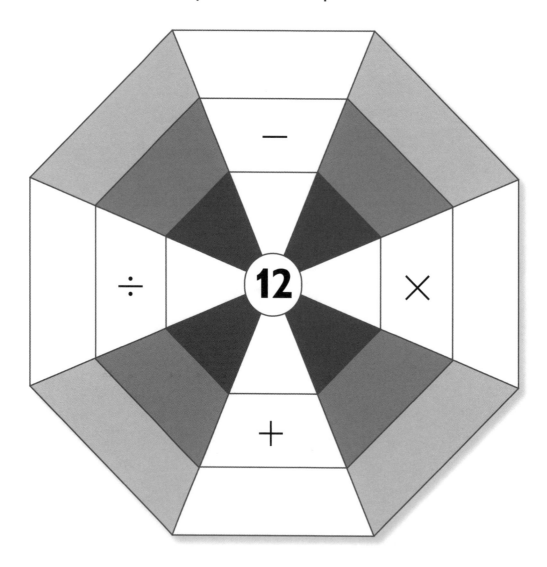

Teacher's notes

This puzzle requires pupils to use their knowledge of addition, subtraction, multiplication and division facts to create the number sentences to make the target number. Ensure that the pupils understand where to enter the numbers on the puzzle – in the white boxes, leaving the shaded boxes blank. Note that the numbers may be entered in one of two ways in each of the addition and multiplication sections. Some pupils may advance very quickly and can be set time challenges before moving on to higher levels.

Name

Date

Look carefully at the puzzle. It has a target number of 14.

You need to write some numbers to make a division with an answer of 14, a subtraction with an answer of 14, an addition with an answer of 14 and a multiplication with an answer of 14.

Here are the numbers you must use: 2 2 6 6 7 8 20 28

Write them in the correct places on the puzzle.

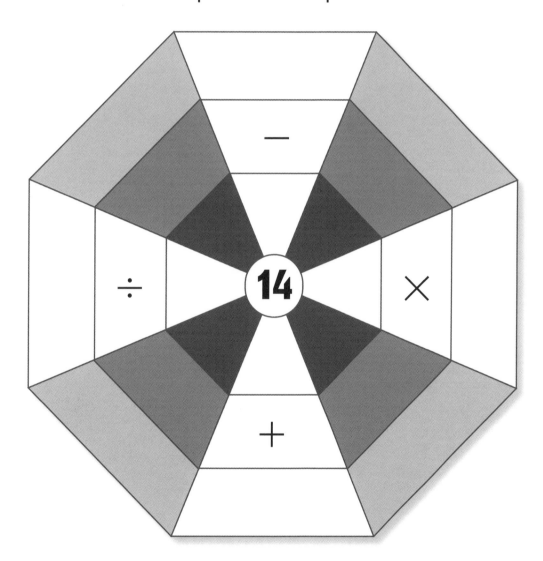

Teacher's notes

This puzzle requires pupils to use their knowledge of addition, subtraction, multiplication and division facts to create the number sentences to make the target number. Ensure that the pupils understand where to enter the numbers on the puzzle – in the white boxes, leaving the shaded boxes blank. Note that the numbers may be entered in one of two ways in each of the addition and multiplication sections. Some pupils may advance very quickly and can be set time challenges before moving on to higher levels.

Name

Date

Look carefully at the puzzle. It has a target number of 15.

You need to write some numbers to make a division with an answer of 15, a subtraction with an answer of 15, an addition with an answer of 15 and a multiplication with an answer of 15.

Here are the numbers you must use: 2 3 3 4 5 11 18 30

Write them in the correct places on the puzzle.

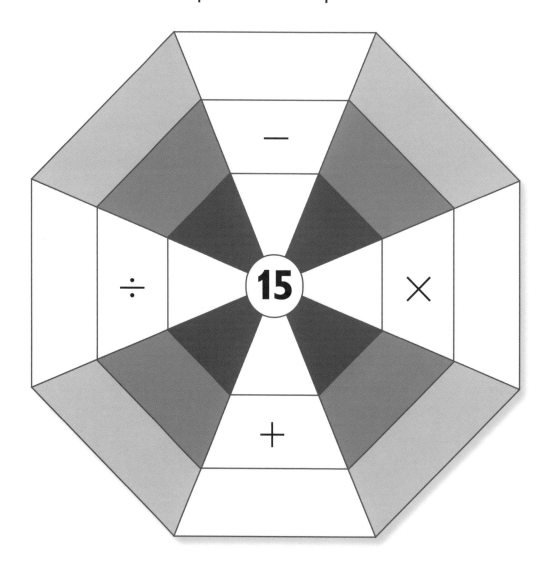

Teacher's notes

This puzzle requires pupils to use their knowledge of addition, subtraction, multiplication and division facts to create the number sentences to make the target number. Ensure that the pupils understand where to enter the numbers on the puzzle – in the white boxes, leaving the shaded boxes blank. Note that the numbers may be entered in one of two ways in each of the addition and multiplication sections. Some pupils may advance very quickly and can be set time challenges before moving on to higher levels.

Name

Date

Look carefully at the puzzle. It has a target number of 16.

You need to write some numbers to make a division with an answer of 16, a subtraction with an answer of 16, an addition with an answer of 16 and a multiplication with an answer of 16.

Here are the numbers you must use: 2 2 4 7 8 9 20 32

Write them in the correct places on the puzzle.

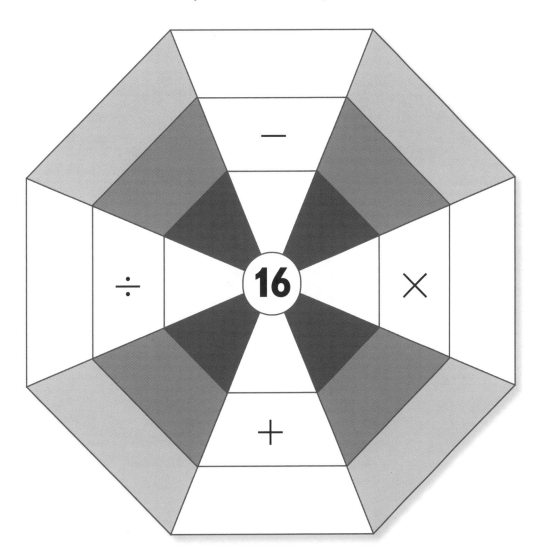

Teacher's notes

This puzzle requires pupils to use their knowledge of addition, subtraction, multiplication and division facts to create the number sentences to make the target number. Ensure that the pupils understand where to enter the numbers on the puzzle – in the white boxes, leaving the shaded boxes blank. Note that the numbers may be entered in one of two ways in each of the addition and multiplication sections. Some pupils may advance very quickly and can be set time challenges before moving on to higher levels.

Name

Date

Look carefully at the puzzle. You need to find the target number that goes in the middle and you need to write numbers in the correct places to make a subtraction sentence, a division sentence, a multiplication sentence and an addition sentence.

Here are the numbers you must use: 2 2 2 2 4 6 8 10 16

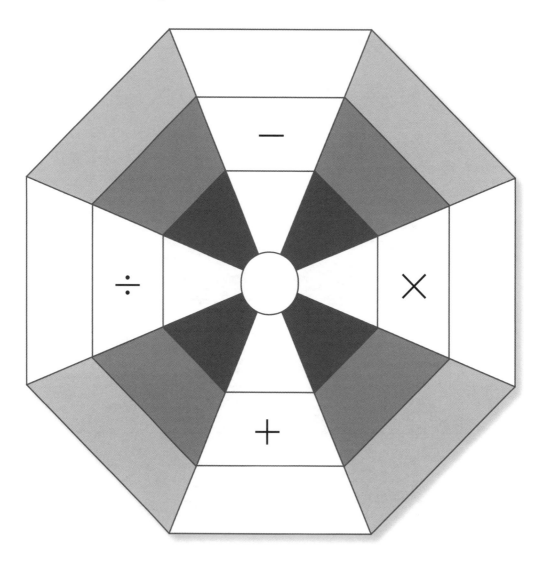

Teacher's notes

Level L is the most difficult level in this book. The puzzle requires pupils to use their knowledge of addition, subtraction, multiplication and division facts to create the number sentences and to find the target number. Ensure that the pupils understand where to enter the numbers on the puzzle – in the white boxes, leaving the shaded boxes blank. Note that the numbers may be entered in one of two ways in each of the addition and multiplication sections.

| **Name** | | **Date** | |

Look carefully at the puzzle. You need to find the target number that goes in the middle and you need to write numbers in the correct places to make a subtraction sentence, a division sentence, a multiplication sentence and an addition sentence.

Here are the numbers you must use: 3 3 3 3 3 6 9 12 27

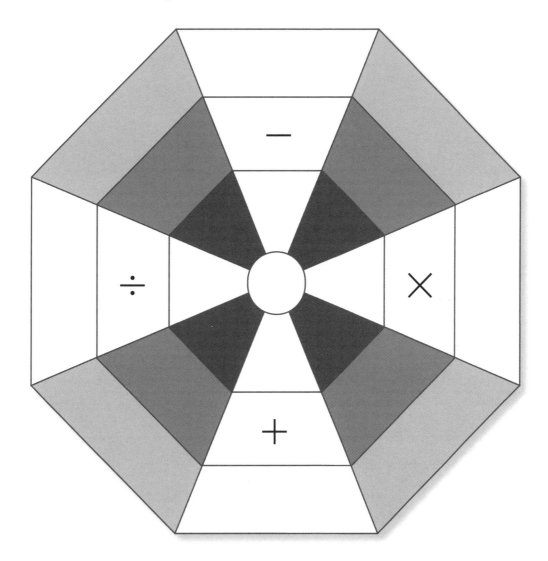

Teacher's notes

Level L is the most difficult level in this book. The puzzle requires pupils to use their knowledge of addition, subtraction, multiplication and division facts to create the number sentences and to find the target number. Ensure that the pupils understand where to enter the numbers on the puzzle – in the white boxes, leaving the shaded boxes blank. Note that the numbers may be entered in one of two ways in each of the addition and multiplication sections.

Name

Date

Look carefully at the puzzle. You need to find the target number that goes in the middle and you need to write numbers in the correct places to make a subtraction sentence, a division sentence, a multiplication sentence and an addition sentence.

Here are the numbers you must use: 2 2 3 3 4 5 6 11 18

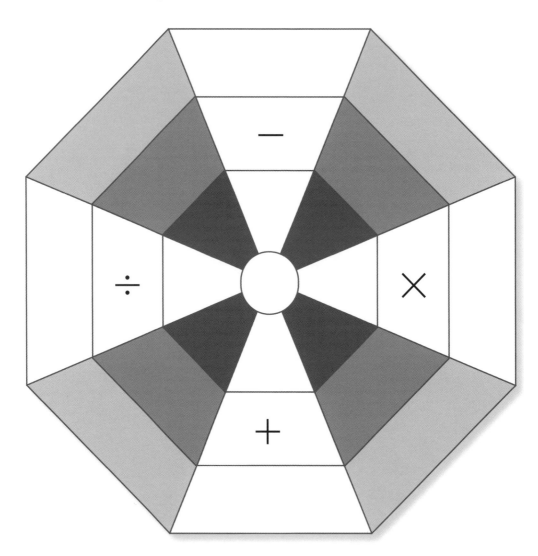

Teacher's notes

Level L is the most difficult level in this book. The puzzle requires pupils to use their knowledge of addition, subtraction, multiplication and division facts to create the number sentences and to find the target number. Ensure that the pupils understand where to enter the numbers on the puzzle – in the white boxes, leaving the shaded boxes blank. Note that the numbers may be entered in one of two ways in each of the addition and multiplication sections.

Name

Date

Look carefully at the puzzle. You need to find the target number that goes in the middle and you need to write numbers in the correct places to make a subtraction sentence, a division sentence, a multiplication sentence and an addition sentence.

Here are the numbers you must use: 2 3 4 5 6 7 12 18 24

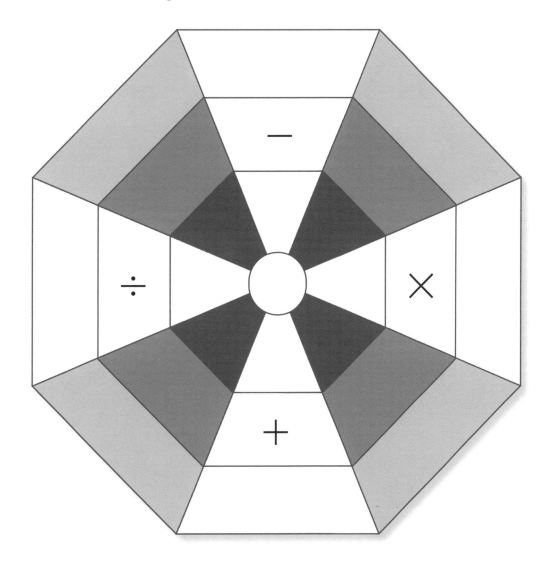

Teacher's notes

Level L is the most difficult level in this book. The puzzle requires pupils to use their knowledge of addition, subtraction, multiplication and division facts to create the number sentences and to find the target number. Ensure that the pupils understand where to enter the numbers on the puzzle – in the white boxes, leaving the shaded boxes blank. Note that the numbers may be entered in one of two ways in each of the addition and multiplication sections.

Name		Date	

Look carefully at the puzzle. You need to find the target number that goes in the middle and you need to write numbers in the correct places to make a subtraction sentence, a division sentence, a multiplication sentence and an addition sentence.

Here are the numbers you must use: 2 2 3 4 5 7 10 14 20

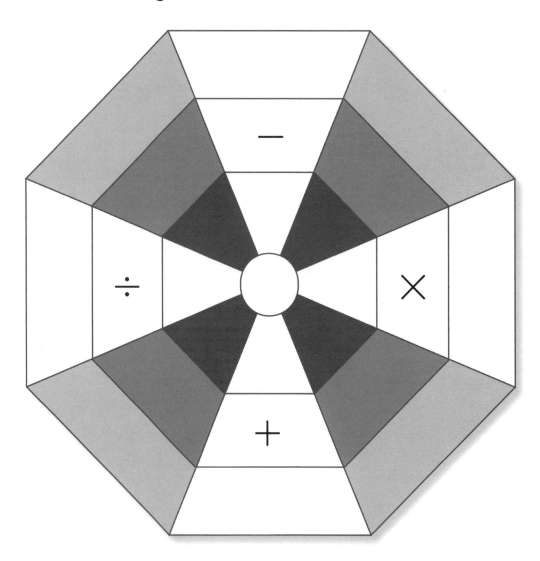

Teacher's notes

Level L is the most difficult level in this book. The puzzle requires pupils to use their knowledge of addition, subtraction, multiplication and division facts to create the number sentences and to find the target number. Ensure that the pupils understand where to enter the numbers on the puzzle – in the white boxes, leaving the shaded boxes blank. Note that the numbers may be entered in one of two ways in each of the addition and multiplication sections.

Andrew Brodie: Maths Mindstretchers 7–9 © A&C Black 2009

Name

Date

Look carefully at the puzzle. You need to find the target number that goes in the middle and you need to write numbers in the correct places to make a subtraction sentence, a division sentence, a multiplication sentence and an addition sentence.

Here are the numbers you must use: 2 3 3 4 4 5 8 12 24

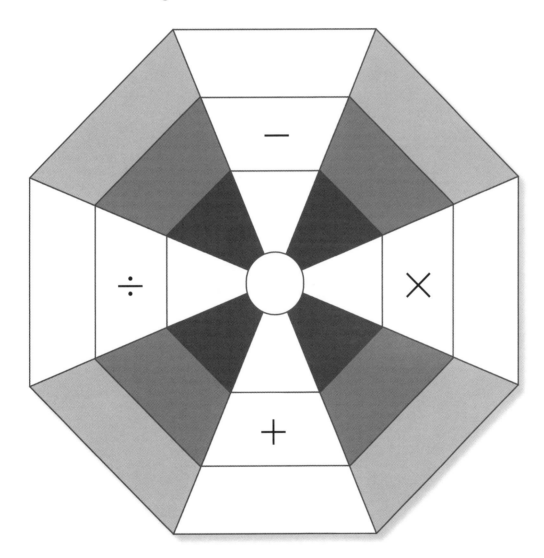

Teacher's notes

Level L is the most difficult level in this book. The puzzle requires pupils to use their knowledge of addition, subtraction, multiplication and division facts to create the number sentences and to find the target number. Ensure that the pupils understand where to enter the numbers on the puzzle – in the white boxes, leaving the shaded boxes blank. Note that the numbers may be entered in one of two ways in each of the addition and multiplication sections.

Name _____ **Date** _____

Look carefully at the puzzle. You need to find the target number that goes in the middle and you need to write numbers in the correct places to make a subtraction sentence, a division sentence, a multiplication sentence and an addition sentence.

Here are the numbers you must use: 1 2 3 4 5 5 6 11 24

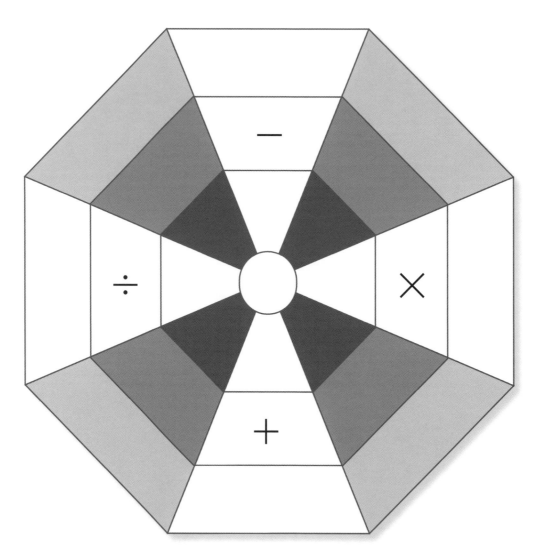

Name

Date

Look carefully at the puzzle. You need to find the target number that goes in the middle and you need to write numbers in the correct places to make a subtraction sentence, a division sentence, a multiplication sentence and an addition sentence.

Here are the numbers you must use: 2   2   2   4   8   12   16   18   32

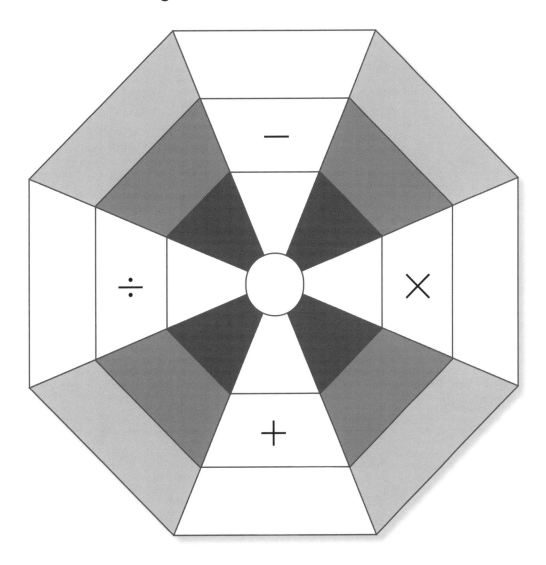

Teacher's notes

Level L is the most difficult level in this book. The puzzle requires pupils to use their knowledge of addition, subtraction, multiplication and division facts to create the number sentences and to find the target number. Ensure that the pupils understand where to enter the numbers on the puzzle – in the white boxes, leaving the shaded boxes blank. Note that the numbers may be entered in one of two ways in each of the addition and multiplication sections.

Name ⬚ **Date** ⬚

Look carefully at the puzzle. You need to find the target number that goes in the middle and you need to write numbers in the correct places to make a subtraction sentence, a division sentence, a multiplication sentence and an addition sentence.

Here are the numbers you must use: 2 2 5 6 7 9 14 20 28

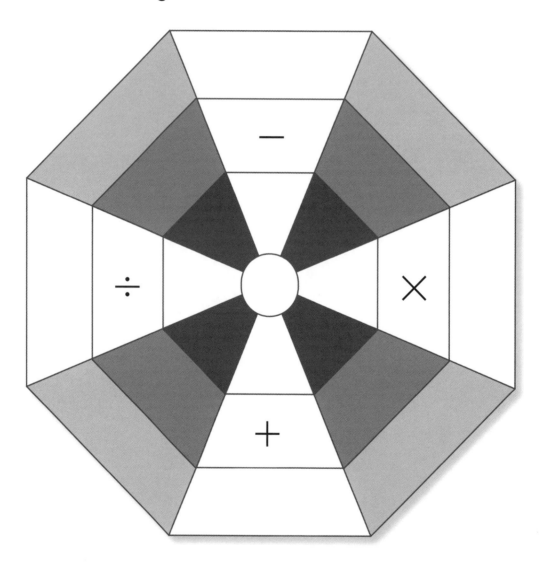

Andrew Brodie: Maths Mindstretchers 7–9 © A&C Black 2009

Name		Date	

Look carefully at the puzzle. You need to find the target number that goes in the middle and you need to write numbers in the correct places to make a subtraction sentence, a division sentence, a multiplication sentence and an addition sentence.

Here are the numbers you must use: 2 2 5 6 7 8 12 20 24

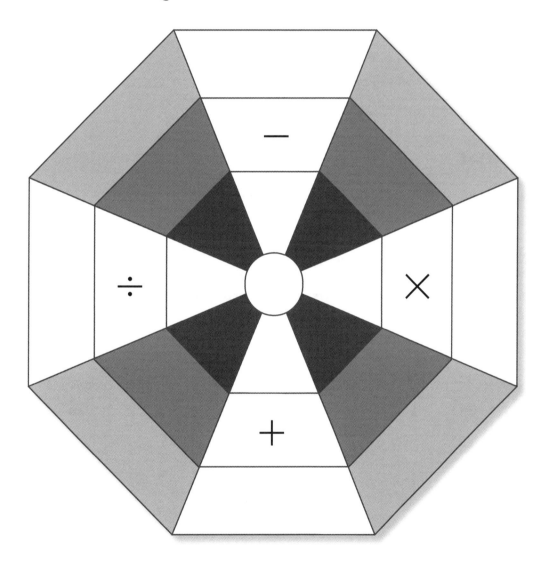

Teacher's notes

Level L is the most difficult level in this book. The puzzle requires pupils to use their knowledge of addition, subtraction, multiplication and division facts to create the number sentences and to find the target number. Ensure that the pupils understand where to enter the numbers on the puzzle – in the white boxes, leaving the shaded boxes blank. Note that the numbers may be entered in one of two ways in each of the addition and multiplication sections.

ANSWERS

Practice of addition and subtraction facts with a target number provided.

Note that pupils can write the additions in either order e.g. in Mindstretcher 1 the first addition can be written as 5 + 3 or 3 + 5.

Mindstretcher 1:

10 − 2 → **8** ← 5 + 3
8 − 3 → **5** ← 4 + 1
11 − 2 → **9** ← 6 + 3
15 − 3 → **12** ← 7 + 5

Mindstretcher 2:

9 − 2 → **7** ← 5 + 2
8 − 2 → **6** ← 5 + 1
12 − 3 → **9** ← 5 + 4
12 − 4 → **8** ← 6 + 2

Mindstretcher 3:

9 − 2 → **7** ← 6 + 1
16 − 6 → **10** ← 7 + 3
13 − 4 → **9** ← 6 + 3
18 − 6 → **12** ← 8 + 4

Mindstretcher 4:

14 − 4 → **10** ← 7 + 3
15 − 3 → **12** ← 8 + 4
20 − 9 → **11** ← 8 + 3
19 − 4 → **15** ← 12 + 3

Mindstretcher 5:

20 − 5 → **15** ← 10 + 5
19 − 3 → **16** ← 12 + 4
18 − 4 → **14** ← 9 + 5
20 − 7 → **13** ← 8 + 5

Practice of addition and subtraction facts, using logical problem solving to find the target number.

Note that pupils can write the additions in either order e.g. in Mindstretcher 6 the first addition can be written as 6 + 3 or 3 + 6.

Mindstretcher 6:

12 − 3 → **9** ← 6 + 3
10 − 3 → **7** ← 6 + 1
12 − 4 → **8** ← 5 + 3
13 − 3 → **10** ← 6 + 4

Mindstretcher 7:

10 − 2 → **8** ← 6 + 2
11 − 2 → **9** ← 6 + 3
9 − 2 → **7** ← 4 + 3
9 − 3 → **6** ← 4 + 2

Mindstretcher 8:

7 − 2 → **5** ← 3 + 2
15 − 5 → **10** ← 5 + 5
11 − 4 → **7** ← 5 + 2
12 − 3 → **9** ← 7 + 2

Mindstretcher 9:

13 − 2 → **11** ← 6 + 5
17 − 3 → **14** ← 8 + 6
18 − 2 → **16** ← 12 + 4
20 − 5 → **15** ← 8 + 7

Mindstretcher 10:

19 − 2 → **17** ← 9 + 8
18 − 5 → **13** ← 8 + 5
31 − 11 → **20** ← 12 + 8
30 − 11 → **19** ← 13 + 6

LEVEL C MINDSTRETCHERS 11–15

Practice of addition and multiplication facts with a target number provided.

Note that pupils can write the additions and the multiplications in either order e.g. in Mindstretcher 11 the first addition can be written as 4 + 2 or 2 + 4 and the first multiplication can be written as 2 × 3 or 3 × 2.

Mindstretcher 11:

(4 + 2) ➡ (6) ⬅ (3 × 2)
(5 + 3) ➡ (8) ⬅ (4 × 2)
(7 + 2) ➡ (9) ⬅ (3 × 3)
(6 + 4) ➡ (10) ⬅ (5 × 2)

Mindstretcher 12:

(8 + 4) ➡ (12) ⬅ (4 × 3)
(9 + 5) ➡ (14) ⬅ (7 × 2)
(8 + 7) ➡ (15) ⬅ (3 × 5)
(9 + 7) ➡ (16) ⬅ (8 × 2)

Mindstretcher 13:

(13 + 5) ➡ (18) ⬅ (6 × 3)
(9 + 3) ➡ (12) ⬅ (6 × 2)
(12 + 6) ➡ (18) ⬅ (9 × 2)
(13 + 3) ➡ (16) ⬅ (4 × 4)

Mindstretcher 14:

(12 + 8) ➡ (20) ⬅ (10 × 2)
(15 + 12) ➡ (27) ⬅ (9 × 3)
(16 + 8) ➡ (24) ⬅ (6 × 4)
(17 + 11) ➡ (28) ⬅ (7 × 4)

Mindstretcher 15:

(12 + 9) ➡ (21) ⬅ (7 × 3)
(15 + 10) ➡ (25) ⬅ (5 × 5)
(11 + 9) ➡ (20) ⬅ (5 × 4)
(13 + 11) ➡ (24) ⬅ (8 × 3)

LEVEL D MINDSTRETCHERS 16–20

Practice of addition and multiplication facts, using logical problem solving to find the target number.

Note that pupils can write the additions and the multiplications in either order e.g. in Mindstretcher 16 the first addition can be written as 7 + 5 or 5 + 7 and the first multiplication can be written as 4 × 3 or 3 × 4.

Mindstretcher 16:

(7 + 5) ➡ (12) ⬅ (4 × 3)
(8 + 6) ➡ (14) ⬅ (7 × 2)
(8 + 8) ➡ (16) ⬅ (4 × 4)
(9 + 6) ➡ (15) ⬅ (5 × 3)

Mindstretcher 17:

(7 + 5) ➡ (12) ⬅ (6 × 2)
(18 + 12) ➡ (30) ⬅ (10 × 3)
(15 + 5) ➡ (20) ⬅ (10 × 2)
(9 + 9) ➡ (18) ⬅ (6 × 3)

Mindstretcher 18:

(12 + 4) ➡ (16) ⬅ (8 × 2)
(13 + 7) ➡ (20) ⬅ (4 × 5)
(15 + 9) ➡ (24) ⬅ (8 × 3)
(17 + 11) ➡ (28) ⬅ (7 × 4)

Mindstretcher 19:

(31 + 9) ➡ (40) ⬅ (8 × 5)
(26 + 9) ➡ (35) ⬅ (7 × 5)
(25 + 7) ➡ (32) ⬅ (8 × 4)
(29 + 7) ➡ (36) ⬅ (6 × 6)

Mindstretcher 20:

(37 + 8) ➡ (45) ⬅ (9 × 5)
(23 + 7) ➡ (30) ⬅ (6 × 5)
(28 + 8) ➡ (36) ⬅ (9 × 4)
(39 + 9) ➡ (48) ⬅ (8 × 6)

Practice of addition, subtraction and multiplication facts with a target number provided.

Note that pupils can write the additions and the multiplications in either order e.g. in Mindstretcher 21 the first addition can be written as 6 + 2 or 2 + 6 and the first multiplication can be written as 4 × 2 or 2 × 4.

Mindstretcher 21:

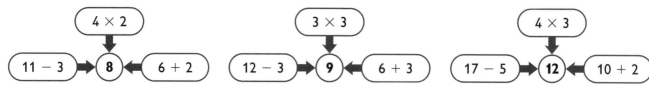

Mindstretcher 22:

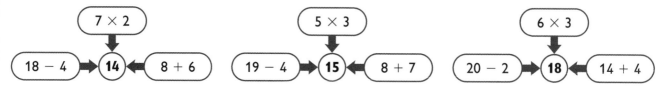

Mindstretcher 23:

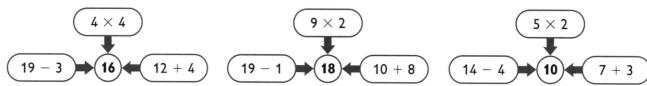

Mindstretcher 24:

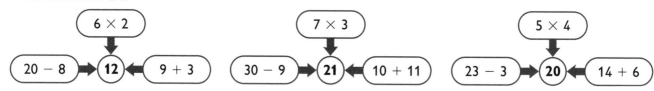

Mindstretcher 25:

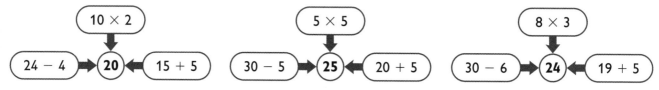

LEVEL F **MINDSTRETCHERS 26–30**

Practice of addition, subtraction and multiplication facts, using logical problem solving to find the target number.

Note that pupils can write the additions and the multiplications in either order e.g. in Mindstretcher 26 the first addition can be written as 6 + 2 or 2 + 6 and the first multiplication can be written as 4 × 2 or 2 × 4.

Mindstretcher 26:

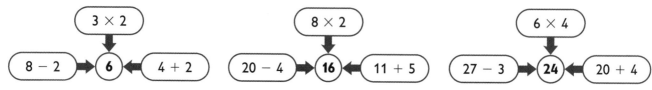

Mindstretcher 27:

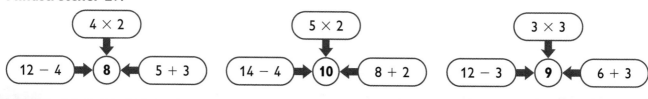

Mindstretcher 28:

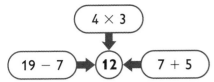

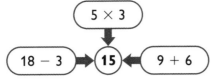

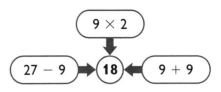

Mindstretcher 29:

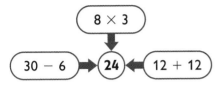

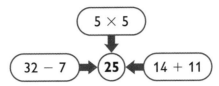

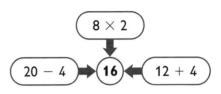

Mindstretcher 30:

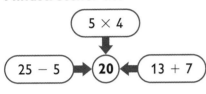

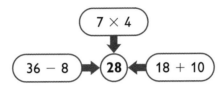

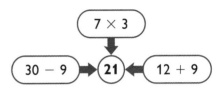

LEVEL G MINDSTRETCHERS 31–35

Practice of multiplication and division facts with a target number provided.
Note that pupils can write the multiplications in either order.

Mindstretcher 31:

$3 \times 3 \rightarrow 9 \leftarrow 18 \div 2$

$4 \times 2 \rightarrow 8 \leftarrow 16 \div 2$

$3 \times 2 \rightarrow 6 \leftarrow 12 \div 2$

$5 \times 2 \rightarrow 10 \leftarrow 20 \div 2$

Mindstretcher 32:

$6 \times 2 \rightarrow 12 \leftarrow 24 \div 2$

$4 \times 2 \rightarrow 8 \leftarrow 24 \div 3$

$3 \times 2 \rightarrow 6 \leftarrow 18 \div 3$

$3 \times 3 \rightarrow 9 \leftarrow 27 \div 3$

Mindstretcher 33:

$5 \times 2 \rightarrow 10 \leftarrow 40 \div 4$

$4 \times 2 \rightarrow 8 \leftarrow 32 \div 4$

$3 \times 2 \rightarrow 6 \leftarrow 24 \div 4$

$4 \times 2 \rightarrow 8 \leftarrow 40 \div 5$

Mindstretcher 34:

$3 \times 2 \rightarrow 6 \leftarrow 30 \div 5$

$3 \times 3 \rightarrow 9 \leftarrow 45 \div 5$

$5 \times 2 \rightarrow 10 \leftarrow 50 \div 5$

$4 \times 3 \rightarrow 12 \leftarrow 24 \div 2$

Mindstretcher 35:

$7 \times 1 \rightarrow 7 \leftarrow 21 \div 3$

$3 \times 2 \rightarrow 6 \leftarrow 36 \div 6$

$4 \times 2 \rightarrow 8 \leftarrow 40 \div 5$

$5 \times 2 \rightarrow 10 \leftarrow 80 \div 8$

LEVEL H MINDSTRETCHERS 36–40

Practice of multiplication and division facts, using logical problem solving to find the target number.

Note that pupils can write the multiplications in either order.

Mindstretcher 36:

$24 \div 3 \rightarrow 8 \leftarrow 4 \times 2$
$24 \div 2 \rightarrow 12 \leftarrow 6 \times 2$
$28 \div 2 \rightarrow 14 \leftarrow 7 \times 2$
$30 \div 2 \rightarrow 15 \leftarrow 5 \times 3$

Mindstretcher 37:

$30 \div 5 \rightarrow 6 \leftarrow 3 \times 2$
$27 \div 3 \rightarrow 9 \leftarrow 3 \times 3$
$32 \div 2 \rightarrow 16 \leftarrow 8 \times 2$
$40 \div 5 \rightarrow 8 \leftarrow 4 \times 2$

Mindstretcher 38:

$36 \div 2 \rightarrow 18 \leftarrow 6 \times 3$
$48 \div 2 \rightarrow 24 \leftarrow 12 \times 2$
$26 \div 2 \rightarrow 13 \leftarrow 1 \times 13$
$28 \div 2 \rightarrow 14 \leftarrow 7 \times 2$

Mindstretcher 39:

$24 \div 2 \rightarrow 12 \leftarrow 4 \times 3$
$32 \div 2 \rightarrow 16 \leftarrow 4 \times 4$
$44 \div 2 \rightarrow 22 \leftarrow 11 \times 2$
$60 \div 2 \rightarrow 30 \leftarrow 15 \times 2$

Mindstretcher 40:

$52 \div 2 \rightarrow 26 \leftarrow 13 \times 2$
$40 \div 2 \rightarrow 20 \leftarrow 10 \times 2$
$36 \div 2 \rightarrow 18 \leftarrow 9 \times 2$
$48 \div 2 \rightarrow 24 \leftarrow 8 \times 3$

LEVEL I MINDSTRETCHERS 41–45

Practice of addition, subtraction and division facts with a target number provided.

Note that pupils can write the additions in either order.

Mindstretcher 41:

$28 \div 4 \downarrow$ $12 - 5 \rightarrow 7 \leftarrow 4 + 3$

$24 \div 3 \downarrow$ $12 - 4 \rightarrow 8 \leftarrow 6 + 2$

$24 \div 2 \downarrow$ $15 - 3 \rightarrow 12 \leftarrow 8 + 4$

Mindstretcher 42:

$30 \div 5 \downarrow$ $8 - 2 \rightarrow 6 \leftarrow 4 + 2$

$16 \div 2 \downarrow$ $18 - 10 \rightarrow 8 \leftarrow 5 + 3$

$35 \div 5 \downarrow$ $13 - 6 \rightarrow 7 \leftarrow 5 + 2$

Mindstretcher 43:

$45 \div 5 \downarrow$ $12 - 3 \rightarrow 9 \leftarrow 7 + 2$

$40 \div 5 \downarrow$ $14 - 6 \rightarrow 8 \leftarrow 7 + 1$

$21 \div 3 \downarrow$ $11 - 4 \rightarrow 7 \leftarrow 6 + 1$

Andrew Brodie: Maths Mindstretchers 7–9 © A&C Black 2009

Mindstretcher 44:

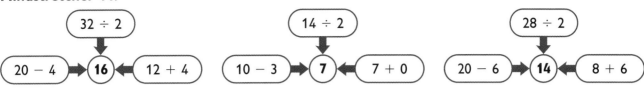

$32 \div 2$ → **16** ; $20 - 4$ → **16** ← $12 + 4$

$14 \div 2$ → **7** ; $10 - 3$ → **7** ← $7 + 0$

$28 \div 2$ → **14** ; $20 - 6$ → **14** ← $8 + 6$

Mindstretcher 45:

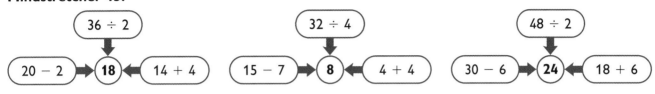

$36 \div 2$ → **18** ; $20 - 2$ → **18** ← $14 + 4$

$32 \div 4$ → **8** ; $15 - 7$ → **8** ← $4 + 4$

$48 \div 2$ → **24** ; $30 - 6$ → **24** ← $18 + 6$

LEVEL J MINDSTRETCHERS 46–50

Practice of addition, subtraction and division facts, using logical problem solving to find the target number.

Note that pupils can write the additions in either order.

Mindstretcher 46:

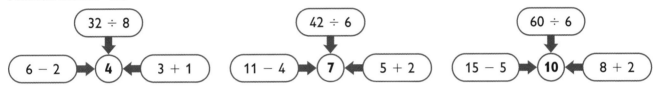

$32 \div 8$ → **4** ; $6 - 2$ → **4** ← $3 + 1$

$42 \div 6$ → **7** ; $11 - 4$ → **7** ← $5 + 2$

$60 \div 6$ → **10** ; $15 - 5$ → **10** ← $8 + 2$

Mindstretcher 47:

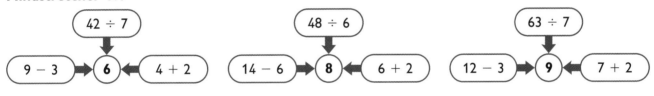

$42 \div 7$ → **6** ; $9 - 3$ → **6** ← $4 + 2$

$48 \div 6$ → **8** ; $14 - 6$ → **8** ← $6 + 2$

$63 \div 7$ → **9** ; $12 - 3$ → **9** ← $7 + 2$

Mindstretcher 48:

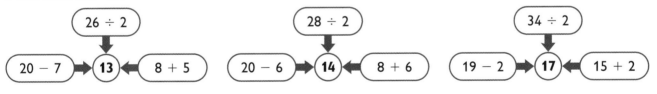

$26 \div 2$ → **13** ; $20 - 7$ → **13** ← $8 + 5$

$28 \div 2$ → **14** ; $20 - 6$ → **14** ← $8 + 6$

$34 \div 2$ → **17** ; $19 - 2$ → **17** ← $15 + 2$

Mindstretcher 49:

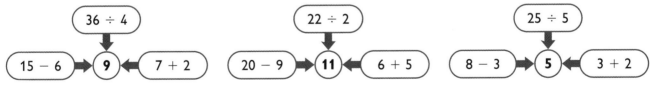

$36 \div 4$ → **9** ; $15 - 6$ → **9** ← $7 + 2$

$22 \div 2$ → **11** ; $20 - 9$ → **11** ← $6 + 5$

$25 \div 5$ → **5** ; $8 - 3$ → **5** ← $3 + 2$

Mindstretcher 50:

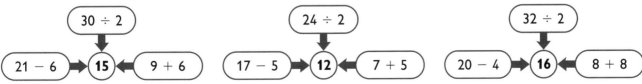

$30 \div 2$ → **15** ; $21 - 6$ → **15** ← $9 + 6$

$24 \div 2$ → **12** ; $17 - 5$ → **12** ← $7 + 5$

$32 \div 2$ → **16** ; $20 - 4$ → **16** ← $8 + 8$

LEVEL K MINDSTRETCHERS 51–60

Practice of all four number operations with a target number provided.

Note that pupils can write the additions and the multiplications in either order. For example, in Mindstretcher 51 the pupils can write 3×2 or 2×3 and $4 + 2$ or $2 + 4$.

Mindstretcher 51:	Target **6**	$18 \div 3$	$13 - 7$	3×2	$4 + 2$
Mindstretcher 52:	Target **8**	$24 \div 3$	$14 - 6$	4×2	$5 + 3$
Mindstretcher 53:	Target **5**	$20 \div 4$	$11 - 6$	1×5	$4 + 1$
Mindstretcher 54:	Target **4**	$20 \div 5$	$10 - 6$	2×2	$3 + 1$
Mindstretcher 55:	Target **9**	$45 \div 5$	$16 - 7$	3×3	$5 + 4$
Mindstretcher 56:	Target **10**	$40 \div 4$	$18 - 8$	5×2	$7 + 3$
Mindstretcher 57:	Target **12**	$24 \div 2$	$20 - 8$	4×3	$7 + 5$
Mindstretcher 58:	Target **14**	$28 \div 2$	$20 - 6$	7×2	$8 + 6$
Mindstretcher 59:	Target **15**	$30 \div 2$	$18 - 3$	5×3	$11 + 4$
Mindstretcher 60:	Target **16**	$32 \div 2$	$20 - 4$	8×2	$9 + 7$

LEVEL L MINDSTRETCHERS 61–70

Practice of all four number operations, using logical problem solving to find the target number.

Note that pupils can write the additions and the multiplications in either order. For example, in Mindstretcher 61 the pupils can write 4×2 or 2×4 and $6 + 2$ or $2 + 6$.

Mindstretcher 61:	Target **8**	$16 \div 2$	$10 - 2$	4×2	$6 + 2$
Mindstretcher 62:	Target **9**	$27 \div 3$	$12 - 3$	3×3	$6 + 3$
Mindstretcher 63:	Target **6**	$18 \div 3$	$11 - 5$	3×2	$4 + 2$
Mindstretcher 64:	Target **12**	$24 \div 2$	$18 - 6$	4×3	$7 + 5$
Mindstretcher 65:	Target **10**	$20 \div 2$	$14 - 4$	5×2	$7 + 3$
Mindstretcher 66:	Target **8**	$24 \div 3$	$12 - 4$	4×2	$5 + 3$
Mindstretcher 67:	Target **6**	$24 \div 4$	$11 - 5$	3×2	$5 + 1$
Mindstretcher 68:	Target **16**	$32 \div 2$	$18 - 2$	8×2	$12 + 4$
Mindstretcher 69:	Target **14**	$28 \div 2$	$20 - 6$	7×2	$9 + 5$
Mindstretcher 70:	Target **12**	$24 \div 2$	$20 - 8$	6×2	$7 + 5$

www.prim-ed.com

G000298267

READING
COMPREHENSION AND WORD READING

Lesson Plans, Texts, Comprehension Activities, Word Reading Activities and Assessments for the Year 4 English Curriculum.

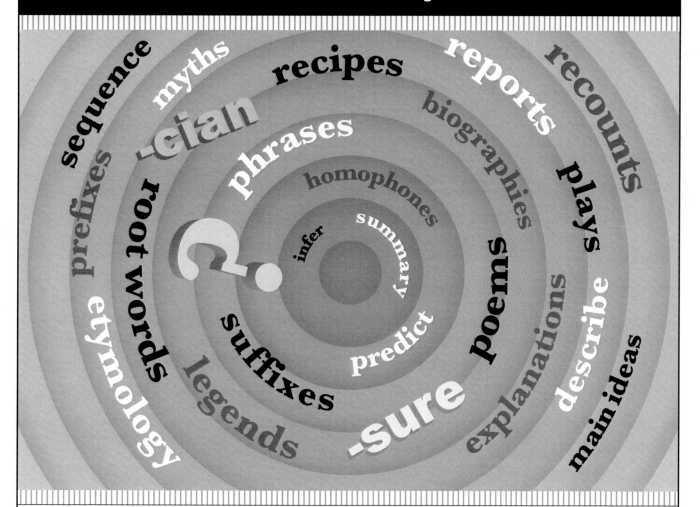

Monitor and track pupil progress with a FREE digital assessment tool.

COMPREHENSION

☑ Wide variety of text genres

☑ Activities to deepen comprehension

☑ Self-assessment for pupils

WORD READING

☑ Focus on word reading elements

☑ Activities to practise word reading skills

☑ Self-assessment for pupils

Reading – Comprehension and Word Reading (Year 4)

Published by Prim-Ed Publishing® 2015
Copyright© R.I.C. Publications® 2015

ISBN 978-1-84654-797-3

PR–2978

Internet websites

In some cases, websites or specific URLs may be recommended. While these are checked and rechecked at the time of publication, the publisher has no control over any subsequent changes which may be made to webpages. It is *strongly* recommended that the class teacher checks *all* URLs before allowing pupils to access them.

View all pages online

Website: http://www.prim-ed.com

Email: sales@prim-ed.com

Foreword

Reading – Comprehension and Word Reading is a six-book series written to support the teaching, learning and assessment of the programmes of study for reading at key stages one and two. The books give equal focus to the dimensions of comprehension and word reading, and the different kinds of teaching and learning experiences needed for each.

Titles in this series are:

- *Reading – Comprehension and Word Reading – Year 1*
- *Reading – Comprehension and Word Reading – Year 2*
- *Reading – Comprehension and Word Reading – Year 3*
- *Reading – Comprehension and Word Reading – Year 4*
- *Reading – Comprehension and Word Reading – Year 5*
- *Reading – Comprehension and Word Reading – Year 6*

Contents

There are 18 six-page units of work within each book, and three formal summative assessment units, one located after every six units.

Each of the 18 units relates to a specific genre of fiction or non-fiction and follows the same format:

A table of **Curriculum Links** is provided, which lists the curriculum objectives covered by the text, comprehension and word reading pupil pages. An outcome is listed for each objective, to aid teacher assessment. Each objective has been allocated a code to aid identification. A table listing these codes and objectives can be found on page xi.

The **Definition of Terms** section includes an explanation of technical literary and grammatical terms. Generally, these terms are not covered in the glossary supplied with the programmes of study for English. They are provided as an aid for the teacher and not for pupils to learn, although teachers may wish to use the information to assist pupils to understand and complete specific activities.

Links to other Curriculum Areas lists any statutory or non-statutory content relating to other programmes of study. This section is omitted if no links are included.

Teacher Page 1

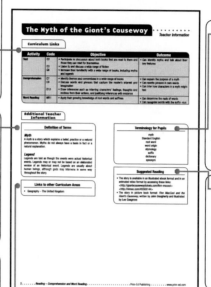

Terminology for Pupils is a list of technical literary and grammatical terms included in the unit. Pupils need to understand and use the terminology to complete the unit's activities.

Suggested Reading includes fiction and non-fiction books and/or digital material that relate to the content of the unit.

The **Notes and Guidance** provide detailed teaching points relating to each of the three pupil activity pages: text; comprehension; and word reading.

There are also assessment activities and answers.

Teacher Pages 2 and 3

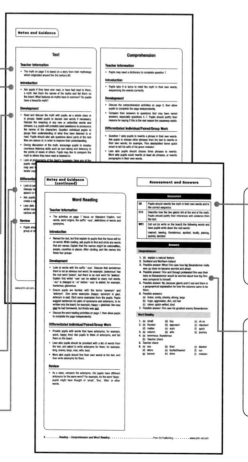

The **Teacher Information** states the content of the copymaster activity and/or any materials the pupils may need.

The **Introduction** provides an activity for the class to complete before commencing the copymaster activity. It might involve a discussion, retelling the text in sequence or rereading the text in search of something specific.

Activities listed in the **Development** section might introduce or revise topics and/or suggest items to discuss, all with the aim of aiding pupils to work on the copymaster activity pages independently.

The **Differentiated Individual/Paired/Group Work** suggests differentiated additional activities related to the pupil activity pages.

The **Review** provides opportunities to discuss and/or share work to assess and conclude each activity.

The **Assessment** table provides assessment activities for the pupil copymaster activity pages.

All the **Answers** are provided for the comprehension and word reading activity pages.

Pupil Page 1

The **genre** of the fiction or non-fiction text the pupils are reading is provided. A list of the text genres is on page x.

The **artwork** illustrates and supports the text.

The **Text focus** of the page is indicated.

Where possible, the **vocabulary in the texts** includes words from the spelling work and the spelling word list outlined in English Appendix 1 for each key stage.

The **learning log** provides an opportunity for pupils to self-assess their reading of the text.

The Myth of the Giant's Causeway – 1
Read this version of the myth.

Long ago, when giants roamed the earth, the Irish giant Finn McCool, who was tired of his Scottish enemy across the sea, decided to do something about it. The giants would often taunt and insult each other across the water and one day Finn became so angry that he gathered up a large clump of earth and hurled it towards his rival. However, the clump missed its target, instead becoming the Isle of Man and leaving the enormous hole to become the great Lough Neagh (the largest lake in the British Isles).

After another occasion of jeering and tormenting, Finn came up with a plan. He gathered many large stone columns and heaved them into the sea. The stones landed side by side, creating a stone bridge or causeway between the two nations.

Soon after, Finn spotted his arch nemesis Benandonner, The Red Man, and shouted a challenge to him. 'Come and fight me and let's settle this once and for all!' Finn stayed to watch The Red Man approach and soon realised his great mistake! As Benandonner came closer, Finn realised just how huge the giant really was ... much bigger than him! Finn skedaddled home quick smart to tell his wife of his grave mistake. By the time he'd finished explaining they could hear the thunderous footsteps of the approaching giant and feel the floor quaking beneath them.

At the giant's booming knock on their door, Finn's wife Oonagh hatched a plan. She shoved Finn into the giant sized bath, covered him in blankets and placed a baby's toy in his hand and a bonnet on his head. She rushed to the door and greeted Benandonner explaining 'What a pity you've just missed Finn! He's away hunting deer. Come in for a rest after your journey and you can wait for his return.' Oonagh offered the giant a drink while he waited.

When he had finished, Oonagh loudly asked him if he'd like to see their baby while he waited for Finn. Not knowing what else to do, Benandonner reluctantly agreed and followed Oonagh's lead through the house.

When she opened the door she greeted her baby, who was sucking his thumb and cooing under the blanket in the bathtub (of course it was Finn McCool himself). The giant Benandonner quickly excused himself, saying he needed to get some air. 'Och', thought the giant, 'if that's the size of the wee laddie I'd hate to see his father. I'll not wait for him to return!' And with that thought, Benandonner broke into a run all the way back home to Scotland. When he heard the giant run off, Finn thanked his quick-thinking and clever wife. As Benandonner thundered back across the causeway he made sure to tear the blocks up to prevent Finn from ever following him.

The remnants of the Giant's Causeway can be seen to this day on the North East coast of Northern Ireland (County Antrim).

My learning log When I read this myth, I could read: ☐ all of it. ☐ most of it. ☐ parts of it.

Pupil Page 2

The **Comprehension focus** of the page is indicated.

Comprehension **questions and activities** relating to the text on *Pupil Page 1* are provided. The comprehension questions may relate to text structure or language features as well as text meaning.

The **learning log** provides an opportunity for pupils to self-assess their completion of the activities.

The Myth of the Giant's Causeway – 2

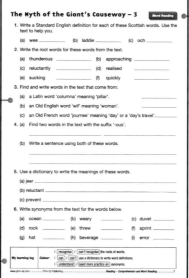

1. This myth began being told to:
   (a) make people laugh. ☐
   (b) explain a natural feature. ☐
   (c) warn children of danger. ☐

2. Which two nations are mentioned in the text?

3. At what point in the story did Finn regret building the Causeway? Explain why.

4. How did Finn and his wife Oonagh trick the giant Benandonner?

5. Do you think this story tells the real version of how the causeway came to be there? Give reasons for your response.

6. Use the text to help you describe the three characters. Think about their physical traits as well as their personalities.
   (a) Finn McCool:
   (b) Benandonner:
   (c) Oonagh:

7. Rewrite the phrase: 'Finn spotted his arch nemesis Benandonner' in your own words.

My learning log While doing these activities: I found it _____ easy. I found it _____ challenging. I found it _____ interesting.

The **answers** are provided on *Teacher Page 3*.

6 · · · · · · Reading – Comprehension and Word Reading · · · · · · · · · · · · · · · · · Prim-Ed Publishing · · · · · · · · www.prim-ed.com

Pupil Page 3

The **Word Reading focus** of the page is indicated.

A list of the word reading concepts covered is on page x.

Word Reading **questions and activities** relating to the text on *Pupil Page 1* are provided. The main focus is the development of new vocabulary.

The **learning log** provides an opportunity for pupils to self-assess their completion of the activities.

The Myth of the Giant's Causeway – 3

1. Write a Standard English definition for each of these Scottish words. Use the text to help you.
   (a) wee _____ (b) laddie _____ (c) och _____

2. Write the root words for these words from the text.
   (a) thunderous _____ (b) approaching _____
   (c) reluctantly _____ (d) realised _____
   (e) sucking _____ (f) quickly _____

3. Find and write words in the text that come from:
   (a) a Latin word 'columna' meaning 'pillar'. _____
   (b) an Old English word 'wif' meaning 'woman'. _____
   (c) an Old French word 'journee' meaning 'day' or a 'day's travel'. _____

4. (a) Find two words in the text with the suffix '-ous'.
   (b) Write a sentence using both of these words.

5. Use a dictionary to write the meanings of these words.
   (a) jeer _____
   (b) reluctant _____
   (c) prevent _____

6. Write synonyms from the text for the words below.
   (a) ocean _____ (b) weary _____ (c) duvet _____
   (d) rock _____ (e) threw _____ (f) sprint _____
   (g) hat _____ (h) beverage _____ (i) error _____

My learning log Colour: I recognise / can't recognise the roots of words. I can / can't use a dictionary to write word definitions. I understand / need more practice on synonyms.

www.prim-ed.com · · · · · · · Prim-Ed Publishing · · · · · · · · · · · · Reading – Comprehension and Word Reading · · · · · · · 7

The **answers** are provided on *Teacher Page 3*.

Digital Assessment Tool

There is a digital assessment tool to accompany each book in the *Reading – Comprehension and Word Reading* series. This will enable teachers to monitor and track pupil progress. Teachers can download this assessment tool from the *Prim-Ed Publishing* website (www.prim-ed.com).

The home page of the download has the following features:

- Instructions for teachers;
- Quick-glance curriculum objectives and codes;
- Assessment by curriculum objectives; and
- Assessment by units in *Reading – Comprehension and Word Reading*.

Clicking the **Instructions for the teacher** icon provides an overview of the features of the download.

Clicking the **Quick-glance curriculum objectives and codes** icon shows the comprehension and word reading objectives from the curriculum and the codes that have been assigned to them in the book.

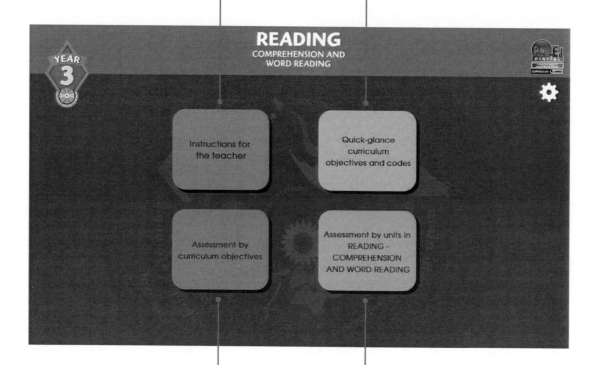

Clicking the **Assessment by curriculum objectives** icon displays each curriculum objective in a linear fashion, with advice and guidance to assess each one (more details are given on page vii).

Clicking the **Assessment by units in *Reading – Comprehension and Word Reading*** icon reveals an overview page allowing the teacher to click on the following options:

- Units (each individual unit in the book can be clicked);
- Formal Assessment (each of the three formal assessments can be clicked);
- Term (the three terms can be clicked); and
- End-of-Year (an overview of the pupil's yearly achievement).

Three categories and colour classifications of pupil progress are used throughout the assessment download. These categories are: working towards expectations (red), meeting expectations (orange) and exceeding expectations (green).

Teachers can assess by:

1. Curriculum objectives

- Click **Assessment by curriculum objectives** on the home page.

- Click on the code of the objective you are assessing. (Refer to the **Curriculum Objectives and Codes** on page xi, or click the quick-glance icon on the home page of the assessment tool and print them out.)

Type the pupils' names into the relevant column and save. This only has to be done once and the names will appear under every objective.

Record a description of the assessment used and the date of the assessment. Where applicable, the assessment activities in each unit of the book can be used to provide the evidence required to help teachers form an accurate picture of each pupil's progress. For example, page 10 presents an assessment activity based on the C5 objective and could be used as part of the evaluation.

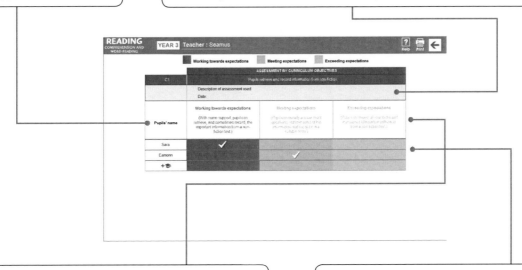

Read the advice and support under each category heading.

Click the box that best applies to each pupil's performance in relation to that objective.

To see a pupil's progress on the curriculum objectives that have been assessed to date, click the pupil's name and the following overview screen will be displayed:

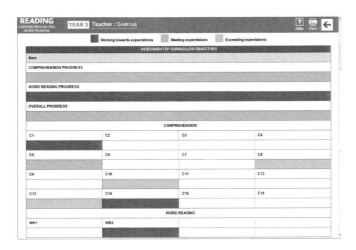

On this screen, which may be printed, the pupil's name is displayed. Progress in both comprehension and word reading are indicated by means of the appropriate colour. An overall progress colour is also displayed. Each curriculum code is displayed at the bottom of this page and the pupil's attainment in relation to this objective is indicated through the relevant colour. This allows teachers to see at a glance the objectives that require additional work.

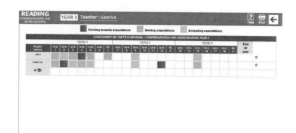

2. Units in *Reading – Comprehension and Word Reading*

- Click **Assessment by units in *Reading – Comprehension and Word Reading*** on the home page.

- Type in pupils' names.

(a) Click on the required unit. For example, by clicking on **Unit 1** the codes of the objectives to be assessed in that unit will appear at the top.

The pupils' names appear down the left-hand side. For each pupil, click the colour that best matches their achievement in relation to that objective. On returning to the page, an average score for that particular unit is displayed (as red, orange or green).

(b) Click on **FA1**, **FA2** or **FA3**, once the pupils have completed the relevant formal assessment. The following screen will be displayed.

Click each question the pupil got correct. A tick mark will be generated. Any questions that are not clicked (i.e. the incorrect ones) automatically receive an incorrect mark. The colour in the overall total bar at the base of the page indicates the pupil's performance.

(c) Click on **TERM** at the end of each term. An end-of-term overview will be displayed, showing a performance colour for both comprehension and word reading.

An overall average is also displayed, showing the combined progress in both comprehension and word reading. The results of the formal assessment for that term are also displayed on this screen. This screen can be printed for use in either pupil profile folders or parent-teacher meetings.

(d) Click on **End-of-Year** at the end of the school year. This will display each pupil's overall progress for the entire school year. A breakdown of progress for each term is displayed, as well as progress in comprehension and word reading over the three terms. An overall average is also generated. This entire page can be printed out and passed on to the next teacher of this pupil.

Three summative assessment units are included in each book, for pupils to take after every six units, or at the teacher's discretion.

The tests are based on the National Curriculum assessment guidelines.

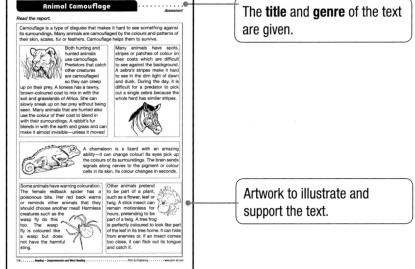

The **title** and **genre** of the text are given.

Artwork to illustrate and support the text.

Comprehension Assessment

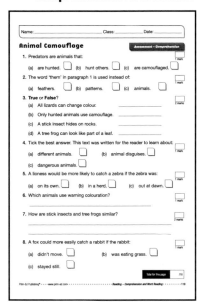

Word Reading Assessment

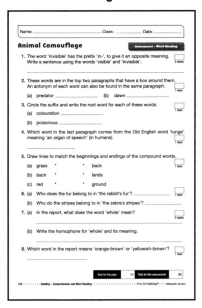

Each question is awarded a mark to a total of 20 marks across the two pages. Inferential questions and multi-part questions are awarded a higher mark than literal questions. Pupils' scores can be recorded on the **Pupil Record Sheet** on page xii. The results of each test can also be recorded on the digital download.

A **Teacher Information** page is provided to accompany each assessment unit.

The **title** and **genre** of the text are given.

The **breakdown of question type/content** and the **mark allocation** are provided in a table. Teachers might choose to photocopy this table for each pupil, ticking/circling the questions answered correctly and recording the marks gained in each assessment and overall.

Answers are provided. Some questions are open-ended and will need to be checked by the teacher.

Text Genres

Unit	Fiction or Non-fiction?	Genre
1. The Myth of the Giant's Causeway	fiction	myth
2. Whuppity Stoorie	fiction	fairy tale
3. Invaders and Settlers Timeline	non-fiction	timeline
4. Make Toad-in-the-Hole	non-fiction	recipe
5. Mr Miacca	fiction	folk tale
6. The Legends of King Arthur's Swords	fiction	legend
7. World Climatic Zones	non-fiction	explanation
8. Great British Artists	non-fiction	biography
9. Brazil	non-fiction	information text
10. Master of all Masters	fiction	folk tale/poem
11. The Hawk and the Grass	fiction	play
12. Boudicca	fiction	legend
13. Romans in Britain	non-fiction	discussion
14. The Ass, the Table and the Stick	fiction	fairy tale
15. St Collen and the Fairy King	fiction	legend
16. A Day in the Indus Valley	fiction	diary
17. A Holiday Suggestion	non-fiction	travel article
18. The Cycle of Water	non-fiction	poem

Word Reading Concepts

Unit 1: The Myth of the Giant's Causeway	Standard English	root words	word origins and meanings	suffix '-ous'	synonyms
Unit 2: Whuppity Stoorie	word meanings	suffix '-ly'	homophones	compound words	antonyms
Unit 3: Invaders and Settlers Timeline	compound words	suffixes '-ing', '-er', '-ed' and '-ion'	word meanings	root words	pronouns
Unit 4: Make Toad-in-the-Hole	root words and suffixes	word origins	prefix 'pre-'	homophones	command verbs
Unit 5: Mr Miacca	word meanings	Standard English	synonyms and antonyms	homophones	suffixes '-ly' and '-ed'
Unit 6: The Legends of King Arthur's Swords	suffix '-ly'	synonyms and antonyms	prefix 're-'	'ou' sound	homophones
Unit 7: World Climatic Zones	homophones	word origins and meanings	prefix 'trans-'	suffixes	root words
Unit 8: Great British Artists	specialist vocabulary	synonyms and antonyms	compound words	'k' sound spelt 'que'	prefix 'pre-' and suffix '-ous'
Unit 9: Brazil	root words	prefixes and suffixes	/ɪ/ sound spelt 'y'	homophones	adjectives
Unit 10: Master of all Masters	word origins and meanings	root words	homophones	antonyms	synonyms
Unit 11: The Hawk and the Grass	suffixes	adjectives	root words	specialist vocabulary	synonyms and antonyms
Unit 12: Boudicca	word origins and meanings	root words	suffix '-ly' and prefix 'in-'	/eɪ/ sound spelt 'ei', 'eigh' or 'ey'	antonyms
Unit 13: Romans in Britain	word origins and meanings	synonyms and antonyms	homophones	prefix 'in-'	suffix '-ation'
Unit 14: The Ass, the Table and the Stick	pronouns	negative prefixes	suffixes	adverbs	synonyms and antonyms
Unit 15: St Collen and the Fairy King	word origins and meanings	homonyms	adjectives and adverbs	suffix '-ly'	possessive apostrophes
Unit 16: A Day in the Indus Valley	word meanings	similes	contractions	/eɪ/ sound spelt 'ei', 'eigh' or 'ey'	antonyms using prefix 'un-'
Unit 17: A Holiday Suggestion	word origins and meanings	compound words	suffixes '-que', '-tion' and '-ous'	'ou' words	homophones
Unit 18: The Cycle of Water	root words	prefix 're-'	suffixes	suffix '-ation'	compound words

Curriculum Objectives and Codes

The following table shows the word reading and comprehension objectives from the reading domain of the English programmes of study. Each objective has been assigned a code. These codes are used throughout the book to assist teachers in planning their work. They are also used in the **Curriculum Links** and **Assessment** tables of the **Teacher Pages**.

Word Reading

WR1	Pupils apply their growing knowledge of root words, prefixes and suffixes (etymology and morphology) as listed in English Appendix 1, both to read aloud and to understand the meaning of new words they meet.
WR2	Pupils read further exception words, noting the unusual correspondences between spelling and sound, and where these occur in the word.

Comprehension

C1	Pupils retrieve and record information from non-fiction.
C2	Pupils participate in discussion about both books that are read to them and those they can read for themselves, taking turns and listening to what others say.
	Pupils develop positive attitudes to reading and an understanding of what they read by:
C3	Listening to and discussing a wide range of fiction, poetry, plays, non-fiction and reference books or textbooks.
C4	Reading books that are structured in different ways and reading for a range of purposes.
C5	Using dictionaries to check the meaning of words that they have read.
C6	Increasing their familiarity with a wide range of books, including fairy stories, myths and legends, and retelling some of these orally.
C7	Identifying themes and conventions in a wide range of books.
C8	Preparing poems and play scripts to read aloud and to perform, showing understanding through intonation, tone, volume and action.
C9	Discussing words and phrases that capture the reader's interest and imagination.
C10	Recognising some different forms of poetry.
	Pupils understand what they read, in books they can read independently, by:
C11	Checking that the text makes sense to them, discussing their understanding and explaining the meaning of words in context.
C12	Asking questions to improve their understanding of a text.
C13	Drawing inferences such as inferring characters' feelings, thoughts and motives from their actions, and justifying inferences with evidence.
C14	Predicting what might happen from details stated and implied.
C15	Identifying main ideas drawn from more than one paragraph and summarising them.
C16	Identifying how language, structure and presentation contribute to meaning.

Summative Assessment Units

The following table should be used to record pupils' scores on the three summative assessment units.

Summative Assessment									
	Why the Flies Bother the Cows			Farm Fresh Restaurant Review			Animal Camouflage		
Pupils' names	Comprehension (___/8)	Word Reading (___/12)	TOTAL (___/20)	Comprehension (___/10)	Word Reading (___/10)	TOTAL (___/20)	Comprehension (___/10)	Word Reading (___/10)	TOTAL (___/20)
	Date:	Date:	Date:	Date:	Date:	Date:	Date:	Date:	Date:

Termly Formative and Summative Assessment

Pupil Record Sheet

The following table should be used to record pupils' formative and summative assessments each term.

Year: **Term:**

Pupils' names	Red — Working towards expectations	Orange — Meeting expectations	Green — Exceeding expectations	Formative	Summative
	Date:	Date:	Date:		

Brief Description of Assessments Used

The Myth of the Giant's Causeway

Curriculum Links

Activity	Code	Objective	Outcome
Text	C2 C3 C6	• Participate in discussion about both books that are read to them and those they can read for themselves • Listen to and discuss a wide range of fiction • Increase their familiarity with a wide range of books, including myths and legends	• Can identify myths and talk about their key features
Comprehension	C7 C9 C13	• Identify themes and conventions in a wide range of books • Discuss words and phrases that capture the reader's interest and imagination • Draw inferences such as inferring characters' feelings, thoughts and motives from their actions, and justifying inferences with evidence	• Can explain the purpose of a myth • Can rewrite phrases in own words • Can infer how characters in a myth might feel
Word Reading	WR1	• Apply their growing knowledge of root words and suffixes	• Can determine the roots of words • Can recognise words with the suffix '-ous'

Additional Teacher Information

Definition of Terms

Myth
A myth is a story which explains a belief, practice or a natural phenomenon. A myth does not always have a basis in fact or a natural explanation.

Legend
Legends are told as though the events were actual historical events. Legends may or may not be based on an elaborated version of an historical event. Legends are usually about human beings, although gods may intervene in some way throughout the story.

Links to other Curriculum Areas

• Geography – The United Kingdom

Terminology for Pupils

myth
Standard English
root word
word origin
etymology
suffix
dictionary
synonym

Suggested Reading

• The story is available in an illustrated ebook format and in an animated video format by accessing these links:
<http://giantscausewaytickets.com/finn-mccool>
<http://vimeo.com/45569144>
• The story in picture book format: *Finn MacCool and the Giant's Causeway*, written by **John Dougherty** and illustrated by **Lee Cosgrove**

Text

Teacher Information

- The myth on page 5 is based on a story from Irish mythology which originated around the 3rd century AD.

Introduction

- Ask pupils if they have ever read, or have had read to them, a myth. Ask them the names of the myths and list them on the board. What features do myths have in common? Do pupils have a favourite myth?

Development

- Read and discuss the myth with pupils, as a whole class or in groups. Assist pupils to decode new words if necessary. Discuss the meaning of any new or unfamiliar words and phrases; e.g. pupils will probably need assistance to pronounce the names of the characters. Question individual pupils to gauge their understanding of what they have listened to or read. Pupils should also ask questions about parts of the text they are unsure of, in order to improve their understanding.

- During discussion of the myth, encourage pupils to employ courteous listening skills such as turn-taking and listening to the points of views of others. Pupils may like to compare the myth to others they have read or listened to.

- Look at photographs of the Giant's Causeway. Have any of the pupils visited this place? Locate the Giant's Causeway on a map and look at its proximity to Scotland. Pupils could also locate Lough Neagh and the Isle of Man.

Differentiated Individual/Paired/Group Work

- Look at cartoon strip versions of myths or other traditional tales. Discuss how text is minimal, and spoken or thought text is in speech or thought balloons.

- Ask pupils to split the text into six main parts. Pupils should create a cartoon strip, in six parts, to retell the myth.

- Less able pupils could create a cartoon strip with four parts, whilst more able pupils should aim to have eight parts for their cartoon strips.

Review

- Pupils should create their best work and share it with their group or class.

Comprehension

Teacher Information

- Pupils may need a dictionary to complete question 7.

Introduction

- Pupils take it in turns to retell the myth in their own words, sequencing the events correctly.

Development

- Discuss the comprehension activities on page 6, then allow pupils to complete the page independently.

- Compare their answers to questions that may have varied answers, especially questions 5–7. Pupils should justify their reasons for saying if this is the real reason the causeway exists.

Differentiated Individual/Paired/Group Work

- Question 7 asks pupils to rewrite a phrase in their own words. Ask pupils to choose other phrases from the text to rewrite in their own words; for example, 'Finn skedaddled home quick smart to tell his wife of his grave mistake.'

- Less able pupils should choose three phrases to rewrite. More able pupils could rewrite at least six phrases, or rewrite paragraphs in their own words.

Review

- As a class, compare pupils' rewritten phrases. Why did they choose the phrases they did?

Word Reading

Teacher Information

- The activities on page 7 focus on Standard English, root words, word origins, the suffix '-ous', definitions of words and synonyms.

Introduction

- Reread the text, but first explain to pupils that the focus will be on words. While reading, ask pupils to find and circle any words that are names. Explain that the names (i.e. proper nouns that start with a capital letter) might be nationalities, people, countries or places. After circling, sort the names into these four groups.

Development

- Look at words with the suffix '-ous'. Discuss that sometimes there is not an obvious root word; for example, 'poisonous' has the root word 'poison', but there is no root word for 'jealous'. Explain that whilst '-ous' can be added to many root words, '-our' is changed to '-or' before '-ous' is added; for example, humorous, glamorous.

- Ensure pupils are familiar with the terms 'synonym' and 'antonym'. Give some examples (happy: synonym is glad, antonym is sad). Elicit some examples from the pupils. Pupils suggest sentences for pairs of synonyms and antonyms, to be written onto the board; for example, happy = glad/sad. Ben was glad he had homework, but Krista was sad.

- Discuss the word reading activities on page 7, then allow pupils to complete the page independently.

Differentiated Individual/Paired/Group Work

- Provide pupils with words that have antonyms; for example, quick, happy, tired. Ask pupils to think of antonyms, and list them on the board.

- Less able pupils should be provided with a list of words from the text, and asked to write antonyms for them; for example, long, enemy, large, man, wife, loud.

- More able pupils should find their own words in the text, and then write antonyms for them.

Review

- As a class, compare the antonyms. Did pupils have different antonyms for the same word? For example, for the word 'large', pupils might have thought of 'small', 'tiny', 'little' or other words.

Assessment

C6	Pupils should rewrite the myth in their own words and in the correct sequence.
C13	Describe how the two giants felt at the end of the myth. Pupils should justify their inferences with evidence from the text.
WR1	Call out (or write on the board) the following words and have pupils write down the root words: roamed, leaving, thunderous, spotted, loudly, placing, quickly, decided

Answers

Comprehension

1. (b) explain a natural feature
2. Scotland and Northern Ireland
3. Possible answer: When Finn saw how big Benandonner really was up close he became worried and afraid.
4. Possible answer: Finn and Oonagh pretended Finn was their baby so Benandonner would be worried about how big Finn was compared to himself.
5. Possible answer: No, because giants aren't real and there is a geographical explanation for how the columns came to be there.
6. Possible answers:
    (a) brave, cocky, cheeky, strong, large
    (b) huge, aggressive, dim, red hair
    (c) clever, quick-witted, kind
7. Possible answer: Finn saw his greatest enemy Benandonner.

Word Reading

1. (a) small   (b) boy   (c) oh no
2. (a) thunder   (b) approach   (c) reluctant
   (d) realise   (e) suck   (f) quick
3. (a) column   (b) wife   (c) journey
4. (a) enormous, thunderous
   (b) Teacher check
5. Teacher check
6. (a) sea   (b) tired   (c) blanket
   (d) stone   (e) hurled/heaved   (f) run
   (g) bonnet   (h) drink   (i) mistake

The Myth of the Giant's Causeway – 1

Read this version of the myth.

Long ago, when giants roamed the earth, the Irish giant Finn McCool, who was tired of his Scottish enemy across the sea, decided to do something about it. The giants would often taunt and insult each other across the water and one day Finn became so angry that he gathered up a large clump of earth and hurled it towards his rival. However, the clump missed its target, instead becoming the Isle of Man and leaving the enormous hole to become the great Lough Neagh (the largest lake in the British Isles).

After another occasion of jeering and tormenting, Finn came up with a plan. He gathered many large stone columns and heaved them into the sea. The stones landed side by side, creating a stone bridge, or causeway, between the two nations.

Soon after, Finn spotted his arch nemesis Benandonner, The Red Man, and shouted a challenge to him. 'Come and fight me and let's settle this once and for all!' Finn stayed to watch The Red Man approach and soon realised his great mistake! As Benandonner came closer, Finn realised just how huge the giant really was ... much bigger than him! Finn skedaddled home quick smart to tell his wife of his grave mistake. By the time he'd finished explaining they could hear the thunderous footsteps of the approaching giant and feel the floor quaking beneath them.

At the giant's booming knock on their door, Finn's wife Oonagh hatched a plan. She shoved Finn into the giant-sized bath, covered him in blankets and placed a baby's toy in his hand and a bonnet on his head. She rushed to the door and greeted Benandonner explaining, 'What a pity you've just missed Finn! He's away hunting deer. Come in for a rest after your journey and you can wait for his return.' Oonagh offered the giant a drink while he waited.

When he had finished, Oonagh loudly asked him if he'd like to see their baby while he waited for Finn. Not knowing what else to do, Benandonner reluctantly agreed and followed Oonagh's lead through the house.

When she opened the door she greeted her baby, who was sucking his thumb and cooing under the blanket in the bathtub (of course it was Finn McCool himself). The giant Benandonner quickly excused himself, saying he needed to get some air. 'Och', thought the giant, 'if that's the size of the wee laddie I'd hate to see his father. I'll not wait for him to return!' And with that thought, Benandonner broke into a run all the way back home to Scotland. When he heard the giant run off, Finn thanked his quick-thinking and clever wife. As Benandonner thundered back across the causeway he made sure to tear the blocks up to prevent Finn from ever following him.

The remnants of the Giant's Causeway can be seen to this day on the north-east coast of Northern Ireland (County Antrim).

| My learning log | When I read this myth, I could read: | ☐ all of it. ☐ most of it. ☐ parts of it. |

The Myth of the Giant's Causeway – 2

1. This myth was told to:

   (a) make people laugh. ⬜

   (b) explain a natural feature. ⬜

   (c) warn children of danger. ⬜

2. Which two countries are mentioned in the text?

   _____

3. At what point in the story did Finn regret building the causeway? Explain why.

   _____

   _____

4. How did Finn and his wife Oonagh trick the giant Benandonner?

   _____

   _____

5. Do you think this story tells the real version of how the causeway came to be there? Give reasons for your response.

   _____

   _____

6. Use the text to help you describe the three characters. Think about their physical traits as well as their personalities.

   (a) Finn McCool: _____

   (b) Benandonner: _____

   (c) Oonagh: _____

7. Rewrite the phrase 'Finn spotted his arch nemesis Benandonner' in your own words.

   _____

   _____

My learning log	While doing these activities:		
	I found Q _____ easy.	I found Q _____ challenging.	I found Q _____ interesting.

The Myth of the Giant's Causeway – 3

1. Write a Standard English definition for each of these Scottish words. Use the text to help you.

   (a) wee _____   (b) laddie _____   (c) och _____

2. Write the root words for these words from the text.

   (a) thunderous _____   (b) approaching _____

   (c) reluctantly _____   (d) realised _____

   (e) sucking _____   (f) quickly _____

3. Find and write words in the text that come from:

   (a) the Latin word 'columna' meaning 'pillar'.   _____

   (b) the Old English word 'wif' meaning 'woman'.   _____

   (c) the Old French word 'journee' meaning a 'day's travel'. _____

4. (a) Find two words in the text with the suffix '-ous'.

   _____   _____

   (b) Write a sentence using both of these words.

   _____

   _____

5. Use a dictionary to write the meanings of these words.

   (a) jeer _____

   (b) reluctant _____

   (c) prevent _____

6. Write synonyms from the text for the words below.

   (a) ocean _____   (b) weary _____   (c) duvet _____

   (d) rock _____   (e) threw _____   (f) sprint _____

   (g) hat _____   (h) beverage _____ (i) error _____

My learning log	Colour:	I recognise / can't recognise the roots of words.
		I can / can't use a dictionary to write word definitions.
		I understand / need more practice on synonyms.

Whuppity Stoorie

Curriculum Links

Activity	Code	Objective	Outcome
Text	C2 C3 C6	• Participate in discussion about both books that are read to them and those they can read for themselves • Listen to and discuss a wide range of fiction • Increase their familiarity with a wide range of books, including fairy stories	• Can identify fairy stories and talk about their key features
Comprehension	C5 C9 C11 C14	• Use dictionaries to check the meaning of words that they have read • Discuss words and phrases that capture the reader's interest and imagination • Check that the text makes sense to them, discuss their understanding and explain the meaning of words in context • Predict what might happen from details stated and implied	• Can explain the meanings of words • Can rewrite phrases in own words • Can answer questions about the text • Can predict what happened to Whuppity Stoorie
Word Reading	WR1 WR2	• Apply their growing knowledge of suffixes • Read further exception words, noting the unusual correspondences between spelling and sound	• Can recognise words with the suffix '-ly' • Can distinguish homophones

Additional Teacher Information

Definition of Terms

Narrative
A narrative is a framework which tells a story. A narrative includes a title, an orientation (setting, time and characters), a complication involving the main character(s), a sequence of events, a resolution to the complication and an ending showing what changed and what the characters have learnt.

Fairy tale
Fairy tales are usually about elves, dragons, hobgoblins, sprites or magical beings and are often set in the distant past. Fairy tales usually begin with the phrase 'Once upon a time ...' and end with the words '... and they lived happily ever after'. Charms, disguises and talking animals may also appear in fairy tales.

Links to other Curriculum Areas
• History – How people lived in the past

Terminology for Pupils

fairy tale
dictionary
phrase
chant
suffix
homophone
compound word
antonym

Suggested Reading

• The story of *Rumpelstiltskin* is available in a YouTube™ video with a voiceover reading. <https://www.youtube.com/watch?v=apZu01nwSvQ>
• Explore the telling of the story on Education Scotland's website. <http://www.educationscotland.gov.uk/scotlandsstories/whuppitystourie/index.asp> Discuss the language used in this version.
• A Collection of Scottish Fairy Tales – *An Illustrated Treasury of Scottish Folk and Fairy Tales* by **Theresa Breslin** and **Kate Leiper**

Text

Teacher Information

- The fairy tale on page 11 is based on a story from Scottish folklore and shares a similar theme with the better-known tale 'Rumpelstiltskin'.

Introduction

- Ask pupils if they are familiar with the fairy tale 'Rumplestiltskin'. Have a discussion about this fairy tale and tell the pupils that they will be reading and discussing another fairy tale that has a similar theme to 'Rumplestiltskin'.

Development

- Read and discuss the text with pupils, as a whole class or in groups. Assist pupils to decode new words if necessary. Discuss the meaning of any new or unfamiliar words and phrases; for example, pupils will probably need assistance to pronounce the names of the characters. Question individual pupils to gauge their understanding of what they have listened to or read. Pupils should also ask questions about parts of the text they are unsure of, in order to improve their understanding.

- During discussion of the fairy tale, encourage pupils to employ courteous listening skills such as turn-taking and listening to the points of views of others. Pupils may like to compare the fairy tale to others they have read or listened to.

- Pupils should have a version of 'Rumpelstiltskin' read to them. They should discuss the similarities and differences between the two fairy tales. The similarities and differences could be written onto the board.

Differentiated Individual/Paired/Group Work

- Pupils should write a review of the two fairy tales, stating which one they prefer and why.

- Less able pupils should state at least two reasons why they prefer one fairy tale to the other, and more able pupils should state at least five reasons. All pupils should justify their reasons with evidence from the text.

Review

- Pupils should read their reviews to their group. The class could vote on which of the two fairy stories is their favourite.

Comprehension

Teacher Information

- Pupils might need a dictionary to complete questions 3 and 7.

Introduction

- Discuss the themes that this fairy tale has in common with many other fairy tales: a tale of woe, an evil character who takes advantage of an unfortunate situation, magic spells, good triumphing over evil, the main character living happily ever after.

Development

- Remind pupils how to use a dictionary efficiently; i.e. alphabetical order and retrieval by 1st, 2nd and 3rd letters. Give each pupil, or pair of pupils, a dictionary. Write words from the text onto the board for pupils to find.

- In paragraph 8, Whuppity Stoorie chants a spell and sprinkles some magic to make the sow well. Discuss the things that might have been in the spell; what words and phrases might Whuppity Stoorie have used? List pupils' suggestions on the board.

- Discuss the comprehension activities on page 12, then allow pupils to complete the page independently.

Differentiated Individual/Paired/Group Work

- Pupils should work in mixed ability groups of three to rehearse the dialogue and act out the story as a play. In each group, one pupil should be the narrator, one the goodwife and one Whuppity Stoorie. Pupils could swap parts, to allow each pupil in the group to play each part.

Review

- In their group, pupils should discuss which part was their favourite to play. Which part was the easiest? hardest? funniest?

Word Reading

Teacher Information

- The activities on page 13 focus on dictionary use, the suffix '-ly', homophones, compound words and antonyms.

Introduction

- Reread the text, but first explain to pupils that the focus will be on words. While reading the text, ask pupils to circle any compound words. Remind pupils that compound words are two words joined together to create a new word.

Development

- Look at words with the suffix '-ly'. Tell pupils that this suffix is added to an adjective to form an adverb. Explain that usually the suffix is added straight onto the end of most root words; for example, sadly, finally. However, there are exceptions, which should also be explained to the pupils:

  (1) If the root word ends in '-y' with a consonant letter before it, the 'y' is changed to 'i', but only if the root word has more than one syllable; for example, happily.

  (2) If the root word ends with '-le', the '-le' is changed to '-ly'; for example, simply.

  (3) If the root word ends with '-ic', '-ally' is added rather than just '-ly'; for example, basically. An exception is 'publicly'.

  (4) The words truly, duly and wholly.

- Ensure pupils are familiar with the term 'homophone'. Give some examples (berry/bury, scene/seen, plain/plane). Elicit some examples from the pupils. Pupils suggest sentences for pairs of homophones, to be written onto the board; for example, main/mane = He is walking down the <u>main</u> road./That horse has a beautiful <u>mane</u>.

- Ensure pupils are familiar with the terms 'synonym' and 'antonym'. Give some examples (happy: synonym is glad, antonym is sad). Elicit some examples from the pupils. Pupils suggest sentences for pairs of synonyms and antonyms, to be written onto the board; for example, happy = glad/sad. Ben was <u>glad</u> he had homework, but Krista was <u>sad</u>.

- Discuss the word reading activities on page 13, then allow pupils to complete the page independently.

Differentiated Individual/Paired/Group Work

- In pairs, pupils should find and list words with an '-ly' suffix. They should then attempt to sort them according to the following table headings.

- More able pupils should aim to create a longer list than less able pupils.

'-ly' suffix	Examples
'-ly' added onto end of root word	carefully, kindly, sadly
'y' changes to 'i' before adding '-ly'	happily, merrily, prettily
'-le' of root word changes to '-ly'	gently, simply, humbly
'-ally' is added to root words ending in '-ic'	basically, frantically

Review

- As a class, compare pupils' lists of '-ly' words.

Assessment

C5	Present the following list of words to the pupils and ask them to write each in a sentence: distraught, cottage, crooked, velvet, sprinkle, protest, spiteful, lighthearted
C14	Ask the pupils to predict what might have happened to Whuppity Stoorie at the end of the text. Pupils should continue the story, writing in the same style. They should add at least one more paragraph to tell what Whuppity Stoorie did next.
WR2	Present the following list of words to the pupils and ask them to write a suitable homophone – a word with the same sound, but different spelling and meaning: berry, break, here, whether, scene, mist, piece, meddle

Answers

Comprehension

1. Teacher check - answers will vary.
2. Teacher check - answers will vary.
3. Very worried and upset
4. Possible answer: Because the pig was sick, and it was her only hope of making any money to support her family.
5. (a) Possible answer: the word 'foolish' implies that the woman will have to pay a great price to the fairy.
   (b) Possible answer: if the woman can guess the fairy's name, she may not lose her son.
6. Teacher check - answers will vary.
7. (a) Possible answer: having difficulties in the future.
   (b) Possible answer: sad stories.
   (c) Possible answer: feeling relieved and unburdened.

Word Reading

1. (b) superior
2. (a) a long stick used as support when walking
   (b) a person's body shape
   (c) a prolonged, high-pitched cry of pain
3. (a) normally, tightly, gratefully, smartly
   (b) joyously   (c) Teacher check
4. (a) wail   (b) heard   (c) right
   (d) son   (e) there   (f) some
   (g) heal   (h) through   (i) for
5. (a) goodwife   (b) anything
   (c) myself   (d) lighthearted
6. (a) hard   (b) ugly   (c) lighter
   (d) future   (e) old   (f) smartly
   (g) quick   (h) husband   (i) worse

Whuppity Stoorie – 1

Read this Scottish version of the fairy tale.

There once was a woman, the goodwife of Kittlerumpit, who was facing some hard times. She was all alone with her infant child as her husband had gone out one day and never returned. To make matters even worse, her only hope of making a living, the pregnant sow she had in the yard, was sick and close to death.

The goodwife became distraught as she worried for her future and the future of her baby. She sat by her cottage with the child in her arms and began to cry and wail in despair.

Looking up for just a moment, the goodwife noticed a strange figure approaching. The figure came closer and the goodwife could make out that it was a small and crooked old woman, very smartly dressed in a green, velvet frock and a crisp, white apron. The goodwife also took note of the large staff the woman used to help her walk. As she approached, the woman spoke to the goodwife.

'Now save your tales of woe. I know all about your husband and your sow and I'm here to tell you I can heal her. Would you like that?'

'Oh yes please!' replied the goodwife gratefully. 'It'll mean so much to myself and the wee one.'

'Aye, very well then. But tell me, what'll you give me in return, I ask?'

'Oh anything, anything at all', the foolish woman responded.

With a quick chant and a sprinkle of magic, the pig was up and eating in no time.

The goodwife felt so relieved and asked the woman, 'How will I ever repay you?'

'Well there's just one thing I'll ask for, your wee bairn.' At the goodwife's cries of protest the woman explained. 'Under the law I live by, I cannot take him until the third day, and not then, if by chance you can tell me my right name.' And off she went with a smug smile.

The goodwife held her baby so tightly and wept the entire first day. On the second day she decided to walk with the wee one in the woods. On and on she walked in a daze until she heard a voice. She spotted the very woman through the trees spinning away on her wheel and babbling to herself.

'Ah a new baby old Whuppity Stoorie'll have at sun up tomorrow!' she said, full of delight.

At that the woman rushed home with a much lighter heart, to rest up before the spiteful fairy returned to claim her beloved son.

The goodwife was a lighthearted woman normally and she decided to play a trick on the ugly old fairy. When she came to collect the baby, the goodwife kept up her crying and wailing and only at the very last moment did she speak the name 'Whuppity Stoorie'. At that, the shocked fairy jumped a mile into the air and when she landed she whirled around and ran off screaming with furious rage. The goodwife laughed and hugged and kissed her baby joyously.

My learning log	When I read this fairy tale, I could read:	☐ all of it.	☐ most of it.	☐ parts of it.

Whuppity Stoorie – 2

1. What do you think happened to the goodwife after this story?

_____

_____

2. What do you think happened to Whuppity Stoorie?

_____

_____

3. Use a dictionary to define the word 'distraught'.

_____

4. Explain why the woman became so worried about the future of herself and her baby.

_____

_____

5. Explain how these phrases can help the reader predict what might happen in the story.

(a) … anything at all', the foolish woman responded.

_____

(b) … and not then, if by chance you can tell me my right name.

_____

6. Write a chant the fairy might have said to make the sow well again.

_____

_____

7. Explain the meanings of the phrases.

(a) facing hard times _____

(b) tales of woe _____

(c) lighter heart _____

My learning log	While doing these activities:		
	I found Q _____ easy.	I found Q _____ challenging.	I found Q _____ interesting.

Whuppity Stoorie – 3

1. The fairy had a 'smug' smile. This means:

   (a) uncertain ☐ (b) superior ☐ (c) lopsided ☐

2. Use a dictionary to write the meanings of these words.

   (a) staff _____

   (b) figure _____

   (c) wail _____

3. (a) Circle the words ending with the suffix '-ly'.

normally	tightly	only	gratefully	smartly	ugly

   (b) Find and write one more word from the text with the suffix '-ly'.

   _____

   (c) Write a sentence using two of these '-ly' words.

   _____

4. Write homophones from the text for the words below.

   (a) whale _____ (b) herd _____ (c) write _____

   (d) sun _____ (e) their _____ (f) sum _____

   (g) heel _____ (h) threw _____ (i) four _____

5. Find four compound words in the text. The first letter is given.

   (a) g_____   (b) a_____

   (c) m_____   (d) I_____

6. Write antonyms from the text for the words below.

   (a) easy _____ (b) pretty _____ (c) heavier _____

   (d) past _____ (e) young _____ (f) scruffily _____

   (g) slow _____ (h) wife _____ (i) better _____

My learning log	*Colour:*	I ⎡can⎤ / ⎡can't⎤ use a dictionary to write word definitions.
		I ⎡can⎤ / ⎡can't⎤ recognise compound words.
		I ⎡understand⎤ / ⎡need more practice on⎤ antonyms.

Invaders and Settlers – Timeline

Curriculum Links

Activity	Code	Objective	Outcome
Text	C2	• Participate in discussion about both books that are read to them and those they can read for themselves	• Can identify timelines and talk about their key features
	C3	• Listen to and discuss a wide range of non-fiction	
	C4	• Read books (texts) that are structured in different ways	
Comprehension	C1	• Retrieve and record information from non-fiction	• Can retrieve and record ideas and information on the various invaders and rulers of Britain
	C5	• Use dictionaries to check the meaning of words that they have read	
	C13	• Draw inferences and justify inferences with evidence	• Can explain the meanings of words
	C15	• Identify main ideas drawn from more than one paragraph and summarise these	• Can infer things about Lindisfarne Island
Word Reading	WR1	• Apply their growing knowledge of root words and suffixes	• Can recognise root words and a range of suffixes

Additional Teacher Information

Definition of Terms

Timeline

A timeline is a visual representation of historical events in the form of a line with date divisions and important events marked on it. It may also be a simple list of important dates and events.

Links to other Curriculum Areas

• Geography – The United Kingdom and Europe
• History – The Roman Empire and its impact on Britain; Britain's settlement by Anglo-Saxons; The Viking and Anglo-Saxon struggle for the Kingdom of England

Terminology for Pupils

timeline
summary
main idea
infer
compound word
suffix
syllable
vowel
consonant
sentence
dictionary
root word

Suggested Reading

• *The Usborne History of Britain* by **Ruth Brocklehurst**
• *Anglo-Saxons and Vikings* by **Hazel Maskell** and **Dr. Abigail Wheatley**
• Two websites with British history timelines including pictures, photographs and more detailed information:
  <http://resources.woodlands-junior.kent.sch.uk/homework/timeline.html>
  <http://primaryhomeworkhelp.co.uk/timeline.html>

Text

Teacher Information

- The timeline on page 17 very briefly outlines the different peoples that invaded and/or settled in Britain from around AD 43 to AD 1066.

Introduction

- The teacher should explain that the timeline shows events in chronological order, starting from the year AD 43.

Development

- Read and discuss the text with pupils, as a whole class or in groups. Assist pupils to decode new words if necessary. Discuss the meaning of any new or unfamiliar words and phrases. For example, pupils will probably need assistance to pronounce the names of the places and people. Question individual pupils to gauge their understanding of what they have listened to or read. Pupils should also ask questions about parts of the text they are unsure of, in order to improve their understanding of it.

- Ask one of the pupils to volunteer. Draw a timeline on the board, starting at their year of birth and ending with the current year, with a line for every year in-between. Interview the pupil to discover what they did during each year of their life. Write their answers onto the timeline; for example, Georgia broke her leg, Georgia's brother Thomas was born, Georgia went on holiday to France. Ask other pupils to help; for example, When we were in Year One we went on a trip to London Zoo. For the years the pupil is too young to remember, pupils should suggest events; for example, Georgia learnt to walk, Georgia spoke her first word.

Differentiated Individual/Paired/Group Work

- Pupils should write a timeline for their own life, like Georgia's.
- Less able pupils could write one event for each year, whilst more able pupils should aim for at least three events per year.

Review

- Pupils should share their timelines in a small group.

Comprehension

Teacher Information

- Some of the questions require that pupils have some historical and geographical knowledge.

Introduction

- Pupils take it in turns to tell, in their own words, what happened at each point on the timeline.

Development

- Discuss the comprehension activities on page 18, before pupils complete the page independently. Compare their answers to questions that may have varied answers, especially question 3. Pupils could work in pairs or small groups to find the information in the text.

Differentiated Individual/Paired/Group Work

- Show pupils artists' images of Lindisfarne Island from the timeline era.
- Pupils should use the information from the text, plus the Internet, to write a fact file about Lindisfarne at the time of the Viking raiders.
- Less able pupils should write five or six facts about Lindisfarne and more able pupils at least twelve.

Review

- Pupils should share the facts they discovered with their group.

Word Reading

Teacher Information

- The activities on page 19 focus on compound words, suffixes, dictionary definitions, root words and pronouns.

Introduction

- Reread the text, but first explain to pupils that the focus will be on words. While reading, ask pupils to find and circle any words that are names; i.e. start with upper case letters. After circling, sort the names into groups, to tell what kind of names they are; for example, countries, kingdoms, continents, religions.

Development

- Discuss and list words which end with the suffix '-ion', specifically the spelling '-tion'. This spelling is used if the root word ends in 't' or 'te'; for example, invention, injection, action, hesitation, completion. Sort the words according to whether the root word ends in 't' or 'te'. There are some exceptions; for example, the words 'attend' and 'intend' both end in 'd', but add the '-tion' suffix to become 'attention' and 'intention'.

- Tell pupils that when a suffix is added to a word with more than one syllable, and the last syllable is stressed and ends in one vowel and one consonant, the consonant is doubled before adding the suffix; for example, controlled, beginner, forgetting.

- Discuss the word reading activities on page 19, then allow pupils to complete the page independently.

Differentiated Individual/Paired/Group Work

- In pairs, pupils should find and list words with the '-ion' suffix; for example, action, comprehension, discussion. They should then sort them according to whether the endings are '-tion', '-sion' or '-ssion' and place them in a table.

- Less able pupils should try and find four words for each column of the table, whilst more able pupils could find a lot more.

- More able pupils could also try and work out why the endings differ: '-tion' is added if the root word ends in 't' or 'te'; '-sion' is added if the root word ends in 'd' or 'se'; and '-ssion' is added if the root word ends in 'ss' or 'mit'.

Review

- As a class, compare pupils' lists of '-ion' words. Which of the suffixes has the greatest number of words?

Assessment

C5	Write a definition for each of the following words from the text: invasion, boundary, shore, longship, monastery, conquer
C15	Ask the pupils to write a synopsis of the timeline. The synopsis needs to include one sentence to explain what happened at each point on the timeline.
WR1	Call out (or write on the board) the following words and have pupils write the root of each word: invasion, occupation, fighting, northern, territories, controlled, arriving, addition

Answers

Comprehension

1. Possible answer: From around AD 43 Britain was invaded and settled by different groups of people who came from across the sea.

2. Approximately. Possible answer: Because it's difficult to know historical dates for certain unless there are official records.

3. Possible answer:

Romans	Anglo-Saxons and Jutes	Vikings	Normans
• invaded Britain 3 times • returned to Italy after around 400 years of occupation • built Hadrian's wall as a northern boundary • defended Britain against raiders from Europe and Ireland	• came from Denmark and Northern Germany around AD 450 • established seven kingdoms across the country	• came to Britain from around AD 793 • raided Lindisfarne Island and killed many monks • began to settle and control lands called The Danelaw • King Canute ruled from 1016-1035	• William of Normandy invaded in 1066 • began 200 years of Norman rule in England
~ 1 970 years ago	~ 1 565 years ago	~ 1 220 years ago	~ 950 years ago

4. Possible answer: The island was unprepared for an attack and it was a religious/Christian place.

5. Britain, Ireland, Italy, Denmark, Germany, England, Norway, France

6. The Danelaw

Word Reading

1. (a) homelands   (b) longships
   (c) timeline/throughout   (d) without

2. (a) forgetting   (b) beginner   (c) preferred
   (d) controlled

3. (a) –ion   (b) Teacher check

4. (a) relating to the Celts or their language
   (b) the geographical and cultural region comprising of Norway, Sweden and Denmark
   (c) a building occupied by a community of monks

5. (a) remain   (b) success   (c) Rome
   (d) north   (e) control   (f) defend

6. The Vikings

7. Possible answer: The words replace 'the Vikings' so the text isn't too repetitive.

Invaders and Settlers – Timeline – 1

Read this historical timeline.

~ AD 43	The third (and at last successful) Roman invasion of Britain results in around 400 years of Roman occupation. After fighting for many years, the Celtic people concede to the Romans. Hadrian's wall marks the northern boundary of Roman-controlled Britain.
~ AD 350–400	Roman soldiers fight off raiders who come over the sea from Europe and Ireland, defending Britain's shores.
~ AD 410	Roman occupation of Britain ends when Romans return to Italy to join the defence of their Empire's other territories against foreign invaders.
~ AD 450	Anglo-Saxon and Jute invaders come from their homelands (present-day Denmark and northern Germany) and settle. British people are unable to defend their lands without the assistance of the Romans.
by ~ AD 600	The Anglo-Saxons and Jutes establish seven Kingdoms which span across the country: Sussex, Kent, Essex, Mercia, East Anglia, Northumbria and Wessex. The Christian religion spreads throughout Britain.
~ AD 793	The first Viking raiders come to Britain from Scandinavia. Vikings sail their longships to Lindisfarne Island where they kill many monks and take the valuables from the monastery.
~ AD 793–1018	Vikings continue to raid and then begin to settle in Britain. Kingdoms fall to the Vikings and a large part of Viking-controlled England becomes known as The Danelaw.
~ AD 1016–1035	King Canute (The Great) becomes the ruler of England (in addition to Denmark and Norway) after arriving with thousands of Viking soldiers to conquer the remaining Anglo-Saxon kingdoms.
AD 1042–1066	King Edward the confessor returns Anglo-Saxon rule to the country.
28 September AD 1066	After Edward's death, William of Normandy (France) invades England and begins a period of around 200 years of Norman rule.

My learning log	When I read this timeline, I could read:	☐ all of it. ☐ most of it. ☐ parts of it.

Invaders and Settlers – Timeline – 2

1. Write a short summary which captures the main idea of the timeline.

_____

_____

_____

2. What does the curly line before the dates mean? Why do you think it is used?

_____

_____

3. Write some information from the text about each different 'group' into the table below. In the last row, write approximately how many years ago this 'group' first came to Britain.

Romans	Anglo-Saxons and Jutes	Vikings	Normans
~ 1 970 years ago	~	~	~

4. What can you infer about Lindisfarne Island from the information in the timeline?

_____

_____

5. List all of the countries mentioned in the timeline.

_____

6. What was the Viking-controlled region of England once known as?

_____

My learning log	While doing these activities:		
	I found Q _____ easy.	I found Q _____ challenging.	I found Q _____ interesting.

Invaders and Settlers – Timeline – 3

1. Find four compound words in the text. The first letter is given.

   (a) h_____

   (b) l_____

   (c) t_____

   (d) w_____

2. When you add a suffix to a word with more than one syllable, and the last syllable is stressed and ends in one vowel and one consonant, double the consonant before adding the suffix.

   (a) forget + ing = _____

   (b) begin + er = _____

   (c) prefer + ed = _____

   (d) control + ed = _____

3. (a) Write the suffix that these three words have in common.

   invasion   occupation   addition   Suffix = _____

   (b) Write these words in sentences.

   invasion: _____

   occupation: _____

4. Use a dictionary to write the meanings of these words.

   (a) Celtic _____

   (b) Scandinavia _____

   (c) monastery _____

5. Write the root word for each of these words from the text.

   (a) remaining _____

   (b) successful _____

   (c) Roman _____

   (d) northern _____

   (e) controlled _____

   (f) defending _____

6. In the text about Vikings (~ AD 793), who do the words 'their' and 'they' refer to?

   _____

7. Explain why these words are used here.

   _____

My learning log	*Colour:*	I can / can't add and spell suffixes correctly.
		I can / can't use a dictionary to write word definitions.
		I understand / need more practice on root words.

Make Toad-in-the-Hole

Curriculum Links

Activity	Code	Objective	Outcome
Text	C2 C3 C4	• Participate in discussion about both books that are read to them and those they can read for themselves • Listen to and discuss a wide range of non-fiction • Read books (texts) that are structured in different ways	• Can identify recipes and talk about their key features
Comprehension	C1 C5	• Retrieve and record information from non-fiction • Use dictionaries to check the meaning of words that they have read	• Can retrieve and record information from a recipe • Can explain the meanings of words
Word Reading	WR1 WR2	• Apply their growing knowledge of root words, prefixes and suffixes • Read further exception words, noting the unusual correspondences between spelling and sound	• Can recognise root words and a range of prefixes and suffixes • Can distinguish homophones

Additional Teacher Information

Definition of Terms

Text
A book or other written or printed work, regarded in terms of its content rather than its physical form.

Recipe
A recipe is a procedure or set of instructions for preparing a particular dish, including a list of the ingredients required. A procedure tells how to make or do something. It uses clear, concise language and command verbs. A recipe is an informational text.

Paragraph
A distinct section of a piece of writing, usually dealing with a single theme and indicated by a new line, indentation or numbering.

Links to other Curriculum Areas

• PSHE — Diet for a healthy lifestyle
• Design and technology – Cooking and nutrition

Terminology for Pupils

recipe
text
paragraph
sentence
heading
dictionary
root word
suffix
prefix
homophone
command verb
instruction

Suggested Reading

• *The International Cookbook for Kids* by **Matthew Locricchio**
• *Quick and Easy Traditional Tea-Time Bakes (Family Favourites Book 1)* [Kindle Edition] by **Christina Wilton**
• *Traditional Old English (British) Recipes* [Kindle Edition] by **B. Thomas-Smith** (teacher reference)
• *The Illustrated Encyclopedia of British Cooking: A Classic Collection of Best-loved Traditional Recipes from the Countries of the British Isles with 1500 Beautiful Step-by-Step Photographs* by **Georgina Campbell** and **Christopher Trotter** (teacher reference)

Text

Teacher Information

- This recipe has also been called 'sausage toad' and 'frog-in-the-hole'. The history of this recipe dates back to 1861 where a similar one was made using cheaper 'bits and pieces' of meat and leftover stewed meat. A 1940s version used during the war used Spam™ instead of sausages. A similar, earlier version dating back to 1747 was called Pigeons-in-a-hole and used pigeon as the meat ingredient.
- Adult supervision is needed if the pupils are going to use the recipe to make the dish. Care should always be taken with hot equipment.
- Recipes are non-fiction texts that impart information. The structure is different to other non-fiction texts.

Introduction

- Colour photographs of toad-in-the-hole (from the Internet) or homemade toad-in-the-hole could be shown (or tasted!) by pupils prior to reading the text. Some pupils may already be familiar with toad-in-the-hole.

Development

- Read and discuss the text with the pupils, as a whole class or in groups. Assist pupils to decode new words if necessary. Question individual pupils to gauge their understanding of what they have listened to or read. Pupils should also ask questions about parts of the text they are unsure of, in order to improve their understanding.
- Discuss the meaning of any new or unfamiliar words and phrases, as some vocabulary is subject-specific relating to recipes, such as 'traditional', 'preparation', 'ingredients', 'casserole', 'approximately' and 'evaluation'.
- Discuss the layout of the procedure/recipe with pupils so they can see how numbered, concise steps make it easier to follow the instructions. The instructions usually begin with an imperative (command) verb.

Differentiated Individual/Paired/Group Work

- Pupils write a procedure for completing a simple food-related task; for example, making a glass of orange cordial, making a cheese sandwich, making a slice of toast.
- Less able pupils could work in pairs to write their instructions.
- More able pupils need to have at least six steps to complete their task.

Review

- Pupils should read their instructions to their group, for the pupils to act out. Do the pupils think the instructions will work? Were they too hard to follow? Were there parts missing?

Comprehension

Teacher Information

- Pupils may need a dictionary to complete questions 4 and 8.

Introduction

- Discuss the structure of the recipe. Talk about why the 'Ingredients' and 'Equipment and Utensils' sections are useful, and why these things need to be collected before making a recipe. Discuss why the steps in the 'Method' section make it easier to follow the recipe.

Development

- Remind pupils how to use a dictionary efficiently; i.e. alphabetical order and retrieval by 1st, 2nd and 3rd letters. Give each pupil, or pair of pupils, a dictionary. Write words from the text onto the board for pupils to find.
- Discuss the comprehension activities on page 24, then allow pupils to complete the page independently. Compare their answers to questions that may have varied answers, especially question 3.

Differentiated Individual/Paired/Group Work

- Give pairs of pupils the twelve points of the recipe, cut up into twelve separate sections, without the number labels. Ask them to place the twelve steps in the correct order.
- Less able pairs could just be given steps 1, 2, 3, 10, 11 and 12 to sequence.

Review

- As a class, discuss whether any of the steps were difficult to place in the correct order. Why was this?

Word Reading

Teacher Information

- The activities on page 25 focus on a variety of suffixes, root words, the prefix 'pre-', homophones and command (imperative) verbs.

Introduction

- Reread the text, but first explain to pupils that the focus will be on words. While reading, ask pupils to find and circle any words that are used to give instructions or commands. Tell pupils these words are called imperative or command verbs. Ask pupils to list the command verbs they found. Why are they often at the start of sentences?

Development

- Look at words with the suffix '-ous'. Discuss that sometimes there is not an obvious root word; for example, 'poisonous' has the root word 'poison', but there is no root word for 'jealous'. Explain that whilst '-ous' can be added to many root words, '-our' is changed to '-or' before '-ous' is added; for example, humorous, glamorous.

- Look at words with the suffix '-ly'. Tell pupils that this suffix is added to an adjective to form an adverb. Explain that usually the suffix is added straight onto the end of most root words; for example, sadly, finally. However, there are exceptions, which should also be explained to the pupils:

  (1) If the root word ends in '-y' with a consonant letter before it, the 'y' is changed to 'i', but only if the root word has more than one syllable; for example, happily.

  (2) If the root word ends with '-le', the '-le' is changed to '-ly'; for example, simply.

  (3) If the root word ends with '-ic', '-ally' is added rather than just '-ly'; for example, basically. An exception is 'publicly'.

  (4) The words truly, duly and wholly.

- Discuss and list words which end with the suffix '-ion', specifically the spelling '-tion'. This spelling is used if the root word ends in 't' or 'te'; for example, invention, injection, action, hesitation, completion. Sort the words according to whether the root word ends in 't' or 'te'. There are some exceptions; for example, the words 'attend' and 'intend' both end in 'd', but add the '-tion' suffix to become 'attention' and 'intention'.

- Ensure pupils are familiar with the term 'homophone'. Give some examples (berry/bury, scene/seen, plain/plane). Elicit some examples from the pupils. Pupils suggest sentences for pairs of homophones, to be written onto the board; for example, main/mane = He is walking down the <u>main</u> road./That horse has a beautiful <u>mane</u>.

- Discuss the word reading activities on page 25, then allow pupils to complete the page independently.

Differentiated Individual/Paired/Group Work

- Tell pupils that the prefix 'pre-' means 'previous to' or 'before'. Ask pupils to find the word beginning with this prefix in the text (preheat). Ask them to explain what 'preheat' means. Pupils should use a dictionary to find more words starting with this prefix. They should write the words in a sentence, using the correct context.

- More able pupils should find more words with the prefix 'pre-' and write more complicated sentences.

Review

- As a class, compare the sentences.

Assessment

C3	Ask the pupils to write at least one reason why each section of the recipe is organised in this way – Ingredients, Equipment and Utensils, Method.
C5	Write a list of words on the board, and ask pupils to write them in alphabetical order: coat, cups, cover, centre, casserole, cook
WR1	Call out (or write on the board) the following words and have pupils write down the suffixes: evaluation, mashed, traditional, poking, mainly, delicious, beaten

Answers

Comprehension

1. (e) the first paragraph
2. ... give instructions for making toad-in-the-hole. (Pupils may also add: to give some background information about the recipe.)
3. Answers will vary.
4. Seasoned flour is flour flavoured with salt and pepper.
5. 65 minutes approximately
6. Answers may suggest that the sausages and batter will burn or stick to the casserole dish.
7. Answers may state that it is easy to read them when they are in a list or it separates what is required from the steps in the 'Method' that show how to make the dish.
8. (a) sausage—minced pork or other meat in a skin that is cylindrical shaped
   (b) recipe—a set of instructions for preparing a dish that includes the ingredients required
   (c) gravy—a sauce made by mixing fat and meat juices with stock and other ingredients
   (d) equipment—the necessary items for a particular purpose
   (e) utensil—a tool, container or other article, especially for household use
9. Cooks may use other containers of a similar size.

Word Reading

1. approximate, -ly, beat, -en, brown, -ed, season, -ed, main, -ly
2. (a) evaluate   (b) poke   (c) main
   (d) mash   (e) prepare   (f) tradition
3. (a) casserole   (b) recipe   (c) pepper
4. (a) pre-   (b) previous to, before
5. (a) delicious   (b) mainly, approximately
   (c) preparation, evaluation
6. (a) read   (b) hole   (c) some
   (d) plain   (e) flour   (f) pour
7. whisk, make, pour, cover, coat, place, preheat, heat, add, place, cook, serve

Make Toad-in-the-Hole – 1

Read the recipe for making toad-in-the-hole.

This traditional British dish consists mainly of sausages and batter. Some people think the name comes from the fact that the cooked dish looks like a toad poking its head out of a hole. It is a very old recipe.

Preparation time: 35 minutes **Cooking time**: 30 minutes **Serves**: 4–6

Ingredients

- 500 grams good-quality sausages
- 1½ cups plain flour
- 3 eggs, beaten
- 1½ cups milk
- 1 tablespoon melted butter
- 1 tablespoon vegetable oil
- salt and pepper to taste

Equipment and Utensils

- large bowl
- whisk
- casserole dish (approximately 20 x 30 cms or 22 x 22 cms)
- frying pan

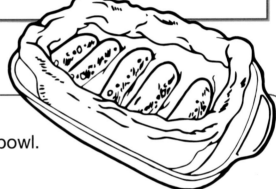

Method

1. Whisk flour, salt and pepper together in bowl.
2. Make a well in centre of seasoned flour.
3. Pour in eggs, milk and butter and whisk until smooth.
4. Cover and stand for 30 minutes.
5. Coat casserole dish with extra vegetable oil.
6. Place empty dish on rack near bottom of oven.
7. Preheat oven to 220° C.
8. Heat tablespoon of oil in frying pan on medium high.
9. Add sausages and brown on at least two sides.
10. Place browned sausages into casserole dish and pour batter over.
11. Cook for about 25–30 minutes until batter is risen and golden.
12. Serve with onion gravy, vegetables and mashed potato.

Test/Evaluation

Do you think this recipe is easy to follow? Do you think the dish will be delicious?

My learning log	When I read this recipe, I could read:	☐ all of it. ☐ most of it. ☐ parts of it.

Make Toad-in-the-Hole – 2

1. Which part of the text gives background information about 'toad-in-the-hole'?

   (a) Ingredients ☐   (b) Equipment and Utensils ☐

   (c) Method ☐   (d) Test/Evaluation ☐

   (e) the first paragraph ☐   (f) the first sentence ☐

2. The purpose of this text is to _____.

3. Do you think the name of this recipe is a suitable one? ⬚ Yes ⬚ No

   Why/Why not? _____

4. What does 'seasoned flour' mean?

   _____

5. How long will it take to make this recipe from start to finish?

   _____

6. What would happen if you placed the sausages and batter in the dish in the oven without coating it first with oil?

   _____

7. Why is it a good idea to put the items under the headings 'Ingredients' and 'Equipment and Utensils' in a list?

   _____

8. Write the dictionary meanings of the following words.

   (a) sausage _____

   (b) recipe _____

   (c) gravy _____

   (d) equipment _____

   (e) utensil _____

9. Why is the word 'approximately' used in regard to the size of the dish?

   _____

My learning log	While doing these activities:		
	I found Q _____ easy.	I found Q _____ challenging.	I found Q _____ interesting.

Make Toad-in-the-Hole – 3

1. Underline the root word and circle the suffix in each word below.

> approximately   beaten   browned   seasoned   mainly

2. Write the root word of each word below.

(a) evaluation _____   (b) poking _____

(c) mainly _____   (d) mashed _____

(e) preparation _____   (f) traditional _____

3. Which word comes from:

(a) the French word 'casse' meaning 'spoon-like container'? _____

(b) the Latin word meaning 'receive' (instructions)? _____

(c) the Greek word 'peperi' meaning 'berry'? _____

4. (a) Write the prefix in the word 'Preheat'. _____

(b) What do you think the prefix in (a) above means?

_____

5. Find and write words in the text with the following suffixes.

(a) –ous   (b) –ly   (c) –ion

_____   _____   _____

_____   _____

6. Write homophones from the text for the words below.

(a) reed _____   (b) whole _____   (c) sum _____

(d) plane _____   (e) flower _____   (f) paw _____

7. Command verbs are used to give instructions. Twelve are used in the 'Method' part of the recipe. Write them below.

_____   _____   _____   _____

_____   _____   _____   _____

_____   _____   _____   _____

My learning log	*Colour:*	I can / can't recognise root words.
		I understand / need more practice on suffixes.
		I can / can't recognise command verbs.

Curriculum Links

Activity	Code	Objective	Outcome
Text	C2 C3 C6	• Participate in discussion about both books that are read to them and those they can read for themselves • Listen to and discuss a wide range of fiction • Increase their familiarity with a wide range of books, including fairy stories	• Can identify folk tales and talk about their key features
Comprehension	C7 C13	• Identify themes in a wide range of books • Draw inferences such as inferring characters' feelings, thoughts and motives from their actions, and justifying inferences with evidence	• Can explain the message of the folk tale • Can infer how characters feel
Word Reading	WR1 WR2	• Apply their growing knowledge of suffixes • Read further exception words, noting the unusual correspondences between spelling and sound	• Can recognise suffixes '-ly' and '-ed' • Can distinguish homophones

Additional Teacher Information

Definition of Terms

Narrative
A narrative is a framework which tells a story. A narrative includes a title, an orientation (setting, time and characters), a complication involving the main character(s), a sequence of events, a resolution to the complication and an ending showing what changed and what the characters have learnt.

Folk tale
Stories which have been passed from one generation to the next (often originally by word of mouth rather than being written down) are folk tales. Folk tales may include sayings, superstitions, social rituals, legends or lore about the weather, animals or plants.

Formal/Informal language
Formal language is used in serious situations, or ones that involve people we don't know well, and often in writing. Informal language is used in more relaxed situations and with people we know well. It is more commonly used when we speak. Each uses particular grammar and vocabulary; for example, informal language often uses contractions, relative clauses without a relative pronoun and ellipsis.

Links to other Curriculum Areas

• PSHE – Common sense, stranger danger and personal safety

Terminology for Pupils

folk tale
formal speech
informal speech
author
adjective
character
Standard English
antonym
synonym
homophone
suffix

Suggested Reading

• This YouTube™ video has a reading of the story: <https://www.youtube.com/watch?v=DbCks4c9hOA>
• *50 Scary Fairy Stories* by **Vic Parker**

Text

Teacher Information

- The folk tale on page 29 is based on a 19th century English folk tale by Joseph Jacobs, a folklorist, literary critic and historian. It is about a boy who, despite his mother's warnings not to, goes around the corner alone and runs into the child-eater Mr Miacca.

Introduction

- Tell pupils that folk tales are stories that have been passed down from one generation to the next.

Development

- Read and discuss the text with pupils, as a whole class or in groups. Assist pupils to decode new words if necessary. Discuss the meaning of any new or unfamiliar words and phrases. Question individual pupils to gauge their understanding of what they have listened to or read. Pupils should also ask questions about parts of the text they are unsure of, in order to improve their understanding of it.
- Discuss the moral or message of the story (Stranger Danger) and how this is still applicable to children today.

Differentiated Individual/Paired/Group Work

- Imagine that when Tommy got home, he decided to tell his mother about what had happened. Pupils should discuss what might happen next.
- Pupils should continue the folk tale, keeping the same style and features of speech.
- Less able pupils should write one or two paragraphs, whilst more able pupils should write at least four.
- The pupils should try and finish their story with a moral.

Review

- Pupils should share their work in a small group.

Comprehension

Teacher Information

- Pupils may need a thesaurus to complete question 4.

Introduction

- Pupils take it in turns to retell the folk tale in their own words, sequencing the events correctly.

Development

- Discuss the way the author has used punctuation and ellipsis to enhance the characters' speech in this text. This will help pupils to answer questions 2 and 3.
- Discuss the comprehension activities on page 30, then allow pupils to complete the page independently.

Differentiated Individual/Paired/Group Work

- Pupils should rewrite the story using short bullet points, only including the most important parts.
- Less able pupils could rewrite the story using 6–8 bullet points. More able pupils should use more bullet points.

Review

- In a group, pupils should share their work.

Word Reading

Teacher Information

- The activities on page 31 focus on definitions of words, Standard English, antonyms, synonyms, homophones and the suffixes '-ly' and '-ed'.

Introduction

- Reread the text, but first explain to pupils that the focus will be on words. While reading, ask pupils to circle any words that they think have more than two syllables. There are not many.

Development

- Ensure pupils are familiar with the terms 'synonym' and 'antonym'. Give some examples (happy: synonym is glad, antonym is sad). Elicit some examples from the pupils. Pupils suggest sentences for pairs of synonyms and antonyms, to be written onto the board; for example, happy = glad/sad. Ben was <u>glad</u> he had homework, but Krista was <u>sad</u>.

- Ensure pupils are familiar with the term 'homophone'. Give some examples (berry/bury, scene/seen, plain/plane). Elicit some examples from the pupils. Pupils suggest sentences for pairs of homophones, to be written onto the board; for example, main/mane = He is walking down the <u>main</u> road./That horse has a beautiful <u>mane</u>.

- Look at words with the suffix '-ly'. Tell pupils that this suffix is added to an adjective to form an adverb. Explain that usually the suffix is added straight onto the end of most root words; for example, sadly, finally. However, there are exceptions, which should also be explained to the pupils:

  (1) If the root word ends in '-y' with a consonant letter before it, the 'y' is changed to 'i', but only if the root word has more than one syllable; for example, happily.

  (2) If the root word ends with '-le', the '-le' is changed to '-ly'; for example, simply.

  (3) If the root word ends with '-ic', '-ally' is added rather than just '-ly'; for example, basically. An exception is 'publicly'.

  (4) The words truly, duly and wholly.

- Discuss the word reading activities on page 31, then allow pupils to complete the page independently.

Differentiated Individual/Paired/Group Work

- Provide pupils with words that have synonyms; for example, quick, happy, tired. Ask pupils to think of synonyms, and list them on the board.

- Less able pupils should be provided with a list of words from the text, and asked to write synonyms for them; for example, bad, wise, huge, little, thoughtful, good.

- More able pupils should find their own words in the text, and then write synonyms for them.

Review

- As a class, compare the synonyms. Did pupils have different synonyms for the same word? For example, for the word 'wise', pupils might have thought of clever, intelligent, knowing, or other words.

Assessment

C3	Pupils should write a review of the folk tale, stating what they like and dislike about it.
C13	Ask the pupils to write how they think Tommy felt during the different parts of the story. They should justify their inferences with evidence from the text.
WR1	Present the following list of root words to the pupils. Ask them to add the suffix '-ly' to each, reminding them of the rules listed in the 'Development' section: final, basic, gentle, prompt, happy, tragic, quick, angry, busy, simple, noble, magic

Answers

Comprehension

1. (c) warn children of danger.
2. Possible answer: Mr and Mrs Miacca don't pronounce the letter 'h' and they cut some words. Their speech is informal.
3. Possible answer: so the reader can get a sense of the characters' accents.
4. Possible answers:
   (a) brave, cheeky, clever, confident, fast
   (b) frightening, big, dangerous, rough
   (c) trusting, obedient, naive
5. Possible answers:
   (a) Tommy's mother would have felt very worried and concerned for her son's safety. She may have reported him missing to the police and/or sent out search parties to look for him.
   (b) Mrs Miacca would have felt surprised and then tricked and disappointed when Tommy didn't return with the pudding. She might have tried to lie to Mr Miacca so she didn't have to admit that she let Tommy go.
   (c) Mr Miacca would have felt angry, hungry and frustrated to find Tommy gone not once but twice. He may have been angry with his wife the first time, and he might have gone looking for Tommy both times.

Word Reading

1. (b) lifted
2. (a) herbs   (b) them   (c) husband
3. (a) tough   (b) relieved   (c) thoughtful
   (d) bad   (e) clever   (f) huge
4. (a) street   (b) frightening   (c) huge
   (d) scarcely   (e) pudding   (f) wise/clever
5. (a) boy   (b) dear   (c) course
   (d) pause   (e) right   (f) meat
   (g) sure   (h) some   (i) him
   (j) ate   (k) not
6. –ly: scarcely, usually, quickly, promptly
   -ed: turned, snapped, dropped, hoisted, pulled, pinched, compared, commented, bothered, exclaimed, called, appeared, answered, asked, explained, tired, relieved, escaped, boiled, ordered, chopped, added, bolted

Mr Miacca – 1

Read this version of the folk tale.

Tommy Grimes was sometimes a good boy and often a bad boy; and he could be a very bad boy! Tommy's mother was always saying to him, 'Dear Tommy, be a good boy and listen to your wise old mother. Don't go out of our street, for if you do Mr Miacca will take you home to eat for his supper.' But because Tommy was, at times, a very bad boy, he of course didn't listen to his mother's wise words of warning. One day he'd scarcely turned the corner out of his street when the huge and frightening Mr Miacca snapped him up, dropped him head first into a sack, hoisted him over his shoulder and took him home.

In his house, Mr Miacca pulled Tommy out of the sack and pinched at his arms and legs. 'You're quite tough compared to the others', he commented, 'but you're all there is for supper and you'll 'ave to do!' After a pause, a bothered looking Mr Miacca exclaimed, 'Blimey! I've forgot the 'erbs and it's rubbish you'll taste without the 'erbs. Sally, come in 'ere to me ... SALLY!' He called out to his wife.

Mrs Miacca soon appeared saying, 'What is it you want dear 'usband?'

'Look 'ere Sally, 'ere's a tough little boy for our supper', said Mr Miacca, 'but I've forgot the 'erbs, so watch 'im while I go fetch 'em will ya?'

'Right you are then, so I will', Mrs Miacca answered as Mr Miacca went off.

Clever Tommy began talking to Mrs Miacca. He asked if they always ate little boys and she explained they usually did. 'What about some pudding?' Tommy asked. 'You must get tired of boy meat all the time?' Mrs Miacca's face lit up and Tommy went on. 'My mother is making a pudding this very day. I'm sure she'd give you some if I ask her. Shall I run and get you some now?'

'Ah what a thoughtful boy you are. Go on now and be sure to be back before Mr Miacca won't you', Mrs Miacca answered.

Tommy ran home, as relieved as a boy could be to have escaped the pot! He was a good boy for many weeks after, but of course that didn't last. Once again Tommy left the street and once again he was quickly snapped up into Mr Miacca's sack.

This time Mr Miacca wasn't taking any chances. He put Tommy under the sofa and sat on it while the pot boiled. Tired of waiting, Mr Miacca ordered, 'Put your leg out now and I'll chop it off to throw in the pot. That'll stop you running off again!' Tommy put out a leg and it was promptly chopped off and added to the pot.

Mr Miacca went to find Sally in the other room and Tommy crept out from under the sofa and bolted home! It was the sofa leg he had put out and not his own!

| **My learning log** | When I read this folk tale, I could read: | ☐ all of it. ☐ most of it. ☐ parts of it. |

Mr Miacca – 2

1. This folk tale is being told to:

   (a) make people laugh. ☐

   (b) explain a natural feature. ☐

   (c) warn children of danger. ☐

2. Explain some of the features of Mr and Mrs Miacca's speech. Is it formal or informal?

   _____

   _____

3. Why has the author dropped the letter 'h' from the speech in the text?

   _____

4. Write some adjectives to describe each character from the story.

   (a) Tommy Grimes: _____

   (b) Mr Miacca: _____

   (c) Mrs Miacca: _____

5. Explain how you think each character felt and acted.

   (a) Tommy's mother when he went missing.

   _____

   _____

   (b) Mrs Miacca when Tommy didn't return with the pudding.

   _____

   _____

   (c) Mr Miacca when he realised that Tommy had escaped.

   _____

   _____

My learning log	While doing these activities:		
	I found Q _____ easy.	I found Q _____ challenging.	I found Q _____ interesting.

1. Mr Miacca 'hoisted' Tommy over his shoulder. Tick the word with the most similar meaning.

   (a) lowered ☐   (b) lifted ☐   (c) lightened ☐

2. Write a Standard English version for each of these words.

   (a) 'erbs: _____   (b) 'em: _____   (c) 'usband: _____

3. Find the antonyms for these words in the text.

   (a) tender _____ (b) worried _____ (c) inconsiderate _____

   (d) good _____ (e) foolish _____ (f) tiny _____

4. Find the synonyms for these words in the text.

   (a) road _____ (b) scary _____ (c) enormous _____

   (d) barely _____ (e) dessert _____ (f) intelligent _____

5. Write homophones from the text for the words below.

   (a) buoy _____   (b) deer _____   (c) coarse _____

   (d) paws _____   (e) write _____

   (f) meet _____   (g) shore _____

   (h) sum _____   (i) hymn _____

   (j) eight _____   (k) knot _____

6. Find the words in the text that have these suffixes and add them to the table.

-ly	-ed		

The Legends of King Arthur's Swords

Curriculum Links

Activity	Code	Objective	Outcome
Text	C2	• Participate in discussion about both books that are read to them and those they can read for themselves	• Can identify legends and talk about their key features
	C3	• Listen to and discuss a wide range of fiction	
	C6	• Increase their familiarity with a wide range of books, including legends	
Comprehension	C5	• Use dictionaries to check the meaning of words that they have read	• Can explain the meanings of words
	C9	• Discuss words and phrases that capture the reader's interest and imagination	• Can explain why they like phrases
			• Can answer questions about the text
	C11	• Check that the text makes sense to them, discuss their understanding and explain the meaning of words in context	• Can predict what Arthur did with Excalibur
	C14	• Predict what might happen from details stated and implied	
Word Reading	WR1	• Apply their growing knowledge of prefixes and suffixes	• Can recognise words with suffix '-ly' and prefix 're-'
	WR2	• Read further exception words, noting the unusual correspondences between spelling and sound	• Can recognise homophones and words with 'ou'

Additional Teacher Information

Definition of Terms

Legend
Legends are told as though the events were actual historical events. Legends may or may not be based on an elaborated version of an historical event. Legends are usually about human beings, although gods may intervene in some way throughout the story.

Text
A book or other written or printed work, regarded in terms of its content rather than its physical form.

Paragraph
A distinct section of a piece of writing, usually dealing with a single theme and indicated by a new line, indentation or numbering.

Language feature
These are the features of language that support meaning. They include sentence structure, noun group/phrase, vocabulary, punctuation and figurative language. Language features and text structures define a text type and shape its meaning. These choices vary according to the purpose of a text, its subject matter, audience and mode of production.

Links to other Curriculum Areas

• History—Britain's settlement by Anglo-Saxons and Scots

Terminology for Pupils

legend
text
phrase
paragraph
direct speech
dictionary
suffix
root word
antonym
bracket
synonym
prefix
sentence
homophone

Suggested Reading

• *The Story of King Arthur and his Knights* (Classic Starts) by **Howard Pyle**
• *Knights* (Penguin Young Readers, L3) by **Catherine Daly-Weir**
• *King Arthur: Excalibur Unsheathed: An English Legend* (Graphic Myths and Legends) by **Jeff Limke** (a graphic novel)

32 . . . . *Reading – Comprehension and Word Reading* . . . . .Prim-Ed Publishing . . . . .www.prim-ed.com

<table>
<tr><td>

Text

Teacher Information

- King Arthur is a legendary British leader from the late 5th and early 6th centuries, who led the defence of Britain against Saxon invaders.

Introduction

- Internet illustrations of King Arthur, his knights and the two swords could be viewed.

Development

- Read and discuss the legends with the pupils, as a whole class or in groups. Assist pupils to decode new words if necessary. Discuss the meaning of any new or unfamiliar words and phrases such as 'squire', 'frantically', 'anvil', 'proclaiming', 'suspiciously', 'saluted', 'rightful', 'lamenting', 'dazzling', 'maiden' and 'promptly'. Question individual pupils to gauge their understanding of what they have listened to or read. Pupils should also ask questions about parts of the text they are unsure of, in order to improve their understanding of it.

Differentiated Individual/Paired/Group Work

- Pupils continue the second legend, to tell what happened after Arthur took hold of Excalibur.
- Less able pupils could write two paragraphs and draw an illustration.
- More able pupils could write at least five paragraphs, in the style of the legend.

Review

- Pupils should share their work in a small group.

</td><td>

Comprehension

Teacher Information

- Pupils might need a dictionary to complete question 9.

Introduction

- Reread the legends. Ask pupils to focus on the sequence of events. Pupils take it in turns to retell the legends in their own words, sequencing the events correctly.

Development

- Discuss possible answers to questions 2 and 6 as they may vary. Pupils need to justify their choice of phrase for question 2.
- Remind pupils how to use a dictionary efficiently; i.e. alphabetical order and retrieval by 1st, 2nd and 3rd letters. Give each pupil, or pair of pupils, a dictionary. Write words from the text onto the board for pupils to find.
- Discuss the comprehension activities on page 36, then allow pupils to complete the page independently.

Differentiated Individual/Paired/Group Work

- Working in mixed ability groups of three, pupils should choose either 'The Sword in the Stone', paragraphs 3 and 4, or 'Excalibur', paragraphs 3 and 4. They should write a short play retelling this part of the legend, and take it in turns to act the parts of the different characters.

Review

- Groups should perform their play to another group or their class.

</td></tr>
</table>

Word Reading

Teacher Information

- The activities on page 37 focus on the suffix '-ly', antonyms, synonyms, the prefix 're-', words with 'ou' and homophones.

Introduction

- Reread the texts, but first explain to pupils that the focus will be on words. While reading the texts, ask pupils to circle any words containing the letters 'ou' (young, house, out, mounted, around, brought, suspiciously, you, would, country). Talk about the sounds the 'ou' makes in the different words.

Development

- Look at words with the suffix '-ly'. Tell pupils that this suffix is added to an adjective to form an adverb. Explain that usually the suffix is added straight onto the end of most root words; for example, sadly, finally. However, there are exceptions, which should also be explained to the pupils:

  (1) If the root word ends in '-y' with a consonant letter before it, the 'y' is changed to 'i', but only if the root word has more than one syllable; for example, happily.

  (2) If the root word ends with '-le', the '-le' is changed to '-ly'; for example, simply.

  (3) If the root word ends with '-ic', '-ally' is added rather than just '-ly'; for example, basically. An exception is 'publicly'.

  (4) The words truly, duly and wholly.

- Ensure pupils are familiar with the terms 'synonym' and 'antonym'. Give some examples (happy: synonym is glad, antonym is sad). Elicit some examples from the pupils. Pupils suggest sentences for pairs of synonyms and antonyms, to be written onto the board; for example, happy = glad/sad. Ben was <u>glad</u> he had homework, but Krista was <u>sad</u>.

- Explain that the prefix 're-' means 'again' or 'back'. How do the words 'remove', 'refresh', 'retrace' and 'return' have these meanings? Can the pupils think of any other words with this prefix? How do they mean 'again' or 'back'?

- The 'ou' words in question 5 should be spoken out loud, so pupils can hear the specific phoneme focused upon.

- Ensure pupils are familiar with the term 'homophone'. Give some examples (berry/bury, scene/seen, plain/plane). Elicit some examples from the pupils. Pupils suggest sentences for pairs of homophones, to be written onto the board; for example, main/mane = He is walking down the <u>main</u> road./That horse has a beautiful <u>mane</u>.

- Discuss the word reading activities on page 37, then allow pupils to complete the page independently.

Differentiated Individual/Paired/Group Work

- Tell pupils that the prefix 're-' means 'again' or 'back'. Ask pupils to find words beginning with this prefix in the text (return, remove, request, released). Ask them to explain what these words mean. Pupils should use a dictionary to find more words starting with this prefix. They should write the words in a sentence, using the correct context.

- More able pupils should find more words with the prefix 're-' and write more complicated sentences.

Review

- As a class, compare the sentences.

Assessment

C2	Ask the pupils to write a review of the two legends. They should provide a synopsis of each and state which legend they prefer, and why.
C5	Present the following list of words to the pupils and ask them to write a definition for each: anvil, sword, honest, borrow, struggle, puzzled, suspicious, salute
WR2	Present the following words to the pupils and ask them to write down a homophone: knight, mane, scent, witch, reign, male, not, groan, ball, site

Answers

Comprehension

1. To relate two legends; To entertain the reader.
2. Answers will vary.
3. Sword 1: in an anvil mounted on a rock;
   Sword 2: in a woman's hand in the middle of a great lake
4. Basically honest, but tried to take advantage of a situation and Arthur's ignorance; Respectful of his father etc.
5. puzzled
6. Answers will vary.
7. Answers may include: to add interest; to break up the narrative; to tell more about the characters etc.
8. There are two titles.
9. (a) with fear, anxiety or other emotion; anxiously
   (b) a heavy iron block on which metals are hammered and shaped
   (c) weeping, wailing; expressing grief

Word Reading

1. (a) frantically, excitedly, suspiciously, kindly, promptly
   (b) frantically
2. Possible answers include:
   (a) led   (b) unkindly, refused
3. (a) confused/perplexed
   (b) cross/annoyed/irritated/irate
   (c) fetch/get
   (d) emerged
4. (a) re-
   (b) Teacher check; again, back
   (c) Teacher check
5. young, trouble, country
6. (a) sent   (b) way   (c) him   (d) which

The Legends of King Arthur's Swords – 1

Read these versions of the legends.

The Sword in the Stone

Young Arthur, who was a squire for his older brother Sir Kay the knight, was sent to collect his sword which they had left behind. Rushing back to the house, Arthur somehow got lost along the way. Frantically worried that he wouldn't hand Kay his sword in time for the games, Arthur had the great fortune to spot a sword jutting out from an anvil mounted on a rock.

Arthur glanced around but saw no one, and as he was an honest boy he knew he'd borrow the sword and return it when the games were finished. Heading over to the anvil, Arthur grabbed the sword's handle and struggled to remove it for a moment before it came free in his hands. Arthur rushed back to his brother with the sword but Kay became angry and asked Arthur why he'd brought him another sword and not his own. When Arthur explained the story, Kay ran to his father excitedly proclaiming, 'I am the new king!' A puzzled Arthur followed.

Sir Ector gazed at Kay suspiciously. 'Where'd you get this sword?' he demanded. Sensing the truth was the best answer, he told his father that Arthur had pulled it from the stone. At this, both men bowed down to Arthur and saluted him as their king.

With Arthur still looking puzzled, Sir Ector asked, 'Did you not read the inscription on the stone? It clearly says "HE WHO REMOVES THIS SWORD WILL BE THE RIGHTFUL KING OF THE LAND".'

From that moment on, Arthur's life would never be the same.

Excalibur

Many years later, after a difficult battle in which this sword was broken in half, Arthur and Merlin were travelling the country. Arthur was lamenting, 'What kind of King has no sword?'

He and Merlin soon came across a great lake where they noticed an unusual sight. From the lake rose a woman's hand, gripping the most dazzling sword Arthur had ever seen. A fair maiden then appeared out of the fog, walking towards them on the lake's surface.

'Here comes the Lady of the Lake', Merlin explained. 'The sword belongs to her and you must ask her if you can take it.'

The lady greeted Merlin and Arthur kindly and agreed to Arthur's request for the sword. She explained it was called Excalibur and would serve Arthur well. She directed the two to a boat on the lake's edge. The men got in and rowed to the sword, which the hand promptly released when Arthur took hold of it.

| **My learning log** | When I read these legends, I could read: | ▢ all of them. | ▢ most of them. | ▢ parts of them. |

The Legends of King Arthur's Swords – 2

1. What is the purpose of these two texts?

   _____

2. (a) Choose and copy a phrase that captures your attention or interest.

   _____

   (b) Explain why you chose this phrase.

   _____

3. Write the location where each sword was found.

   SWORD 1: _____

   SWORD 2: _____

4. How would you describe the character of Sir Kay?

   _____

5. Which word, in paragraph two of the first legend, tells you that Arthur did not understand what it meant to have pulled the sword out of the stone?

   _____

6. What do you think Arthur did with Excalibur once he took it from the lake?

   _____

   _____

7. Why do you think direct speech was used in the texts?

   _____

8. What language feature on page 35 tells you that there are two different legends about Arthur?

   _____

9. What are the dictionary meanings of the following words?

   (a) frantically _____

   (b) anvil   _____

   (c) lamenting _____

My learning log	While doing these activities:		
	I found Q _____ easy.	I found Q _____ challenging.	I found Q _____ interesting.

The Legends of King Arthur's Swords – 3

1. (a) Write the five words in the text with the suffix '-ly'.

_____ _____ _____ _____ _____

  (b) If the root word ends with '-ic', '-ally' is added rather than just '-ly'. Which word above has the suffix '-ally'? _____

2. Write antonyms for the words in brackets to change the meaning.

  (a) A puzzled Arthur (followed) _____.

  (b) The lady greeted Merlin and Arthur (kindly) _____

    and (agreed to) _____ Arthur's request for the sword.

3. Write a synonym for each word below.

  (a) puzzled _____   (b) angry   _____

  (c) collect _____   (d) appeared _____

4. (a) Circle the prefix that these words have in common.

    remove   retrace   return

  (b) What does this prefix mean? _____

  (c) Write a sentence using each word.

    remove: _____

    retrace: _____

    return: _____

5. Circle the words with the /ʌ/ sound spelt 'ou'; for example, touch, double.

| young | mounted | country | house | trouble | cloud |

6. Which words from the text are homophones for the following words?

  (a) scent _____   (b) weigh _____

  (c) hymn _____   (d) witch _____

My learning log	**Colour:**	I understand / need more practice on synonyms and antonyms.
		I know / don't know the meaning of the prefix 're-'.
		I can / can't recognise homophones.

Why the Flies Bother the Cows

Read the Nigerian folk tale.

Many moons ago, the rich and hospitable Queen of Calabar regularly put on lavish feasts for all of the domestic animals in her kingdom. Of course, the wild beasts were never invited, because the Queen couldn't trust them to behave in a civilised manner.

At one of these feasts, the table was crowded with animal guests. The Queen asked the cow to sit at the head of the table because she was the biggest animal present. It was the cow's job to serve the guests. She felt privileged to be given this responsibility. The cow did a great job of serving. However, she forgot about the fly sitting at the other end of the table because he was so small.

When the small but very hungry fly noticed that he had been overlooked, he politely called out to the cow to ask for his share but the cow hushed him and said, 'Be quiet my friend, you must have patience.'

When the second course arrived and the fly was once again forgotten, he called out to the cow once more. However, instead of serving him, the cow merely pointed to her eye and said to the fly, 'Look here, you will get your food later. I said to have some patience.'

Eventually all of the courses were served and the fly, who the cow hadn't given any food to, went home to bed hungry and reasonably angry, with an empty, growling stomach.

The fly decided that this was not acceptable, so the next day he went to see the Queen to explain what had happened at the feast. The fly recounted the events of the night before and the Queen came to a decision. 'As the cow presided over the feast and didn't give you your share, but instead pointed to her eye, in the future you can get your food from a cow's eyes.'

This is why whenever you see cows you will also see flies feeding from their eyes, because the Queen of Calabar ordered it so.

Why the Flies Bother the Cows

1. Why didn't the Queen invite the wild animals to the feast? Tick one.

☐ 1 mark

She was afraid of them. ☐   They ate too much. ☐

They wouldn't behave. ☐   They lived far away. ☐

2. Find and copy the two adjectives in paragraph 1 that describe the Queen of Calabar.

☐ 1 mark

_____   _____

3. Sequence these events from 1 to 4.

☐ 1 mark

(a)   The fly went home, hungry and angry.   ☐

(b)   The cow was seated at the head of the table.   ☐

(c)   The fly politely asked to be served some dinner.   ☐

(d)   The Queen told the fly where to get his food from.   ☐

4. Tick the best answer. This text was written for the reader to:

☐ 1 mark

learn about animals. ☐   enjoy a story with a moral. ☐

learn about Nigeria. ☐

5. Explain the main message of this story in your own words.

☐ 1 mark

_____

_____

6. Write a word that you think would describe how the fly felt after he

☐ 1 mark

spoke with the Queen. _____

7. Do you think the Queen's decision was fair? Explain why or why not.

☐ 2 marks

_____

_____

_____

Total for this page	/8

Why the Flies Bother the Cows

1. Which word in paragraph 2 means 'honoured and special'?

    [   ] 1 mark

2. Which word in the folk tale means 'friendly and welcoming'?

    [   ] 1 mark

3. The Queen said 'the cow presided over the feast'. What does this phrase mean?

    _____ 2 marks

    _____

4. Only the 'domestic animals' were invited to the feast. Domestic animals ...

    1 mark

    (a) live alongside humans. ☐   (b) live in the wild. ☐   (c) live in zoos. ☐

5. Find and write the synonyms for these words in the text.

    1 mark

    (a) often _____   (b) tiny _____

    (c) starving _____   (d) furious _____

6. The word 'crowded' is in paragraph 2. Find its antonym in paragraph 5.

    [   ] 1 mark

7. Circle the words that have the same 'ou' sound as 'touch' and 'double'.

    1 mark

    | you | about | could | cousin | recount |

8. Find and write the homophones for these words in the text.

    2 marks

    (a) coarse _____   (b) bean _____

    (c) knight _____   (d) grate _____

9. Tick the words made from each root word.

    1 mark

    (a) travel: travelled ☐   travelling ☐

    (b) excite: excited ☐   exciting ☐

10. Circle the prefix and underline the suffix in this word.

    1 mark

    recounted

| Total for this page | /12 | Total for this assessment | /20 |

Why the Flies Bother the Cows

Genre: Folk tale

Breakdown of question type/content and mark allocation

Comprehension			Word Reading		
Q 1.	Finding information	1 mark	Q 1.	Word meanings	1 mark
Q 2.	Understanding adjectives	1 mark	Q 2.	Word meanings	1 mark
Q 3.	Sequencing	1 mark	Q 3.	Phrase meanings	2 marks
Q 4.	Choosing best answer	1 mark	Q 4.	Phrase meanings	1 mark
Q 5.	Identifying moral	1 mark	Q 5.	Synonyms	1 mark
Q 6.	Inferring	1 mark	Q 6.	Antonyms	1 mark
Q 7.	Giving opinion	2 marks	Q 7.	'ou' sounds	1 mark
			Q 8.	Homophones	2 marks
			Q 9.	Root words	1 mark
			Q 10.	Prefixes and suffixes	1 mark
	Sub-total			Sub-total	
				Record the pupil's total result for this assessment.	

Assessment – Why the Flies Bother the Cows

Comprehension ....*Page 39*

1. because they wouldn't behave
2. rich, hospitable
3. (b), (c), (a), (d)
4. enjoy a story with a moral.
5. Teacher check
6. Possible answers: content, satisfied, heard, happy
7. Possible answer: I think the Queen's decision was unfair as all cows were made to suffer for the mistake of only one.

Word Reading ....*Page 40*

1. privileged
2. hospitable
3. Teacher check; The cow was the leader or boss of the feast, as she was serving the food.
4. (a) live alongside humans.
5. (a) regularly   (b) small   (c) hungry   (d) angry
6. empty
7. could, cousin
8. (a) course   (b) been   (c) night   (d) great
9. (a) travelled, travelling   (b) excited, exciting
10. recounted

World Climatic Zones

Curriculum Links

Activity	Code	Objective	Outcome
Text	C2 C3	• Participate in discussion about both books that are read to them and those they can read for themselves • Listen to and discuss a wide range of non-fiction	• Can identify explanatory texts and talk about their key features
Comprehension	C1 C5 C7 C11 C12 C16	• Retrieve and record information from non-fiction • Use dictionaries to check the meaning of words that they have read • Identify themes and conventions in a wide range of books • Check that the text makes sense to them, discuss their understanding and explain the meaning of words in context • Ask questions to improve understanding of a text • Identify how language, structure and presentation contribute to meaning	• Can answer questions about a non-fiction text • Can explain the meanings of words • Can recognise language features of text • Can answer questions about the text • Can ask questions to clarify understanding • Can recognise language features in a text
Word Reading	WR1 WR2	• Apply their growing knowledge of root words, prefixes and suffixes • Read further exception words, noting the unusual correspondences between spelling and sound	• Can recognise root words, prefix 'trans-' and a range of suffixes • Can distinguish homophones

Additional Teacher Information

Definition of Terms

Explanation
An explanation is a framework that outlines how something occurs, works or is made.

Text
A book or other written or printed work, regarded in terms of its content rather than its physical form.

Formal/Informal language
Formal language is used in serious situations or ones that involve people we don't know well, and often in writing. Informal language is used in more relaxed situations and with people we know well. It is more commonly used when we speak. Each uses particular grammar and vocabulary. For example, informal language often uses contractions, relative clauses without a relative pronoun and ellipsis.

Paragraph
A distinct section of a piece of writing, usually dealing with a single theme and indicated by a new line, indentation or numbering.

Language features
These are the features of language that support meaning. They include sentence structure, noun group/phrase, vocabulary, punctuation and figurative language. Language features and text structures define a text type and shape its meaning. These choices vary according to the purpose of a text, its subject matter, audience and mode of production.

Links to other Curriculum Areas

• Geography—Human and physical geography: describe and understand key aspects of physical geography including climate zones

Terminology for Pupils

explanation
opening paragraph
bullet point
rhyming word
text
phrase
question
dictionary
word origin
suffix
root word
consonant
syllable

Suggested Reading

• *What is Climate?* (Science Slam: Weather Wise) by **Ellen Lawrence**
• *On the Same Day in March: A Tour of the World's Weather* by **Marilyn Singer**
• Visit <http://www.kbears.com/climates.html> for an interactive world climate map. This version uses the classifications 'tropical', 'dry', 'mild', 'continental', 'polar' and 'mountain'.

Text

Teacher Information

- The informative text explains the factors that affect world climatic zones: latitude; altitude; winds; distance from the sea; and ocean currents. Pupils will need to have knowledge of relevant geographical vocabulary.

Introduction

- Look at the map on page 45 and discuss the names and features of the six climatic zones. Which climatic zone do the pupils live in? Have any of the pupils travelled to another climatic zone? What was the weather like? How did the weather impact on the plant life, animals and clothes/daily lives of the people living there?

Development

- Read and discuss the text with the pupils, as a whole class or in groups. Assist pupils to decode new words if necessary. Discuss the meaning of any new or unfamiliar words and phrases such as 'average', 'zone', 'regions', 'latitude', 'equator', 'temperatures', 'experience', 'landmasses', 'moisture', 'evaporates', 'territories', 'transport' and 'current'. Question individual pupils to gauge their understanding of what they have listened to or read. Pupils should also ask questions about parts of the text they are unsure of, in order to improve their understanding.

Differentiated Individual/Paired/Group Work

- Pupils choose one of the six climatic zones on the map. They should write a fact file, describing the climatic zone. Pupils should include a list of the countries within the climatic zone, the average weather there, the type of vegetation and animals, and the impact of the weather on the daily lives and clothing of the people who live there.

- More able pupils should aim to have a lengthier fact file that contains more geographical vocabulary.

Review

- Pupils should present their fact files neatly, including illustrations and/or diagrams, and display them in the classroom.

Comprehension

Teacher Information

- Pupils may need a dictionary to complete questions 3 and 4.

Introduction

- Pupils take it in turns to summarise each paragraph in their own words.

Development

- Remind pupils how to use a dictionary efficiently; i.e. alphabetical order and retrieval by 1st, 2nd and 3rd letters. Give each pupil, or pair of pupils, a dictionary. Write words from the text onto the board for pupils to find.

- Discuss the comprehension activities on page 46, then allow pupils to complete the page independently.

Differentiated Individual/Paired/Group Work

- Pupils create a glossary for some of the geographical vocabulary in the explanation; for example, flora, fauna, latitude, equator, temperature, polar regions, altitude, sea level, landmass, coastal regions, moisture, evaporates, precipitation, tropics, ocean currents.

- Less able pupils could create a glossary for six words; more able pupils for all 15 words.

Review

- As a class, compare pupils' definitions of the words. Which words were the hardest and easiest to define?

Word Reading

Teacher Information

- The activities on page 47 focus on definitions of words, dictionary usage, a range of suffixes and root words.

Introduction

- Reread the text, but first explain to pupils that the focus will be on words. While reading, ask pupils to find and circle words ending in '-er'. (larger, colder, further, cooler, thinner, lower, milder, hotter, wetter). Explain to pupils that words that end in '-er', if being used to compare something to one other thing, are called 'comparatives'. Ask pupils if they know the word ending that is used to compare something to more than one other thing (-est). Tell pupils these words are called 'superlatives'. Can pupils see any superlatives in the text? (lowest, highest).

Development

- Ensure pupils are familiar with the term 'homophone'. Give some examples (berry/bury, scene/seen, plain/plane). Elicit some examples from the pupils. Pupils suggest sentences for pairs of homophones, to be written onto the board; for example, main/mane = He is walking down the <u>main</u> road./That horse has a beautiful <u>mane</u>.

- Look at words with the suffix '-ly'. Tell pupils that this suffix is added to an adjective to form an adverb. Explain that usually the suffix is added straight onto the end of most root words; for example, sadly, finally. However, there are exceptions, which should also be explained to the pupils:

  (1) If the root word ends in '-y' with a consonant letter before it, the 'y' is changed to 'i', but only if the root word has more than one syllable; for example, happily.

  (2) If the root word ends with '-le', the '-le' is changed to '-ly'; for example, simply.

  (3) If the root word ends with '-ic', '-ally' is added rather than just '-ly'; for example, basically. An exception is 'publicly'.

  (4) The words truly, duly and wholly.

- Discuss the word reading activities on page 47, then allow pupils to complete the page independently.

Differentiated Individual/Paired/Group Work

- Explain that the prefix 'trans-' means 'carry across'. Ask pupils how the word 'transport' has this meaning.

- Pupils should use a dictionary to find other words with this prefix. They should write the words in a sentence, using the correct context.

- More able pupils should find more words with the prefix 'trans-' and write more complicated sentences.

Review

- As a class, compare the sentences.

	Assessment	
C1	Ask the pupils to write a short summary of this explanation in bullet points. The summary should explain what climate is, and include a description of the five factors that affect climate.	
C12	Pupils should write a list of questions they would like to have answered about the six climatic zones.	
WR2	Say the following words out loud. Tell pupils to write them into two lists, according to whether they have the suffix '-ture' or '-sure': adventure, treasure, measure, moisture, creature, assure, furniture, picture, pleasure, enclosure	

Answers

Comprehension

1. The following should be ticked: an opening paragraph, paragraphs of information, maps and images
2. latitude, altitude, winds, distance from the sea, ocean currents
3. (a) vegetation   (b) animals
   (c) thinner   (d) rain
   (e) invisible lines running horizontally across the earth's surface
   (f) height above sea level
4. spread over a wide area
5. The air is thinner and cannot hold heat as easily.
6. Coastal regions get more rain because moisture from the sea forms clouds and falls as rain or evaporates before it reaches the inland regions.
7. Answers will vary.
8. Polar regions would get hotter because the sun's rays would have a shorter distance to travel.

Word Reading

1. (a) affected—influenced or touched by something; effected—caused to happen; bring about
   (b) current—a body of water or air moving in a different direction;
   currant—a small dried fruit made from a grape
2. (a) Latin—trans (across), portare (carry); transport– carry across
   (b) Answers may include: transfer, transit, translate, transplant
3. evaporate<u>s</u>, colde<u>r</u>, disperse<u>d</u>, climat<u>ic</u>, precipita<u>tion</u>, thinne<u>r</u>, temperature<u>s</u>, territorie<u>s</u>, hotte<u>r</u>
4. (a) –ly   (b) easily, easy
5. (a) equator   (b) horizon/horizontal
   (c) add/addition/additional
   (d) pole
6. (a) moisture   (b) Teacher check

World Climatic Zones – 1

Read the explanation.

Climate is the average weather of a place over many years. Climatic zones differ around the world. They have an impact on the types of vegetation (flora), the weather, the animals (fauna) and the daily lives of people in the region. The climate of a place is affected by:

Latitude

Lines of latitude (invisible lines running horizontally across the earth's surface) tell us how far a place is from the equator (0°). Places close to the equator experience similar, warm temperatures year round. This is because the sun's rays are dispersed over larger areas of land as you move away from the equator. Additionally, polar regions are colder because the sun's rays have further to travel compared to Equatorial regions.

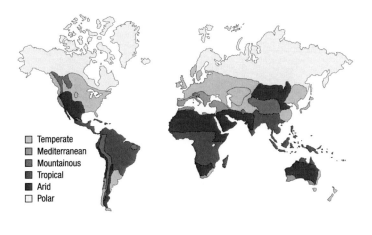

- Temperate
- Mediterranean
- Mountainous
- Tropical
- Arid
- Polar

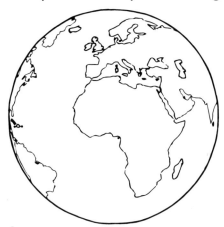

Altitude

Altitude means height above sea level. Places that are at high altitudes experience cooler weather as the air is thinner (less dense) and cannot hold heat as easily.

Winds

Winds that blow from cold areas will lower temperatures and winds that blow from hot areas will increase temperatures. Winds from the sea often bring rain.

Distance from the sea

Landmasses heat up and cool down more quickly than the sea. Therefore, coastal regions have a lower temperature range (difference between lowest and highest) than inland areas. Coastal areas experience milder winters and cooler summers compared with the colder winters and hotter summers of inland territories. Coastal areas are also wetter as the moisture from the sea (which forms clouds) often evaporates before it reaches inland.

Ocean currents

Currents transport warm water and precipitation (rain) from the equator north and south towards the poles and cold water from the poles back to the tropics. Without currents, temperatures would be more extreme—very hot at the equator and much colder towards the poles.

| My learning log | When I read this explanatory text, I could read: | ☐ all of it. | ☐ most of it. | ☐ parts of it. |

World Climatic Zones – 2

1. Which language features are included in the text? Tick them.

   • an opening paragraph ☐   • bullet points ☐

   • paragraphs of information ☐   • maps and images ☐

   • a table sorting information ☐   • lines that end in rhyming words ☐

   • the words 'Once upon a time …' and '… they lived happily ever after' ☐

2. Write five things that affect the climate of a place.

   _____

3. Use words from the text to give the meanings of the following words and phrases.

   (a) flora _____   (b) fauna _____

   (c) less dense _____   (d) precipitation _____

   (e) lines of latitude _____

   (f) altitude _____

4. The word 'dispersed' means _____.

5. What causes cooler weather at high altitudes?

   _____

6. Which regions get more rain—coastal or inland regions? Explain why.

   _____

   _____

7. Choose one paragraph that was difficult to understand. Write one question that will give you more information and help you understand it.

   _____

8. What do you think would happen if polar regions were suddenly tilted closer to the sun?

   _____

   _____

My learning log	While doing these activities:		
	I found Q _____ easy.	I found Q _____ challenging.	I found Q _____ interesting.

World Climatic Zones – 3

1. Use a dictionary to find the difference between each pair of words.

   (a) affected _____

       effected _____

   (b) current _____

       currant _____

2. (a) Use a dictionary to find out the origin and meaning of the word 'transport'.

       _____

   (b) Write two other words that begin with 'trans-'.

       _____   _____

3. Underline the suffix in each word below.

   evaporates   colder   dispersed   climatic

   precipitation   thinner   temperatures   territories   hotter

4. (a) Circle the suffix that these words have in common.

quickly	horizontally	easily	accidentally

   (b) If the root word ends in a consonant and 'y', the 'y' is changed to 'i'.
       (Only if the word has more than one syllable!)

       Which word above follows this rule?   _____

       What is this word's root word?   _____

5. Write the root word for each word below.

   (a) equatorial   _____   (b) horizontally   _____

   (c) additionally _____   (d) polar   _____

6. (a) Find and write a word from the text with the suffix '-ture'. _____

   (b) Write this word in a sentence.

       _____

My learning log	**Colour:**	I can / can't recognise homophones and near-homophones.
		I know / don't know the origins and meanings of words.
		I understand / need more practice on suffixes.

Great British Artists

Curriculum Links

Activity	Code	Objective	Outcome
Text	C2 C3	• Participate in discussion about both books that are read to them and those they can read for themselves • Listen to and discuss a wide range of non-fiction	• Can identify biographies and talk about their key features
Comprehension	C1 C5 C15	• Retrieve and record information from non-fiction • Use dictionaries to check the meaning of words that they have read • Identify main ideas drawn from more than one paragraph and summarise them	• Can answer questions about a non-fiction text • Can explain the meanings of words • Can write about the painting styles of artists
Word Reading	WR1 WR2	• Apply their growing knowledge of suffixes • Read further exception words, noting the unusual correspondences between spelling and sound	• Can recognise the suffix '-ous' • Can recognise 'que' words

Additional Teacher Information

Definition of Terms

Biography
A biography is an account of someone's life written by someone else.

Text
A book or other written or printed work, regarded in terms of its content rather than its physical form.

Bullet point
Each of several items in a list, preceded by a bullet symbol for emphasis.

Opinion
A view or judgement formed about something, not necessarily based on fact or knowledge.

Links to other Curriculum Areas

• Art and Design – Great artists

Terminology for Pupils

explanation
flow chart
text
biography
sentence
dictionary
bullet point
synonym
antonym
phrase
compound word
suffix

Suggested Reading

• *Discovering Great Artists: Hands-On Art for Children in the Styles of the Great Masters* (Bright Ideas for Learning) by **Mary Ann F. Kohl**
• *Rembrandt* (Getting to Know the World's Greatest Artists) by **Mike Venezia** (a series featuring Monet, Van Gogh, Picasso, Da Vinci, Degas, Renoir and others)
• *Exploring Landscape Art with Children* (Come Look with Me) by **Gladys S. Blizzard**

Text

Teacher Information

- Gainsborough may be considered a pre- or early Romantic artist, as opposed to Constable and Turner whose works fall into the category of Romanticism. Romanticism was an artistic movement that flourished in France and Britain in the early decades of the nineteenth century until the mid-nineteenth century. Artworks focused on imagination and emotion. They often showed violent and terrifying images of nature such as storms causing shipwrecks and other struggles of man against the power of nature.
- While Thomas Gainsborough gained great acclaim for his portrait painting, landscape painting was his true love. Portrait painting enabled Gainsborough to support his family when his landscapes were not selling well.
- Constable's 'six footers' were large-scale paintings (about six foot by four and a half) of a series of views on the River Stour. They include *The Hay Wain* (1820–1), *Hadleigh Castle* (1829) and *Salisbury Cathedral from the Meadows* (1831). The preliminary sketches associated with these large-scale paintings had never been done before and are now world-famous. They are as finely executed as the final paintings.
- The art of Joseph Mallord William Turner is considered by some to be a forerunner to Impressionism because his later works border on being abstract. As 'the painter of light', he used colour and light to bring depth to his paintings.

Introduction

- Look at images of the artists' most famous paintings. Discuss the types of paintings they produced. Pupils should state which paintings they like the best, and why.

Development

- Read and discuss the text with the pupils, as a whole class or in groups. Assist pupils to decode new words if necessary. Discuss the meaning of any new or unfamiliar words and phrases such as 'exhibited', 'notorious', 'established', 'merchant', 'techniques', 'lectured', 'preliminary', 'print maker', 'architects', 'topographical draughtsmen', 'engraved' and 'catastrophes'. Question individual pupils to gauge their understanding of what they have listened to or read. Pupils should also ask questions about parts of the text they are unsure of, in order to improve their understanding.

Differentiated Individual/Paired/Group Work

- Pupils should choose the painting that they like the most. They should research when it was painted and other relevant background information.
- Pupils should write a report about their favourite painting. They should use their research and give reasons why it is their favourite artwork.
- More able pupils should produce more detailed reports, with additional information and art-related vocabulary.

Review

- Pupils should share their work in a small group.

Comprehension

Teacher Information

- Pupils may need a dictionary to complete question 4.

Introduction

- Pupils take it in turns to summarise the biographies of each artist in their own words.

Development

- Remind pupils how to use a dictionary efficiently; i.e. alphabetical order and retrieval by 1st, 2nd and 3rd letters. Give each pupil, or pair of pupils, a dictionary. Write words from the text onto the board for pupils to find.
- Pupils complete the comprehension activities on page 52 independently.

Differentiated Individual/Paired/Group Work

- Pupils should write a list of things that at least two of the three artists have in common; for example, All three artists painted landscapes, Gainsborough and Constable were both born in Suffolk.
- Less able pupils could create a list of four things the artists have in common, whilst more able pupils should aim for eight.

Review

- As a class, compare pupils' lists.

Word Reading

Teacher Information

- The activities on page 53 focus on specialist vocabulary, synonyms, antonyms, compound words, the /k/ sound spelt 'que', the suffix '-ous' and word origins.

Introduction

- Reread the text, but first explain to pupils that the focus will be on words. While reading, ask pupils to circle words that are the names of occupations. Discuss which of these occupations are still common today.

Development

- Ensure pupils are familiar with the terms 'synonym' and 'antonym'. Give some examples (happy: synonym is glad, antonym is sad). Elicit some examples from the pupils. Pupils suggest sentences for pairs of synonyms and antonyms, to be written onto the board; for example, happy = glad/sad. Ben was glad he had homework, but Krista was sad.

- Tell pupils that words ending in '-que' have a 'k' sound and are French in origin. Say some '-que' words aloud, and have pupils repeat them, to hear the sound. For example, technique, boutique, unique, antique.

- Look at words with the suffix '-ous'. Discuss that sometimes there is not an obvious root word; for example, 'poisonous' has the root word 'poison', but there is no root word for 'jealous'. Explain that whilst '-ous' can be added to many root words, '-our' is changed to '-or' before '-ous' is added; for example, humorous, glamorous.

- Tell pupils that the prefix 'pre-' means 'previous to' or 'before'. Ask pupils to find the word beginning with this prefix in the text (preliminary). Ask them to explain what 'preliminary' means. Pupils should suggest other words that start with this prefix.

- Discuss the word reading activities on page 53, then allow pupils to complete the page independently.

Differentiated Individual/Paired/Group Work

- Pupils should find and discuss the compound words in the text.

- Pupils should think of other compound words that contain the words 'sun', 'light', 'work' and 'ship', and write a list for each word.

- More able pupils should write a longer list than less able pupils.

Review

- As a class, compare pupils' lists of words. Which of the words has the greatest number of compound words? Was it easier to find compound words with the chosen word at the beginning or end? Why do pupils think this is?

Assessment

C1	Ask the pupils to write a list of ten things they learnt from the biographies. Were there any facts in the text that they already knew?
C5	Ask the pupils to write definitions of the following words: biography, portrait, merchant, notorious, lively, architect, exhibition, catastrophe
WR2	Present the following list of words to the pupils and ask them to sort them according to whether they have a 'gue' or 'que' ending: technique, antique, analogue, tongue, boutique, unique, league, catalogue, barbeque

Answers

Comprehension

1. ... give brief biographies of three landscape painters.
2. Answers may include six of the following: name, date of birth and death, birthplace, when and where studied, painting style, notable achievements, famous paintings.
3. Gainsborough—merged human figures with landscapes; used observations of nature to paint, not formal rules.
   Constable—brilliant colour and lively brushwork to show light and movement in clouds and sky.
   Turner—'painter of light'—emphasised light and colour in paintings.
4. (a) inspired—filled with the urge to do something creative
   (b) notorious—famous or well-known for some bad quality or deed
   (c) preliminary— preceding or done in preparation for something
   (d) topographical—relating to the arrangement or accurate representation of the physical features of an area
5. To become well-known (or make a name for himself) so that he could continue to work as an artist.
6. Many brief points of information can be included.
7. Gainsborough and Turner

Word Reading

1. Answers may include any from the following list: landscape, portrait(s), artists, engraving, painted, painter, figure, painting, oil, watercolour, techniques, colour, brushwork, light, sketches, water colourist, sketched, pencil, exhibit.
2. Answers will include eight from the following list: landscape painter, portrait painter, weaver, merchant, water colourist, printmaker, barber, wig maker, architect, topographical draughtsman.
3. (a) favourite—best-liked
   (b) lively—energetic
   (c) observations—ideas
4. good fortune
5. watercolour, brushwork, printmaker, draughtsmen, fishermen, shipwrecks, sunlight
6. (a) techniques
   (b) Answers could include: antique, boutique, unique.
7. notorious, famous
8. Latin 'prae' meaning 'before' and 'limen' meaning 'threshold'; 'pre-' means 'before'.

Great British Artists – 1

Read the explanation in the flow chart.

There is no doubt that Britain has produced some of the greatest artists in the world. Read short biographies of three of them.

Thomas Gainsborough (1727–1788)

- Landscape and portrait painter
- Born in Sudbury, Suffolk, son of a weaver
- 1740 – studied engraving in London
- 1769 – founding member of Royal Academy
- 1769 – exhibited portraits of well-known or notorious people
- 1780 – painted portraits of King George III and his queen; became Royal Family's favourite painter
- Established 18th century British landscape school
- Merged figures in portraits with landscape; painted from observations of nature rather than formal rules of art
- Most famous paintings – *Girl with Pigs* (1781–2), *The Blue Boy* (1770) and *Portrait of Mrs Graham* (1775)

John Constable (1776–1837)

- Oil and watercolour landscape painter
- Born in East Bergholt, Suffolk, son of a merchant
- 1799 – studied at Royal Academy
- 1819 – first important painting – *The White Horse* sold
- Inspired by Thomas Gainsborough
- Developed techniques of brilliant colour and lively brushwork to show light and movement of clouds and the sky
- Lectured at Royal Academy
- Painted large scale landscapes called 'six footers' with full-scale preliminary oil sketches
- Most famous paintings—*Dedham Vale* (1802) and *The Hay Wain* (1821)

J.M.W. Turner (1775–1851)

- Landscape painter, water colourist and printmaker
- Born Covent Garden, London, son of a barber and wig maker
- 1785 – First engraved plates done
- 1786 – Sketched town and surroundings of Margate
- 1789 – Pencil sketches of Berkshire landscape
- Drew for architects and topographical draughtsmen
- 1789 – Entered Royal Academy aged 14; first exhibit at 15
- 1796 – First oil painting – *Fishermen at Sea* – exhibited
- Called the 'Painter of Light'; painted shipwrecks, fires, storms, sunlight, rain, fog, natural catastrophes
- Most famous paintings – *The Fighting Temeraire* (1839) and *Snow Storm* (1842)

| **My learning log** | When I read these biographies, I could read: ☐ all of them. ☐ most of them. ☐ parts of them. |

Great British Artists – 2

1. The purpose of the texts is to _____

   _____.

2. Name six common things that are recorded in the biography of each artist.

   _____

   _____

   _____

3. Write one sentence about the painting style (the way each painted) of each artist.

   • Gainsborough _____

   _____

   • Constable _____

   _____

   • Turner _____

   _____

4. Write the dictionary meaning of each word.

   (a) inspired   _____

   (b) notorious   _____

   (c) preliminary   _____

   (d) topographical   _____

5. Why do you think Gainsborough painted portraits of well-known or notorious people in his early career?

   _____

6. Why were bullet points used for the main part of the text?

   _____

7. Which two artists both did engravings?

   _____

My learning log	While doing these activities:		
	I found Q _____ easy.	I found Q _____ challenging.	I found Q _____ interesting.

Great British Artists – 3

1. Write six words from the text that relate to art and painting.

   _____ _____ _____ _____ _____ _____

2. Write eight words that are occupations of the 18th and 19th centuries.

   _____ _____ _____ _____

   _____ _____ _____ _____

3. Underline the synonym for each word.

   (a) **favourite:**   taste   best-liked   worst

   (b) **lively:**   energetic   friendly   quiet

   (c) **observations:**   stubborn   studies   ideas

4. In the phrase 'natural catastrophes', which antonym could be used to replace 'catastrophes' to give it the opposite meaning? Circle it.

   | disasters | good fortune | emergencies | climate |

5. Find and write seven compound words in the text.

   _____ _____ _____ _____

   _____ _____ _____

6. (a) Find and write a word with the /k/ sound spelt 'que'. _____

   (b) Can you think of any other words with this ending?

   _____

7. Write two words in the text with the suffix '-ous'.

   _____   _____

8. Use a dictionary to find the origin of the word 'preliminary' and explain what the prefix 'pre-' means in the word.

   _____

   _____

My learning log	**Colour:**	I [can] / [can't] sort words by topic.
		I [understand] / [need more practice on] synonyms and antonyms.
		I [know] / [don't know] about compound words.

Brazil

Curriculum Links

Activity	Code	Objective	Outcome
Text	C2 C3	• Participate in discussion about both books that are read to them and those they can read for themselves • Listen to and discuss a wide range of non-fiction	• Can identify non-fiction information texts and talk about their key features
Comprehension	C1 C5 C11	• Retrieve and record information from non-fiction • Use dictionaries to check the meaning of words that they have read • Check that the text makes sense to them, discuss their understanding and explain the meaning of words in context	• Can answer questions about a non-fiction text • Can explain the meanings of words
Word Reading	WR1 WR2	• Apply their growing knowledge of root words, prefixes and suffixes • Read further exception words, noting the unusual correspondences between spelling and sound	• Can recognise root words and a range of prefixes and suffixes • Can recognise homophones and the /ɪ/ sound spelt 'y'

Additional Teacher Information

Definition of Terms

Text
A book or other written or printed work, regarded in terms of its content rather than its physical form.

Report
A report is a written document describing the findings of an individual or group. A report may take the form of a newspaper report, sports or police report, or a report about an animal, person or object.

Table
A set of facts or figures systematically displayed, especially in columns.

Paragraph
A distinct section of a piece of writing, usually dealing with a single theme and indicated by a new line, indentation or numbering.

Terminology for Pupils

information
report
table
dictionary
phrase
root word
prefix
suffix
homophone

Suggested Reading

• *Brazil: The Land* (Lands, Peoples and Cultures) by **Malika Hollander**
• *Spotlight on Brazil* (Spotlight on My Country) by **Bobbie Kalman**
• *Brazil* by **Michael Dah**

Links to other Curriculum Areas

• Geography – Locational knowledge: locate the world's countries, using maps to focus on South America, concentrating on their environmental regions, key physical and human characteristics, countries and major cities; Place knowledge: understand geographical similarities and differences through the study of human and physical geography of a region within South America; Human and physical geography: describe and understand key aspects of physical geography (biomes, rivers); human geography (types of settlement)

Text

Teacher Information

- Brazil is the largest country in South America, and the fifth largest country in the world. With a population of over 200 million people, it has the fifth largest population in the world.

Introduction

- Look at a large map of South America with the pupils, either as a poster or in atlases. Ask pupils to locate Brazil, and read the names of the neighbouring countries. Reread the text and highlight the names of places that are mentioned. Find these places on the map (Amazon River, Iguazu Falls, Pantanal, Sao Paulo, Rio de Janeiro and Brasilia).

Development

- Read and discuss the text with the pupils, as a whole class or in groups. Assist pupils to decode new words if necessary. Discuss the meaning of any new or unfamiliar words and phrases such as 'accounting for', 'uncontacted peoples', 'traditional', 'discharge', 'volume', 'ancestors', 'cascades', 'region', 'tropical', 'wetland', 'species', 'architecture', 'population', 'redeemer', 'populous' and 'colonial'. Question individual pupils to gauge their understanding of what they have listened to or read. Pupils should also ask questions about parts of the text they are unsure of, in order to improve their understanding.

Differentiated Individual/Paired/Group Work

- Choose one of the three places listed in the 'Physical Geography' section. Use the Internet and other resources to write a report to tell about this place. A map and illustrations should be included.
- More able pupils should produce a more detailed report.

Review

- Pupils should present their work neatly and display it in the classroom.

Comprehension

Teacher Information

- Pupils may need a dictionary to complete questions 5 and 8.
- Answers for the natural features in the table for question 4 have been split into Amazon River and Rainforest, and Iguazu Falls and Iguazu River but teachers may accept these combined.
- Pupils need to be familiar with the terms 'flora' and 'fauna' to complete question 8.

Introduction

- Pupils take it in turns to summarise each section in their own words.

Development

- Remind pupils how to use a dictionary efficiently; i.e. alphabetical order and retrieval by 1st, 2nd and 3rd letters. Give each pupil, or pair of pupils, a dictionary. Write words from the text onto the board for pupils to find.
- Discuss the comprehension activities on page 58, then allow pupils to complete the page independently.

Differentiated Individual/Paired/Group Work

- As a class, discuss pupils' answers to question 6, which asks why the Pantanal should be protected. Research problems the Amazon Rainforest is experiencing and why it should also be protected. Pupils should write a list of points in favour of protecting the Amazon Rainforest.
- Less able pupils should write a list of 4–5 reasons, whilst more able pupils should create a more comprehensive list.

Review

- As a class, compare pupils' lists of reasons.

Word Reading

Teacher Information

- The activities on page 59 focus on root words, the prefixes 'un-' and 'dis-', the suffix '-ian', homophones and adjectives.

Introduction

- Reread the text, but first explain to pupils that the focus will be on words. While reading, ask pupils to circle words that are proper nouns; i.e. the names of continents, countries, rivers, nationalities etc. Explain that as these are names they should always start with a capital letter.

Development

- Look at words with the prefixes 'un-' and 'dis-'. Discuss how adding these prefixes makes the words negative; for example, 'do' becomes 'undo' and 'obey' becomes 'disobey'. Write sentences containing the pairs of words; for example, Peter was <u>kind</u> to Marissa, but <u>unkind</u> to me.

- Discuss the names given to people from different countries; i.e. their nationalities. The nationalities in question 3 all end in '-ian'. Can the pupils think of other endings that are used for nationalities? Write a list on the board.

- Words with the /ɪ/ sound spelt 'y' elsewhere than at the end of words should be spoken out loud and learnt as needed; for example, physical, gym, myth, mystery.

- Ensure pupils are familiar with the term 'homophone'. Give some examples (berry/bury, scene/seen, plain/plane). Elicit some examples from the pupils. Pupils suggest sentences for pairs of homophones, to be written onto the board; for example, main/mane = He is walking down the <u>main</u> road./That horse has a beautiful <u>mane</u>.

- Discuss the word reading activities on page 59, then allow pupils to complete the page independently.

Differentiated Individual/Paired/Group Work

- Pupils should look at the text and identify the three nationalities (Brazilian, Argentinian and Portuguese). Explain that a range of suffixes are used for nationalities, including '-ian' and '-ese'.

- Pupils should research and write a list of other nationalities with these suffixes.

- More able pupils could try and discover whether nationalities from certain parts of the world are more likely to have certain endings than others; for example, the '-ish' suffix is mainly used for European nations and '-i' for nations in the Middle East.

Review

- As a class, compare pupils' lists of nationalities. Which suffix has the greatest number of nationalities?

Assessment

C5	Ask the pupils to write definitions for the following words from the text:
	border, species, discharge, ancestors, tropical, rare, hyacinth, tourist
C12	Ask the pupils to write a list of questions they would like to know about Brazil.
	Afterwards they could research the answers.
WR1	Present the following list of words to the pupils and ask them to identify each word's prefix:
	uncontacted, redeem, discharge, misbehave, inactive, autograph, superstar, impossible, submarine, preheat

Answers

Comprehension

1. Physical Geography; Human Geography
2. Nile
3. No; The capital of Brazil is Brasilia which is the fourth most populous city; Sao Paulo has the largest population.
4. Natural Features of Brazil (6): Amazon River; Amazon Rainforest; Iguazu Falls; Iguazu River; Pantanal Wetland Area; Ipanema Beach
   Man-made Features of Brazil (7): Sao Paulo; Octavio Frias de Oliveira Bridge; Rio de Janiero; Christ the Redeemer statue; Brasilia; Juscelino Kubitschek Bridge; Cathedral of Brasilia
5. (a) discharge—release; let go
   (b) traditional— long-established; acting as part of a tradition
   (c) cascades—pour down rapidly in vast quantities
   (d) colonial—relating to or characteristic of a colony
6. The Pantanal area should be protected because it is the home of many rare species of birds and animals. If it is destroyed, the rare species would disappear.
7. Tribes/Groups of people who have lived without the contact of white people or other tribes.
8. fauna
9. It covers a large land area of the world; It has 200 million people.

Word Reading

1. populate
2. uncontacted, discharge
3. (a) Ecuadorian (b) Peruvian (c) Australian
   (d) Italian (e) Belgian (f) Egyptian
   (g) Iranian (h) Norwegian (i) Russian
4. (a) -al; tradition (b) -age; per cent
   (c) -ing; account (d) -al; tropic
   (e) -ly; part (f) -al; nature
   (g) -er; old (h) -ure; architect
5. myth, gymnasium
6. (a) some (b) for
   (c) new (d) by
7. (a) large (b) world's known/rare
   (c) many, high-rise (d) modern/colonial
   (e) two, modern (f) populous/largest/other/older

Brazil – 1

Read the information report.

Brazil is the world's fifth largest country and the largest country in South America. It shares borders with all other countries on the continent except Chile and Ecuador. Home to over 200 million people, Brazil's population ranks fifth in the world. Brazil has some interesting natural and man-made geographical features.

Physical Geography

Amazon River and Rainforest

- The Amazon is home to millions of plant, animal, bird and fish species accounting for a large percentage of all the world's known species.

- The river is the world's second longest after the Nile and is the largest river in the world by discharge of water volume.

- The Amazon is still home to a small number of 'uncontacted peoples' who live traditional lives as their ancestors have done for thousands of years.

Iguazu Falls and River

- The falls are located on the border of Brazil and Argentina.

- The river's water cascades over the cliffs, falling 60–80 metres.

- The falls bring many tourists to the region, on both the Brazilian and Argentinian sides.

Pantanal

- The world's largest tropical wetland area is home to many rare species such as the giant river otter, the hyacinth macaw and the maned wolf.

- It is located mostly in Brazil and partly in Bolivia and Paraguay.

Human Geography

Sao Paulo

- Founded by the Portuguese in 1554, Sao Paulo is the largest city in Brazil and has a population of around 20 million people.

- The Octavio Frias de Oliveira Bridge, completed in 2008, is an example of modern architecture in the city.

Rio de Janiero

- Founded by the Portuguese in 1565, this city was Brazil's capital from 1793–1960.

- Ipanema Beach is a natural feature lined with many high-rise buildings and often visited by locals and tourists.

- The enormous statue, Christ the Redeemer, was built from 1922 and completed in 1931. It stands on a mountain top overlooking the city.

Brasilia

- This city was constructed to become Brazil's new capital from 1960 and is now the country's fourth most populous city.

- The Juscelino Kubitschek Bridge and Cathedral of Brasilia are two modern structures. They are very different from the colonial architecture found throughout Brazil's other older cities.

My learning log	When I read this report, I could read:	☐ all of it. ☐ most of it. ☐ parts of it.

Brazil – 2

1. What two categories has the information about Brazil been sorted into?

_____   _____

2. The longest river in the world is the _____.

3. Is the capital of Brazil the city with the largest population? Explain.

_____

_____

4. Complete the table.

Natural Features of Brazil (6)	Man-made Features of Brazil (7)

5. Match the dictionary meanings to the correct words.

(a) discharge   •   •   long-established; acting as part of a tradition

(b) traditional   •   •   relating to or characteristic of a colony

(c) cascades   •   •   release; let go

(d) colonial   •   •   pour down rapidly in vast quantities

6. Why should the tropical wetland area of the Pantanal be protected?

_____

7. What does the phrase 'uncontacted peoples' mean?

_____

8. Which word describes the giant river otter, the hyacinth macaw and the maned wolf? Underline it.   flora   fauna

9. Why is Brazil the fifth largest country in the world?

_____

My learning log	While doing these activities:		
	I found Q _____ easy.	I found Q _____ challenging.	I found Q _____ interesting.

Brazil – 3

1. The root word for 'population' and 'populous' is _____.

2. The prefixes 'un-' and 'dis-' give words an opposite meaning.
   Find two words in the text with these prefixes.

   _____   _____

3. If you are Brazilian, it means you come from Brazil. Many nationalities have the suffix '-ian'. Research and write the nationalities of people from the following countries. (Be careful, some change their spelling!)

   (a) Ecuador _____   (b) Peru _____   (c) Australia _____

   (d) Italy _____   (e) Belgium _____   (f) Egypt _____

   (g) Iran _____   (h) Norway _____   (i) Russia _____

4. Underline the prefix and/or suffix and write the root word for each word.

   (a) traditional _____   (b) percentage _____

   (c) accounting _____   (d) tropical _____

   (e) partly _____   (f) natural _____

   (g) older _____   (h) architecture _____

5. The word 'physical' has an /ɪ/ sound spelt 'y'. Circle the words with the same 'y' sound.

   | geography | myth | country | gymnasium |

6. Write a homophone for each word that can be found in the text.

   (a) sum _____   (b) four _____

   (c) knew _____   (d) bye _____

7. Write a descriptive word or phrase from the text for each noun.

   (a) _____ percentage   (b) _____ species

   (c) _____ buildings   (d) _____ architecture

   (e) _____ structures   (f) _____ city

My learning log	**Colour:**	I [can] / [can't] recognise the prefixes 'un-' and 'dis-'.
		I [know] / [don't know] the suffixes used for some nationalities.
		I [can] / [can't] recognise adjectives in a text.

Master of all Masters

Curriculum Links

Activity	Code	Objective	Outcome
Text	C2	• Participate in discussion about both books that are read to them and those they can read for themselves	• Can identify poems and talk about their key features
	C3	• Listen to and discuss a wide range of poetry	
	C6	• Increase their familiarity with a wide range of books	
Comprehension	C5	• Use dictionaries to check the meaning of words that they have read	• Can explain the meanings of words
	C9	• Discuss words and phrases that capture the reader's interest and imagination	• Can talk about the most interesting words in a poem
	C10	• Recognise some different forms of poetry	• Can recognise rhyme in a poem
	C13	• Draw inferences such as inferring characters' feelings, thoughts and motives from their actions, and justifying inferences with evidence	• Can infer why characters do certain things
			• Can summarise a verse from a poem
	C15	• Identify main ideas and summarise them	
Word Reading	WR1	• Apply their growing knowledge of root words	• Can recognise root words
	WR2	• Read further exception words, noting the unusual correspondences between spelling and sound	• Can recognise homophones

Additional Teacher Information

Definition of Terms

Folk tale

A folk tale is a story passed from one generation to the next by word of mouth rather than being written down. A folk tale may include sayings, superstitions, social rituals, legends or lore about the weather, animals or plants.

Poem

A piece of writing in which the expression of feelings and ideas is given intensity by particular attention to diction (sometimes involving rhyme), rhythm and imagery.

Narrative

A narrative is a text that tells a story. It includes a title, orientation (setting, time and characters), complication to main character(s), series of events, resolution to complication and ending.

Rhyme

A group of lines that form a unit in a poem or song; a stanza.

Verse

Free verse is an open form of poetry which does not use consistent metre patterns, rhyme or any other musical pattern. It often follows the rhythm of natural speech.

Links to other Curriculum Areas

• History—common words and phrases relating to the passing of time; similarities and differences between ways of life in different periods (Revision of Key Stage 1 concepts)

Terminology for Pupils

folk tale
poem
free verse
narrative
rhyme
phrase
verse
dictionary
root word
homophone
antonym
synonym

Suggested Reading

• *Master of All Masters: An English Folk Tale* illustrated by **Marcia Sewall**

Text

Teacher Information

- 'Master of all Masters' is an English folk tale. This version is based on the narrative by Joseph Jacobs, folklorist, literary critic and historian who compiled and edited a number of books of English, Celtic, Indian and European fairy and folk tales.

Introduction

- The names for various common objects and names of the 1890s (abode, couch, master, pantaloons) could provide a humorous oral activity for pupils as they reread or dramatise the poem.
- Some discussion may derive from the poem about informal language for everyday objects.

Development

- Read and discuss the text with the pupils, as a whole class or in groups. Assist pupils to decode new words if necessary. Discuss the meaning of any new or unfamiliar words and phrases; e.g. servant, elderly, engaged, master, pantaloons, diction and slackers. Question individual pupils to gauge their understanding of what they have listened to or read. Pupils should also ask questions about parts of the text they are unsure of, in order to improve their understanding.
- Discuss the rhyming pattern of the poem; i.e. for each stanza, lines 1 and 2 and lines 3 and 4 rhyme.

Differentiated Individual/Paired/Group Work

- As a class, list the nonsense words that the Master allocated to everyday objects.
- Pupils should choose some classroom objects and create nonsense word names for them; for example, pencil, pencil sharpener, light bulb.
- Less able pupils should aim to create 6–8 nonsense words, and more able pupils a longer list.

Review

- Pupils should say some of their nonsense words to the class. Can the other pupils guess the classroom object from the nonsense word?

Comprehension

Teacher Information

- Pupils may need a dictionary to complete question 7.

Introduction

- Pupils should discuss the use of the nonsense and old-fashioned vocabulary. Which words do the pupils most like, or find the most interesting, and why?

Development

- Remind pupils how to use a dictionary efficiently; i.e. alphabetical order and retrieval by 1st, 2nd and 3rd letters. Give each pupil, or pair of pupils, a dictionary. Write words from the text onto the board for pupils to find.
- Discuss the comprehension activities on page 64, then allow pupils to complete the page independently.

Differentiated Individual/Paired/Group Work

- Pupils should work in mixed ability groups of three to produce a dramatisation of the poem. The three parts should be the narrator, the Master and the servant girl. Pupils should take it in turns to play the three parts.

Review

- As a class, pupils should discuss their performances. Which part was the hardest/most fun to play? Did pupils have difficulty pronouncing any of the words?

Word Reading

Teacher Information

- The activities on page 65 focus on vocabulary, root words, homophones, synonyms and antonyms.

Introduction

- Reread the text, but first explain to pupils that the focus will be on words. While reading, ask pupils to circle any nonsense words. Discuss what these nonsense words might mean.

Development

- Ensure pupils are familiar with the term 'homophone'. Give some examples (berry/bury, scene/seen, plain/plane). Elicit some examples from the pupils. Pupils suggest sentences for pairs of homophones, to be written onto the board; for example, *main/mane* = He is walking down the <u>main</u> road./That horse has a beautiful <u>mane</u>.

- Ensure pupils are familiar with the terms 'synonym' and 'antonym'. Give some examples (happy: synonym is glad, antonym is sad). Elicit some examples from the pupils. Pupils suggest sentences for pairs of synonyms and antonyms, to be written onto the board; for example, happy = glad/sad. Ben was <u>glad</u> he had homework, but Krista was <u>sad</u>.

- Discuss the word reading activities on page 65, then allow pupils to complete the page independently.

Differentiated Individual/Paired/Group Work

- In pairs, pupils should find and list words with the '-ed' suffix; for example, climbed, cried, danced. They should then sort them according to how the suffix was added and place them in a table.

- Less able pupils should try and find five words for each column of the table, whilst more able pupils could find a lot more.

'-ed' added straight onto end of root words	Root words ending in 'y' change to 'i'	Root words ending in 'e' drop the 'e'
called	replied	engaged
discussed	dried	continued
hissed	cried	named

Review

- As a class, compare pupils' lists of '-ed' words. Which of the suffixes has the greatest number of words?

C3	Ask the pupils to write a short review of the poem. The review needs to include a short synopsis of the poem and give the pupil's opinion of it.
C5	Write the following words on the board and ask pupils to write them in alphabetical order: servant, slackers, she, speech, seek, squibs, services, show
WR1	Write the following words on the board and ask pupils to write their root words: employment, looking, called, replies, continued, newly, learnt, arrival

Answers

Comprehension

1. (b) and (c) should be ticked
2. Answers will vary.
3. Answers may include: In an emergency, the quickest way to relate information should be used; It is a bit ridiculous to use fancy or unusual words when a few simple ones could relate the same information more quickly when necessary.
4. Answers will vary.
5. Answers will vary but may state that the old man knew that the cat's tail was on fire and he needed to get water to save the house from being burnt down; He got out of bed, put on his trousers, and got water to put the fire out.
6. Teacher check
7. (a) diction—the choice and use of words and phrases in speech and writing.
   (b) pantaloons— men's close-fitting trousers fastened below the calf or at the foot.
8. The words at the end of the first and second; and third and fourth lines of each verse rhyme.

Word Reading

1. home/house
2. trousers
3. (a) engage (b) employ (c) point (d) continue
4. barnacle, squibs and crackers, white-faced simminy, high topper mountain, cockalorum, pondalorum
5. (a) fare (b) their/they're (c) knight (d) thyme (e) tale (f) knead (g) too/two (h) plaice (i) four (j) sum (k) berry (l) peace
6. (a) elderly (b) many (c) long (d) arrival (e) high (f) night
7. (a) grin (b) seek (c) things (d) begin (e) replied (f) maid

Master of all Masters – 1

Read the folk tale in the form of a poem.

Master of all Masters

Once long ago a servant girl went to a nearby fair

To seek employment from one of the people there.

At last an elderly man—a funny-looking gent

Engaged her services so to his home she went.

Upon her arrival at his abode, he gave her quite a speech

About the names he called his things—the names he had to teach.

'What will you call me?' he asked. 'That is the place to begin.'

'Master or mister or whatever you please', she replied with a grin.

'Master of all masters it is!' he said, and pointing to his bed,

'A bed or couch is called a barnacle', he said.

'What about my pantaloons?' he asked. 'Breeches or trousers', the maid replied.

'Squibs and crackers is their name. Please use those words!' he cried.

And so the lesson continued with many words discussed.

The cat was the 'white-faced simminy'; 'hot cockalorum' the fire that hissed.

'Pondalorum' named water and the house the 'high topper mountain'.

That very night the servant girl had to use her newly-learnt diction.

'Master of all masters, get out of your barnacle!' she yelled. 'Put on your squibs and crackers!

This is no time for anyone here to show that they are slackers!

The white-faced simminy has on its tail a spark of hot cockalorum.

To save your 'high topper mountain' you need to get some pondalorum!

—That's all!'

My learning log	When I read this poem, I could read:	☐ all of it. ☐ most of it. ☐ parts of it.

Master of all Masters – 2

1. What form of poem is the one on page 63?

   (a) free verse ☐   (b) narrative ☐   (c) rhyming ☐

2. Which words are the most interesting in the poem and why?

   _____

   _____

3. What do you think this folk tale in poetry form is trying to teach the reader?

   _____

   _____

4. Why do you think the old gentleman wanted the servant girl to use the words and phrases that he liked using for common objects?

   _____

   _____

5. What do you think happened after the servant girl used the words and phrases to warn the old man about the fire danger?

   _____

   _____

6. In your own words, relate what the servant girl was telling the old gentleman in verse five.

   _____

   _____

   _____

7. Use a dictionary to write the meanings of the following words.

   (a) diction   _____

   (b) pantaloons _____

8. What is the pattern of the poem?

   _____

My learning log	While doing these activities:		
	I found Q _____ easy.	I found Q _____ challenging.	I found Q _____ interesting.

Master of all Masters - 3

1. The old man took the servant girl to his 'abode'.

   This means he took her to his _____.

2. Which word from the old Irish word 'triús' means 'an outer garment covering the body from the waist to the ankles, with a separate part for each leg'?

   _____

3. Write the root words for each word.

   (a) engaged _____   (b) employment _____

   (c) pointing _____   (d) continued _____

4. Which words that the old gentleman used for objects are used only in

   this folk tale? _____

   _____

   _____

5. Write a homophone for each word.

   (a) fair _____   (b) there _____   (c) night _____

   (d) time _____   (e) tail _____   (f) need _____

   (g) to _____   (h) place _____   (i) for _____

   (j) some _____   (k) bury _____   (l) piece _____

6. Which words from the text are antonyms of the words below?

   (a) young _____   (b) few _____   (c) short _____

   (d) departure _____   (e) low _____   (f) day _____

7. Which words from the text are synonyms of the words below?

   (a) smile _____   (b) search for _____

   (c) possessions _____   (d) start _____

   (e) answered _____   (f) servant girl _____

My learning log	***Colour:***	I can / can't recognise root words.
		I can / can't read nonsense words.
		I understand / need more practice on synonyms and antonyms.

The Hawk and the Grass

Curriculum Links

Activity	Code	Objective	Outcome
Text	C2	• Participate in discussion about both books that are read to them and those they can read for themselves	• Can identify plays and talk about their key features
	C3	• Listen to and discuss a wide range of plays	
	C6	• Increase their familiarity with a wide range of books	
Comprehension	C5	• Use dictionaries to check the meaning of words that they have read	• Can explain the meanings of words
	C11	• Check that the text makes sense to them, discuss their understanding and explain the meaning of words in context	• Can answer questions about the text
	C13	• Draw inferences such as inferring characters' feelings, thoughts and motives for their actions	• Can explain why a character looks panicked
Word Reading	WR1	• Apply their growing knowledge of root words and suffixes	• Can recognise root words and a range of suffixes
	WR2	• Read further exception words, noting the unusual correspondences between spelling and sound	

Additional Teacher Information

Definition of Terms

Play
A play is a specific piece of drama, usually enacted on a stage by a number of actors dressed in make-up and appropriate costumes.

Text
A book or other written or printed work, regarded in terms of its content rather than its physical form.

Opinion
A view or judgement formed about something, not necessarily based on fact or knowledge.

Descriptive
Serving or seeking to describe.

Author
A writer of a book, article or document.

Formal/Informal language
Formal language is used in serious situations or ones that involve people we don't know well, and often in writing. Informal language is used in more relaxed situations and with people we know well. It is more commonly used when we speak. Each uses particular grammar and vocabulary. For example, informal language often uses contractions, relative clauses without a relative pronoun and ellipsis.

Links to other Curriculum Areas

• Science—Living things and their habitats (recognise that living things can be grouped in a variety of ways); Animals including humans (construct and interpret a variety of food chains, identifying producers, predators and prey)

Terminology for Pupils

play
text
dictionary
suffix
sentence
root word
synonym
antonym

Suggested Reading

• *What are Food Chains and Webs?* (Science of Living Things) by **Bobbie Kalman**
• *Pass the Energy, Please!* by **Barbara Shaw McKinney**
• *Hawks* (Birds) by **Cecilia Pinto McCarthy**

Text

Teacher Information

- This short play is an imaginative way to impart information. Pupils are introduced to prey, producers and primary and secondary consumers.

Introduction

- Teachers may select pupils to read or 'act out' the parts of the two main characters in the play. They should use intonation, tone, volume, gestures and body language to support their play reading.

Development

- Read and discuss the text with the pupils, as a whole class or in groups. Assist pupils to decode new words if necessary. Discuss the meaning of any new or unfamiliar words and phrases; e.g. imperious, regally, producers and consumers. Question individual pupils to gauge their understanding of what they have listened to or read. Pupils should also ask questions about parts of the text they are unsure of, in order to improve their understanding.

Differentiated Individual/Paired/Group Work

- Working in mixed ability pairs, pupils should read the play, using intonation, tone, volume, gestures and body language to support their play reading.

Review

- Pupils should discuss the parts of the play they found the easiest and most difficult to perform, and give reasons why.

Comprehension

Teacher Information

- Pupils will need to understand food chains and the vocabulary producers, consumers and prey.
- Pupils will need a dictionary to complete question 6.

Introduction

- Discuss the features of a play; for example, setting, list of characters and stage directions. Another play should be looked at, which has all these features.

Development

- Pupils describe what is going to happen to each character in the play. Will they be eaten or will they eat another?
- Discuss the meaning of fiction and non-fiction. Why could this play be described as being a mixture of both?
- Discuss the comprehension activities on page 70, then allow pupils to complete the page independently.

Differentiated Individual/Paired/Group Work

- Pupils should use the information given by the Grass in paragraph 9 (the longest paragraph), to create a food chain. The food chain needs to include: The source of energy (sun); producers (plants and grass); plant-eating consumers (insects and rabbits); and meat-eating consumers (hawks).
- More able pupils could add other plants and animals into the food chain at the various levels.

Review

- As a class, discuss food chains that can be found in other ecosystems; for example, a pond, the ocean.

Word Reading

Teacher Information

- The activities on page 71 focus on the suffixes '-ous' and '-ly', root words, vocabulary, synonyms and antonyms.

Introduction

- Reread the text, but first explain to pupils that the focus will be on words. While reading, ask pupils to find and circle words they feel are technical or scientific vocabulary referring to food chains.

Development

- Look at words with the suffix '-ous'. Discuss that sometimes there is not an obvious root word; for example, 'poisonous' has the root word 'poison', but there is no root word for 'jealous'. Explain that whilst '-ous' can be added to many root words, '-our' is changed to '-or' before '-ous' is added; for example, humorous, glamorous.
- Look at words with the suffix '-ly'. Tell pupils that this suffix is added to an adjective to form an adverb. Explain that usually the suffix is added straight onto the end of most root words; for example, sadly, finally. However, there are exceptions, which should also be explained to the pupils:
  (1) If the root word ends in '-y' with a consonant letter before it, the 'y' is changed to 'i', but only if the root word has more than one syllable; for example, happily.
  (2) If the root word ends with '-le', the '-le' is changed to '-ly'; for example, simply.
  (3) If the root word ends with '-ic', '-ally' is added rather than just '-ly'; for example, basically. An exception is 'publicly'.
  (4) The words truly, duly and wholly.
- Ensure pupils are familiar with the terms 'synonym' and 'antonym'. Give some examples (happy: synonym is glad, antonym is sad). Elicit some examples from the pupils. Pupils suggest sentences for pairs of synonyms and antonyms, to be written onto the board; for example, happy = *glad/sad*. Ben was glad he had homework, but Krista was sad.
- Discuss the word reading activities on page 71, then allow pupils to complete the page independently.

Differentiated Individual/Paired/Group Work

- Pupils should write a list of suffixes that can be added to a given list of root words. The suffixes should include -ed, -ing, -ly and -er. The root words could be: warm, kind, loud, speak, heat and control.
- As an additional challenge, more able pupils could think of a root word to which all four of these suffixes can be added.

Review

- As a class, compare pupils' lists of words. Discuss the results of the challenge activity.

Assessment

C3	Ask the pupils to write a short play about the food chain using the following characters: sun, grass, rabbit, hawk.
C5	Present the following list of words to the pupils and ask them to write a definition for each: hawk, branch, imperious, lush, shrew, mercy, survive, convince
WR1	Present the following list of root words to the pupils and ask them to write them into two lists, according to whether they can add the suffix '-ly' or '-ous': slight, loud, mountain, fame, regal, vary, calm, firm, poison, danger

Answers

Comprehension

1. (a), (b) and (c) should be ticked
2. (a) producer   (b) consumer   (c) consumer   (d) consumer
3. to show who is speaking
4. The insects and rabbits would have no food and would die; then the food for the larger consumers would decrease and they may die out too.
5. ... impart simple information about food chains in a different, more interesting manner/structure.
6. (a) lush—very rich; healthy; impressive
   (b) bask—lie in the warmth and light for recreation and pleasure
   (c) imperious—bossy; dominating
7. Answers may include that the hawk will be hunted or killed by the hunter.
8. Answers may include: The hawk realises that he is not so powerful after all; He realises that he depends on others to survive.
9. A food chain is a series of organisms (plants and animals) that each depend on the next as a source of food.

Word Reading

1. imperious, obvious
2. (a) loudly, regally, calmly, firmly, exactly, slightly
   (b) Teacher check
3. Teacher check
4. (a) powerful   (b) depends   (c) speaking
   (d) warmth   (e) stretches   (f) hunter
   (g) loudly   (h) decided
5. energy, consumer, producer
6. The words make the hawk seem like a king.
7. (a) excellent/great   (b) forest   (c) powerful
   (d) warmth   (e) snatch   (f) under
8. (a) prey   (b) true   (c) sure
   (d) stretches   (e) sitting   (f) high

The Hawk and the Grass – 1

Read the short play.

Scene:	The hawk is sitting on a high branch of a tree in the forest, scouting the fields for prey and looking imperious. The grass beneath the tree is lush and green. The grass stretches towards the sun basking in its warmth.
Hawk:	It is an excellent day to survey my kingdom. (*squawks loudly and regally*)
Grass:	What do you mean YOUR kingdom? Who decided that you were the ruler of everything? (*speaking calmly but firmly*)
Hawk:	Well, it's obvious. All the animals fear me. I can fly down and snatch a mouse, shrew, hare or rabbit whenever I am hungry. All ground creatures are under my control.
Grass:	I wouldn't be so sure about that! Your life depends on others! Without living things like me, you wouldn't survive!
Hawk:	What rubbish! I look after myself. I'm a great hunter. Other animals are at my mercy! I don't depend on anyone or anything!
Grass:	That's not exactly true! You're just another part of the food chain. Listen while I explain how a food chain works.
Hawk:	Oh hurry up! Get on with it! Nothing you can say will convince me that another living thing is as important as me!
Grass:	The sun is the source of energy for all living things in a food chain. Energy from the sun makes plants grow. Plants, like me, change light energy into food so we can grow. We are producers of food for others. Plant eaters like insects and rabbits eat grass to get energy. They are the consumers. Then, creatures like you, who are also consumers, eat the other consumers. In short, your life depends on the sun and other living things like me. I guess that doesn't make you so powerful after all. In fact, without me, you would be powerless!
Hawk:	That can't be true! I control my own life! (*looks slightly panicked*) And even if it is true, I'm still the last consumer in the food chain.
Grass:	Tell that to the hunter! (*waves blades of grass towards a pair of hunting boots approaching*)

My learning log	When I read this play, I could read:	☐ all of it.	☐ most of it.	☐ parts of it.

The Hawk and the Grass – 2

1. What kind of text is the play? Tick more than one.

   (a) imaginative ☐   (b) informative ☐   (c) persuasive ☐

   (d) narrative ☐   (e) poetry ☐   (f) folk tale ☐

2. Next to each creature write either producer or consumer.

   (a) grass _____   (b) rabbit _____

   (c) insect _____   (d) hawk _____

3. Why are the names 'Hawk' and 'Grass' used repeatedly?

   _____

4. What would happen if there was no grass for the insects and rabbits to eat?

   _____

   _____

5. The purpose of this short play is to _____

   _____.

6. Write the dictionary meanings of the words below.

   (a) lush   _____

   (b) bask   _____

   (c) imperious _____

7. What do you think will happen to the hawk? _____

   _____

8. Why do you think the hawk 'looks slightly panicked' near the end of the play?

   _____

   _____

9. A food chain is _____

   _____.

My learning log	While doing these activities:		
	I found Q _____ easy.	I found Q _____ challenging.	I found Q _____ interesting.

The Hawk and the Grass – 3

1. Find and write two words from the text with the suffix '-ous'.

_____   _____

2. (a) Find and write six words from the text with the suffix '-ly'.

_____ _____ _____ _____ _____ _____

(b) Use two of these words in a sentence.

_____

_____

3. The grass uses the words 'powerful' and 'powerless' in one sentence. Write another sentence that uses both these words.

_____

_____

4. Underline the root word and circle the suffix.

(a) powerful   (b) depends   (c) speaking   (d) warmth

(e) stretches   (f) hunter   (g) loudly   (h) decided

5. Underline three words that relate to the food chain.

| energy | consumer | producer | control | kingdom |

6. Why does the author use the words 'imperious', 'kingdom', 'regally' and 'ruler' to describe the hawk?

_____

7. Write the synonym in the text for each word.

(a) fabulous _____   (b) wood _____   (c) strong _____

(d) heat _____   (e) grab _____   (f) beneath _____

8. Write the antonym in the text for each word.

(a) predator _____   (b) false _____   (c) unsure _____

(d) shrinks _____   (e) standing _____   (f) low _____

My learning log	**Colour:**	I can / can't recognise a range of suffixes.
		I know / don't know words relating to the food chain.
		I understand / need more practice on synonyms and antonyms.

Boudicca

Curriculum Links

Activity	Code	Objective	Outcome
Text	C2 C3 C6	• Participate in discussion about both books that are read to them and those they can read for themselves • Listen to and discuss a wide range of fiction • Increase their familiarity with a wide range of books, including legends	• Can identify legends and talk about their key features
Comprehension	C5 C14 C15	• Use dictionaries to check the meaning of words that they have read • Predict what might happen from details stated and implied • Identify main ideas drawn from more than one paragraph and summarise them	• Can explain the meanings of words • Can predict what might have happened to Boudicca if she had been captured • Can list differences between armies
Word Reading	WR1 WR2	• Apply their growing knowledge of root words, prefixes and suffixes • Read further exception words, noting the unusual correspondences between spelling and sound	• Can recognise root words, the prefix 'in-' and the suffix '-ly' • Can recognise homophones and words spelt 'ei', 'eigh' and 'ey'

Additional Teacher Information

Definition of Terms

Legend
Legends are told as though the events were actual historical events. Legends may or may not be based on an elaborated version of an historical event. Legends are usually about human beings, although gods may intervene in some way throughout the story.

Text
A book or other written or printed work, regarded in terms of its content rather than its physical form.

Story
An account of imaginary or real people and events told for entertainment.

Paragraph
A distinct section of a piece of writing, usually dealing with a single theme and indicated by a new line, indentation or numbering.

Links to other Curriculum Areas

• History—the Roman Empire and its impact on Britain; British resistance

Terminology for Pupils

legend
text
dictionary
paragraph
vocabulary
root word
suffix
adjective
adverb
consonant
syllable
prefix
antonym

Suggested Reading

• *Boudicca* (Famous People, Famous Lives) by **Emma Fischel**
• <http://www.bbc.co.uk/schools/primaryhistory/romans/rebellion/>
• *Literacy and History – The Celts* by **Marion Redmond** (published by Prim-Ed Publishing – additional teacher background information)

Text

Teacher Information

- This text is a legend which provides information about the Celtic queen, Boudicca. Informational texts may take many forms, such as legends.
- The site of the final battle between Boudicca's army and the Romans is uncertain, but it is referred to as The Battle of Watling Street.
- The Romans occupied Britain until AD 410. Following the harsh actions on the Britons by Suetonius, Nero considered withdrawing from the territory. Instead, he replaced the governor, Suetonius, with a leader who governed in a less ruthless manner. After the rebellion, many Britons adopted Roman dress, lifestyles and wrote or spoke Latin.

Introduction

- Teachers may wish to add geography links by having the pupils locate the territory of the Iceni tribe, Camulodunum (Colchester in Essex), Londinium (London) and Verulamium (an ancient town southwest of the city of St Albans in Hertfordshire).

Development

- Read and discuss the text with the pupils, as a whole class or in groups. Assist pupils to decode new words if necessary. Discuss the meaning of any new or unfamiliar words and phrases; e.g. justice, confiscate, taxed, natural, fierce, demolished, manoeuvre, rebellion and temple. Question individual pupils to gauge their understanding of what they have listened to or read. Pupils should also ask questions about parts of the text they are unsure of, in order to improve their understanding.

Differentiated Individual/Paired/Group Work

- Pupils write an alternative ending to the legend, to tell what might have happened if the Romans had captured Boudicca.
- Less able pupils could write two paragraphs and draw an illustration.
- More able pupils could write more paragraphs, in greater detail, in the style of the legend.

Review

- Pupils should share their work in a small group.

Comprehension

Teacher Information

- Pupils might need a dictionary to complete question 2.

Introduction

- Reread the legend. Ask pupils to focus on the sequence of events. Ask them to discuss the order of events in the legend.

Development

- Remind pupils how to use a dictionary efficiently; i.e. alphabetical order and retrieval by 1st, 2nd and 3rd letters. Give each pupil, or pair of pupils, a dictionary. Write words from the text onto the board for pupils to find.
- Discuss possible answers to question 4 as they may vary.
- Discuss the comprehension activities on page 76, then allow pupils to complete the page independently.

Differentiated Individual/Paired/Group Work

- Pupils summarise the legend using bullet points.
- Less able pupils could summarise the legend in ten bullet points, whilst more able pupils should summarise in more detail, using more bullet points.

Review

- As a class, ask pupils to summarise the legend in just five or six bullet points. Which points do they feel are the most important and need including?

Word Reading

Teacher Information

- The activities on page 77 focus on word origins, root words, the suffix '-ly', the prefix 'in-' and antonyms.

Introduction

- Reread the text, but first explain to pupils that the focus will be on words. While reading, ask pupils to find and circle words with the suffix '-ly'.

Development

- Look at words with the suffix '-ly'. Tell pupils that this suffix is added to an adjective to form an adverb. Explain that usually the suffix is added straight onto the end of most root words; for example, sadly, finally. However, there are exceptions, which should also be explained to the pupils:

  (1) If the root word ends in '-y' with a consonant letter before it, the 'y' is changed to 'i', but only if the root word has more than one syllable; for example, happily.

  (2) If the root word ends with '-le', the '-le' is changed to '-ly'; for example, simply.

  (3) If the root word ends with '-ic', '-ally' is added rather than just '-ly'; for example, basically. An exception is 'publicly'.

  (4) The words truly, duly and wholly.

- Tell pupils that the prefix 'in-' can mean both 'not' and 'in'/'into'. Find the word starting with 'in-' in the text, and decide which meaning it has.

- Explain to pupils that the sound /eɪ/ can be spelt in three different ways: 'ei', 'eigh' and 'ey'. Practise saying words with these spellings with the pupils. Ask pupils to find words with these spellings in the text.

- Ensure pupils are familiar with the terms 'synonym' and 'antonym'. Give some examples (happy: synonym is glad, antonym is sad). Elicit some examples from the pupils. Pupils suggest sentences for pairs of synonyms and antonyms, to be written onto the board; for example, happy = glad/sad. Ben was glad he had homework, but Krista was sad.

- Discuss the word reading activities on page 77, then allow pupils to complete the page independently.

Differentiated Individual/Paired/Group Work

- Pupils should be given a selection of 'in-' words. They should sort them into two lists, according to whether the prefix has the meaning 'not' or 'in'/'into'. The list of words could include:

  NOT: inaccurate, inaccessible, inconvenient, inexpensive, intolerant, invisible.

  IN/INTO: inside, inhabitant, intruder, indoors, insert, inhale.

- More able pupils could write some of the 'in-' words in sentences.

Review

- As a class, compare pupils' lists of words. Can they use them in sentences? For example, The intruder stole an inexpensive necklace.

	Assessment
C5	Write the following words on the board and ask pupils to write each one in a sentence: warrior, justice, peace, equally, confiscate, slave, fierce, manoeuvre
C15	Pupils should summarise paragraphs 5 and 6, ensuring the main ideas are included.
WR2	Say the following words to the pupils, and ask them to write them into three lists, according to whether they are spelt with an 'ei', 'eigh' or 'ey': vein, weigh, they, foreign, eight, obey, neighbour, prey, beige

Answers

Comprehension

1. (a) a legend
   (b) to give information about the life of Boudicca
2. (a) heroine—a woman admired for courage, outstanding achievements or noble qualities
   (b) justice—being fair and reasonable
   (c) confiscate— take away or seize someone's property with authority
   (d) demolished—pulled or knocked down
   (e) manoeuvre—move around with skill and care
3. The Britons were a large force; The Romans were small in number./The Romans were well-trained and skilled in combat; The Britons were not.
4. Answers should state that she probably would have been killed.
5. Paragraphs 1 and 7
6. The Romans were taking the land of the Britons; They were making them slaves and prisoners and killing them; They were destroying their way of life and culture.
7. Answers will vary. Some pupils may tick all or some of the bullet points.

Word Reading

1. (a) rebel
   (b) to fight against a government or leader
2. warrior
3. tribe
4. easy, -ly
5. equally, <u>heavily</u>, totally, <u>easily</u>
6. (a) inhabitants   (b) in/into
7. (a) reign/their   (b) neighbouring/eighty   (c) they
8. (a) win   (b) daughters   (c) tall
   (d) north   (e) freedom   (f) peace

Boudicca – 1

Read the legend.

Boudicca was a Celtic warrior queen. She was a heroine and fighter for freedom and justice.

In AD 43, the Roman empire first spread to England. When the Romans conquered southern England, they allowed Prasutagus, the king of the Iceni tribe to continue to reign. They hoped he would keep peace between the Romans and Britons.

When Prasutagus died, he left his kingdom to be ruled equally by his daughters and the Roman emperor, Nero. Prasutagus hoped this would allow his family, tribe and kingdom to live in peace. The Romans, however, decided to confiscate the property of all the tribesmen and rule themselves. The royal family and their relatives became prisoners or slaves. Many people were killed or flogged including the family of Prasutagus–his wife, Boudicca, and his children.

Around AD 60 or 61, the Roman army was in the north fighting rebels. Boudicca started to gather together other tribes. They had been taxed heavily, driven off their lands or forced to become slaves by the Romans. The Celtic culture, too, was being destroyed. Boudicca was a natural leader. She was tall, intelligent and fierce. The neighbouring tribes were happy to join her rebellion.

Boudicca and her army marched to Camulodunum, the Roman Britain capital. They destroyed the Roman temple and killed all the inhabitants. The city was totally demolished. Roman legions sent to help were wiped out. The cities of Londinium and Verulamium were destroyed next. Tens of thousands of people were killed–no prisoners or slaves were taken.

Meanwhile, the Roman governor, Suetonius, was gathering his forces. Almost ten thousand Roman soldiers faced over two hundred thousand Britons. Boudicca, from her chariot, gave a stirring speech, vowing to win or die. However, the Roman soldiers were well-trained and skilled in combat. The Britons could not manoeuvre easily with their long swords. They also fought without armour. Almost eighty thousand Britons died compared to about four hundred Romans. Boudicca fled to her kingdom. She is thought to have poisoned herself and her daughters so they could not be captured.

Even though Boudicca was not victorious, she will always be remembered as a national heroine. A bronze statue of Boudicca and her daughters in their chariot stands in London near the Houses of Parliament.

| My learning log | When I read this legend, I could read: | ☐ all of it. ☐ most of it. ☐ parts of it. |

Boudicca – 2

1. (a)   What type of text is the story about Boudicca?

    _____

   (b)   What is the purpose of the text?

    _____

2. Use a dictionary to write the meanings of the following words.

    (a)   heroine   _____

    (b)   justice   _____

    (c)   confiscate   _____

    (d)   demolished _____

    (e)   manoeuvre _____

3. What were the main differences between the army of the Britons and the Roman army?

    _____

    _____

    _____

4. What do you think would have happened to Boudicca if she had been captured?

    _____

5. Which paragraphs tell why Boudicca is an important person in history?

    _____

6. Why did Boudicca build an army to fight the Romans?

    _____

    _____

7. Tick the things in the text that help you understand it.

    • dates ☐   • events like battles in order ☐   • time words ☐

    • names of people and places ☐   • military vocabulary ☐

My learning log	While doing these activities:		
	I found Q _____ easy.	I found Q _____ challenging.	I found Q _____ interesting.

Boudicca – 3

1. (a) What word does the word 'rebellion' come from? _____

   (b) What does the word answer to (a) mean? _____

2. Which word in paragraph 1 comes from the French word 'werreior' meaning to 'make war'?

   _____

3. Which word in paragraph 2 means 'a group made up of families or communities who have the same religion, family ties, culture and language, with a chosen leader'?

   _____

4. Write the root word and the suffix in the word 'easily'.

   root word: _____   suffix: _____

5. The suffix '-ly' is added to an adjective to form an adverb. If the root word ends in '-y', with a consonant letter before it, the 'y' is changed to 'i'. (Only if the word has more than one syllable.)

   Write four words from the text with this suffix. Circle the two words with this spelling change.

   _____   _____   _____   _____

6. The prefix 'in-' can mean 'not' and 'in'/'into'.

   (a) Find and write the word with this prefix in the text. _____

   (b) Does it mean 'not' or 'in'/'into'? _____

7. The /eɪ/ sound can be spelt 'ei', 'eigh' or 'ey'. Find some words in the text with these sounds and spellings.

   (a) ei = _____   (b) eigh = _____   (c) ey = _____

8. Write the antonyms in the text for these words.

   (a) lose   _____   (b) sons   _____

   (c) short   _____   (d) south   _____

   (e) slavery   _____   (f) war   _____

My learning log	**Colour:**	I know / don't know about the origins of words.
		I understand / need more practice on root words and suffixes.
		I can / can't read words with spellings 'ei', 'eigh' and 'ey'.

Read the review.

Farm Fresh Restaurant

234 Alexander Road, Harrington

Open: Tuesday to Sunday for lunch and dinner

Star rating: ★★★★✫

Prices: smaller plates £5–£12;

mains £14–£21

Fresh and fabulous!

With its grand opening weekend happening a fortnight ago, Farm Fresh Restaurant has started to get into the swing of things. We arrived to find most of the tables occupied and were greeted by a friendly staff member and promptly shown to our table.

The restaurant's decor fits with the farm fresh theme, with the place looking like a large and welcoming farmhouse. The herb and vegetable planters spread around the restaurant add a burst of colour, and show you how fresh some of the ingredients really are!

Packed with healthy and delicious choices, the menu offers large meals for the hungry and smaller plates for people seeking a lighter option. To go with your meal or snack you can choose from a huge range of fresh and natural juices and smoothies.

My dining partner and I were very impressed with our delicious and healthy meals, that arrived after a very short wait. My salad had a very tasty dressing and my companion said that her fish was cooked perfectly and smothered in a delightful sauce.

The juices complemented the meal nicely and we even had room to try two of their fantastic fruity desserts. We left very satisfied, promising that we would return soon!

Smoothies and juices

Main courses

Desserts

Farm Fresh Restaurant Review

Assessment – Comprehension

1. What is the purpose of the box in the top-left corner of this review?

   2 marks

   _____

2. The opening times of this restaurant are:

   1 mark

   _____

3. Write a short description of how the restaurant looks.

   2 marks

   _____

   _____

4. Tick **Fact** or **Opinion**.

   Fact **Opinion**

   1 mark

   (a) There are herb and vegetable planters. ☐ ☐

   (b) The sauce on the fish is delightful. ☐ ☐

   (c) The restaurant is in Harrington. ☐ ☐

5. Tick **True** or **False**.

   True **False**

   1 mark

   (a) The author ordered fish. ☐ ☐

   (b) Meals are priced from £5–£21. ☐ ☐

   (c) The author didn't like the restaurant. ☐ ☐

6. Tick the best answer. This text was written for the reader to:

   1 mark

   (a) find out about the author's opinion of a restaurant. ☐

   (b) find out about the recipes and menu items. ☐

   (c) find out about when the restaurant was opened. ☐

7. Does this review appeal to you? Would you like to visit this restaurant? Explain why or why not.

   2 marks

   _____

   _____

Total for this page	/10

Farm Fresh Restaurant Review

1. Look at the root words below. Find and write the changed forms in the text (root word + suffix).

   ☐ 2 marks

   (a) welcome _____   (b) impress _____

   (c) delight _____   (d) satisfy _____

2. What does the word 'companion' mean in the text?

   ☐ 1 mark

   _____

3. Find a word in the review that is a homophone for these words.

   Write a sentence for each.

   ☐ 2 marks

   (a) weight _____

   _____   _____

   (b) source _____

   _____   _____

4. Match each word to a meaning.

   ☐ 2 marks

   (a) menu   •   •   taken up by people

   (b) decor   •   •   added something to

   (c) occupied   •   •   list of foods

   (d) complemented •   •   colours and furnishings

5. Find and write two words from the text with the suffix '-ous'.

   ☐ 2 marks

   _____   _____

6. The customers were 'promptly' shown to their table.

   Which word is the best antonym for 'promptly'? Tick one.

   ☐ 1 mark

   (a) leisurely ☐   (b) clumsily ☐   (c) quickly ☐

Total for this page	/10	Total for this assessment	/20

Farm Fresh Restaurant Review

Genre: Review

Breakdown of question type/content and mark allocation

Comprehension			Word Reading		
Q 1.	Understanding text features	2 marks	Q 1.	Root words and suffixes	2 marks
Q 2.	Finding information	1 mark	Q 2.	Word meanings	1 mark
Q 3.	Identifying main idea	2 marks	Q 3.	Homophones	2 marks
Q 4.	Identifying facts and opinions	1 mark	Q 4.	Word meanings	2 marks
Q 5.	Identifying true and false statements	1 mark	Q 5.	Suffix '-ous'	2 marks
Q 6.	Choosing best answer	1 mark	Q 6.	Antonyms	1 mark
Q 7.	Giving opinion	2 marks			
	Sub-total			Sub-total	
				Record the pupil's total result for this assessment.	

Assessment Answers

Assessment – Farm Fresh Restaurant Review

Comprehension .... *Page 79*

1. Possible answer: It gives information about where the restaurant is, when it is open and the prices of its meals.
2. Tuesday to Sunday for lunch and dinner.
3. Possible answer: The restaurant looks like a large farmhouse, there are herb and vegetable planters inside.
4. (a) Fact   (b) Opinion   (c) Fact
5. (a) False   (b) True   (c) False
6. (a) Find out about the author's opinion of a restaurant.
7. Possible answer: I wouldn't like to go to this restaurant because I don't really like eating fruit and vegetables.

Word Reading .... *Page 80*

1. (a) welcoming   (b) impressed   (c) delightful   (d) satisfied
2. Teacher check; somebody who accompanies, a partner or friend.
3. (a) wait; Teacher check sentences.
   (b) sauce; Teacher check sentences.
4. (a) menu – list of foods
   (b) decor – colours and furnishings
   (c) occupied – taken up by people
   (d) complemented – added something to
5. fabulous, delicious
6. (a) leisurely

Romans in Britain

Curriculum Links

Activity	Code	Objective	Outcome
Text	C2 C3 C6	• Participate in discussion about both books that are read to them and those they can read for themselves • Listen to and discuss a wide range of fiction • Increase their familiarity with a wide range of books	• Can identify discussion texts and talk about their key features
Comprehension	C5 C9 C13 C14	• Use dictionaries to check the meaning of words that they have read • Discuss words and phrases that capture the reader's interest and imagination • Draw inferences such as inferring characters' feelings, thoughts and motives from their actions, and justifying inferences with evidence • Predict what might happen from details stated and implied	• Can explain the meanings of words • Can choose interesting sentences and justify choices • Can infer how Caesar felt after a failed invasion • Can predict what might happen if a similar situation were to occur again
Word Reading	WR1 WR2	• Apply their growing knowledge of root words, prefixes and suffixes • Read further exception words, noting the unusual correspondences between spelling and sound	• Can recognise root words, the prefix 'in-' and the suffix '-tion' • Can recognise homophones

Additional Teacher Information

Definition of Terms

Discussion
A conversation or debate about a specific topic.

Text
A book or other written or printed work, regarded in terms of its content rather than its physical form.

Opinion
A view or judgement formed about something, not necessarily based on fact or knowledge.

Formal/Informal language
Formal language is used in serious situations or ones that involve people we don't know well, and often in writing. Informal language is used in more relaxed situations and with people we know well. It is more commonly used when we speak. Each uses particular grammar and vocabulary. For example, informal language often uses contractions, relative clauses without a relative pronoun and ellipsis.

Links to other Curriculum Areas

• History—The Roman Empire and its impact on Britain; Julius Caesar's attempted invasion in 55–54 BC

Terminology for Pupils

discussion
text
sentence
dictionary
synonym
antonym
homophone
prefix
suffix

Suggested Reading

• *Who was Julius Caesar?* by Nico Medina
• *The Life of Julius Caesar* (Stories from History) by **Dr. Nicholas Saunders** (a graphic novel for advanced pupils or as a teacher reference)
• <http://www.bbc.co.uk/schools/primaryhistory/romans/invasion/>

Text

Teacher Information

- This text is a discussion between two pupils about the invasion of Britain by Caesar. The discussion, being a conversation, gives many different ideas with some agreement between the two speakers. This is different to a debate as speakers do not take on opposing views or opinions.

- After two invasions of Britain, Caesar never returned. It was almost a century later, in AD 43, that another Roman invasion under Emperor Claudius finally succeeded in successfully invading Britain. Between 55 BC and AD 43 links between the two countries continued through trade.

Introduction

- Provide images of the military equipment mentioned in the text, and discuss how the equipment worked; for example, catapult, sling, archer, armoured war elephant and chariot.

Development

- Read and discuss the text with the pupils, as a whole class or in groups. Assist pupils to decode new words if necessary. Discuss the meaning of any new or unfamiliar words and phrases; e.g. military, invaded, defence, armoured, slingers, tactic, accomplishments and geography. Question individual pupils to gauge their understanding of what they have listened to or read. Pupils should also ask questions about parts of the text they are unsure of, in order to improve their understanding.

Differentiated Individual/Paired/Group Work

- In mixed ability groups, pupils should use the Internet to research facts about Julius Caesar.
- Each group should produce a fact sheet about Caesar's personal life and military achievements.

Review

- Each group should present their fact sheet to the rest of the class.

Comprehension

Teacher Information

- Pupils will need a dictionary to complete question 4.

Introduction

- Discuss the structure of the text and how the speech balloons and heads assist the reader.

Development

- Remind pupils how to use a dictionary efficiently; i.e. alphabetical order and retrieval by 1st, 2nd and 3rd letters. Give each pupil, or pair of pupils, a dictionary. Write words from the text onto the board for pupils to find.

- Discuss possible answers to question 8, which requires pupils to give an opinion and back it up.

- Discuss the comprehension activities on page 86, then allow pupils to complete the page independently.

Differentiated Individual/Paired/Group Work

- In mixed ability groups, pupils should summarise each speech balloon, in as few words as possible, but without losing the meaning.

Review

- Pupils should share some of their summaries with the class. The class should discuss whether the summary was short but inclusive of all the details.

Word Reading

Teacher Information

- The activities on page 87 focus on word origins, synonyms, antonyms, homophones, the prefix 'in-' and the suffix '-ation'.

Introduction

- Reread the text, but first explain to pupils that the focus will be on words. While reading, ask pupils to circle homophones.

Development

- Ensure pupils are familiar with the terms 'synonym' and 'antonym'. Give some examples (happy: synonym is glad, antonym is sad). Elicit some examples from the pupils. Pupils suggest sentences for pairs of synonyms and antonyms, to be written onto the board; for example, happy = *glad/sad*. Ben was glad he had homework, but Krista was sad.

- Ensure pupils are familiar with the term 'homophone'. Give some examples (*berry/bury, scene/seen, plain/plane*). Elicit some examples from the pupils. Pupils suggest sentences for pairs of homophones, to be written onto the board; for example, *main/mane* = He is walking down the main road./That horse has a beautiful mane.

- Tell pupils that the prefix 'in-' can mean both 'not' and 'in'/'into'. Find the words starting with 'in-' in the text, and decide which meanings they have.

- Tell pupils that the suffix '-ation' is added to verbs to form nouns. An example from the text is inform/information. Rules that have already been learnt for adding suffixes also apply to this suffix.

- Discuss the word reading activities on page 87, then allow pupils to complete the page independently.

Differentiated Individual/Paired/Group Work

- Provide pupils with words that have antonyms; for example, slow, sad. Ask pupils to think of antonyms, and list them on the board.

- Less able pupils should be provided with a list of words from the text, and asked to write antonyms for them; for example, great, true, large, dry, clever.

- More able pupils should find their own words in the text, and then write antonyms for them.

Review

- As a class, compare the antonyms. Did pupils have different antonyms for the same word? For example, for the word 'large', pupils might have thought of 'small', 'tiny', 'little' or other words.

Assessment

C3	Write a review of the discussion text. Include what they like and dislike about it, and whether they think it is a good genre for providing factual, historical information.
C5	Ask the pupils to write the following words from the text in alphabetical order: leader, land, lot, large, leadership, lead, links, landforms
WR2	Write the following homophone pairs on the board and have pupils write a sentence containing each: grate/great, tale/tail, whether/weather, flee/flea, seen/scene, sent/scent

Answers

Comprehension

1. Answers may indicate that Caesar was a great military leader.
2. Each person speaks in turn, giving ideas, thoughts and opinions.
3. Answers will vary.
4. (a) defence—the action of defending from or resisting attack
   (b) catapult—a weapon with a lever and ropes for throwing missiles
   (c) tactic—an action or strategy to achieve a specific end
   (d) military— relating to or characteristic of soldiers or armed forces
5.-6. Answers will vary.
7. The cliffs gave the Britons a good position to defend their land against the Romans; The bad weather brought tides that destroyed Caesar's ships.
8. Answers will vary.

Word Reading

1. Old French; cart or wheeled vehicle
2. (a) amazing   (b) weather   (c) tales
   (d) mistakes   (e) scared/terrified (f) ships
3. (a) failure   (b) leader   (c) man
   (d) true   (e) dry   (f) gathered
4. (a) sea, shore   (b) weather, bean
5. Teacher check
6. Teacher check
7. information

Romans in Britain – 1

Read the discussion between two pupils.

Dane

Caesar was a great military leader. He showed good leadership when he invaded Britain. He had already conquered Gaul. He wanted to make sure the Britons didn't help the Gauls against him. He also wanted to see if the tales about Britain were true. Britain was supposed to have lots of pearls, lead, gold and tin.

Cassian

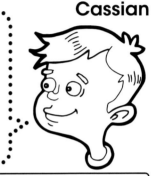

Yes, but he invaded Britain twice—once in 55 BC and again in 54 BC! The first time was a failure. He only got as far as the coast. The cliffs gave the Britons a good defence against the invaders. Then, when he tried to land further up the coast, he had to use catapults and slings to drive off the Britons. Even the tides swamped his ships!

Okay, so he didn't know much about Britain's weather, landforms or tides but he didn't give up. Even though he didn't discover any riches, he planned another invasion in 54 BC. He gathered information about Britain from Romans he sent there. He took a larger force and designed special ships. There were about 800 ships!

I agree that he learnt from some of his mistakes but such a large force would have scared off anyone! Don't forget that after he moved inland, he got a message that the tides and storms had damaged some of his ships (again)!

Alright! So he was a better soldier on dry land than in the sea! You know that he used an armoured war elephant carrying archers and slingers in a tower to make the Britons flee! The Britons had never seen such an animal before! They must have been terrified! It was a clever tactic! The tribes soon surrendered.

I know Caesar had some amazing accomplishments. He learnt a lot about the ways Britons fought using chariots. He discovered a lot about the geography and climate of Britain and extended Roman trade links to more countries. I think you could say that Caesar was a great man, not just a great military leader!

| **My learning log** | When I read this discussion text, I could read: | ☐ all of it. | ☐ most of it. | ☐ parts of it. |

Romans in Britain – 2

1. This text is trying to tell people that Caesar was _____

_____.

2. There is a pattern in the order of speaking in the discussion. What is it?

_____.

3. (a) Copy the most interesting sentence from the text.

_____

_____

(b) Why did you choose this sentence? _____

_____

4. Use a dictionary to find the meanings of these words.

(a) defence _____

(b) catapult _____

(c) tactic _____

(d) military _____

5. How do you think Caesar felt when his first invasion of Britain failed?

_____

6. After reading the text, what is your opinion of Caesar?

_____

_____

7. What things caused Caesar's first invasion to fail?

_____

_____

8. Do you think the Britons would surrender if they faced an armoured elephant in battle again? [**Yes**] [**No**] Why?

_____

My learning log	While doing these activities:		
	I found Q _____ easy.	I found Q _____ challenging.	I found Q _____ interesting.

Romans in Britain – 3

1. Where does the word 'chariot' come from and what does it mean?

   _____

2. Write synonyms from the text for the words below.

   (a) spectacular _____   (b) climate _____

   (c) stories _____   (d) errors _____

   (e) frightened _____   (f) boats _____

3. Write antonyms from the text for the words below.

   (a) success _____   (b) follower _____

   (c) woman _____   (d) false _____

   (e) wet _____   (f) scattered _____

4. Circle the correct homophones in these sentences.

   (a) From out at (see / sea) he could see the (sure / shore).

   (b) The sunny (weather / whether) helped the (been / bean) to grow.

5. Write sentences using the following homophones.

   (a) flee _____

        flea _____

   (b) sent _____

        scent _____

6. The prefix 'in-' can mean 'not' and 'in'/'into'. Write a sentence containing each 'in-' word.

   (a) invaded: _____

   (b) inland: _____

7. The suffix '-ation' is added to verbs to make nouns.

   Find a word in the text with this suffix. _____

My learning log	*Colour:*	I [understand] / [need more practice on] synonyms and antonyms.
		I [know] / [don't know] about homophones.
		I [recognise] / [don't recognise] words with the prefix 'in-'.

The Ass, the Table and the Stick

Curriculum Links

Activity	Code	Objective	Outcome
Text	C2 C3 C6	• Participate in discussion about both books that are read to them and those they can read for themselves • Listen to and discuss a wide range of fiction • Increase their familiarity with a wide range of books, including fairy stories	• Can identify fairy stories and talk about their key features
Comprehension	C5 C11 C12 C13 C15	• Use dictionaries to check the meaning of words that they have read • Check that the text makes sense to them, discuss their understanding and explain the meaning of words in context • Ask questions to improve their understanding of a text • Draw inferences such as inferring characters' feelings, thoughts and motives for actions, and justify inferences with evidence • Identify main ideas drawn from more than one paragraph and summarise them	• Can explain the meanings of words • Can answer questions about the text • Can ask questions to find out more about bridge building • Can infer why Jack acted as he did • Can summarise paragraphs
Word Reading	WR1 WR2	• Apply their growing knowledge of prefixes and suffixes • Read further exception words, noting the unusual correspondences between spelling and sound	• Can recognise words with a range of prefixes and suffixes

Additional Teacher Information

Definition of Terms

Text

A book or other written or printed work, regarded in terms of its content rather than its physical form.

Fairy tale

A fairy tale is a short story usually featuring fantasy characters such as elves, dragons, hobgoblins, sprites or magical beings and is often set in the distant past. A fairy tale usually begins with the phrase 'Once upon a time …' and ends with the words '… and they lived happily ever after'. Charms, disguises and talking animals may also appear in a fairy tale.

Links to other Curriculum Areas

• PSHE – Personal, social, health and economic education

Terminology for Pupils

fairy tale
text
dictionary
paragraph
sentence
pronoun
prefix
suffix
vowel
consonant
syllable
adverb
root word
synonym
antonym

Suggested Reading

• *The Table, the Donkey and the Stick* by **Paul Galdone**
• <http://www.sacred-texts.com/neu/eng/eft/eft40.htm>
This website contains the version used as a reference.

Text

Teacher Information

- There are a number of different versions of this tale. In some versions, there are three brothers who have to feed their father's goat. This is the version shown in the first bullet point of 'Suggested Reading' on page 88. Pupils may be interested in listening to, or reading, different versions of the tale and discussing the similarities and differences.

Introduction

- Discuss the themes that this fairy tale has in common with many other fairy tales: a young man leaving home to seek his fortune; the man working hard to be tricked by a bad person; the man taking revenge on the bad person; the young man living happily ever after.

Development

- Read and discuss the text with the pupils, as a whole class or in groups. Assist pupils to decode new words if necessary. Discuss the meaning of any new or unfamiliar words and phrases such as fortune, swapped, permission, joiner, wages, club, harshly and maiden. Question individual pupils to gauge their understanding of what they have listened to or read. Pupils should also ask questions about parts of the text they are unsure of, in order to improve their understanding.

Differentiated Individual/Paired/Group Work

- Pupils should write another paragraph, following the same format, to insert in the story between paragraph 3 (when he received the table) and paragraph 4 (when he received the club). What work did Jack do? What did he receive in payment? What magical quality did the item have?

- More able pupils should write a longer paragraph, with more detail, which mimics the style of the original.

Review

- Pupils should share their paragraph in a small group.

Comprehension

Teacher Information

- Pupils may need a dictionary to complete question 2.

Introduction

- Pupils take it in turns to summarise each paragraph in their own words.

Development

- Remind pupils how to use a dictionary efficiently; i.e. alphabetical order and retrieval by 1st, 2nd and 3rd letters. Give each pupil, or pair of pupils, a dictionary. Write words from the text onto the board for pupils to find.

- Discuss the comprehension activities on page 92, then allow pupils to complete the page independently.

Differentiated Individual/Paired/Group Work

- Pupils should form small, mixed ability groups of three or four, to make up impromptu plays to dramatise the fairy tale. Pupils should be encouraged to use intonation, tone, volume and action in their play.

Review

- Each group should perform their fairy tale to the rest of the class.

Word Reading

Teacher Information

- The activities on page 93 focus on pronouns, the prefixes 'un-' and 'dis-', suffixes, adverbs, synonyms and antonyms.

Introduction

- Reread the text, but first explain to pupils that the focus will be on words. While reading, ask pupils to circle words with the prefixes 'un-' and 'dis-'.

Development

- Look at words with the prefixes 'un-' and 'dis-'. Discuss how adding these prefixes makes the words negative; for example, 'do' becomes 'undo' and 'obey' becomes 'disobey'. Write sentences containing the pairs of words; for example, Peter was <u>kind</u> to Marissa, but <u>unkind</u> to me.

- Tell pupils that when a suffix is added to a word with more than one syllable, and the last syllable is stressed and ends in one vowel and one consonant, the consonant is doubled before adding the suffix; for example, controlled, beginner, forgetting.

- Ensure pupils are familiar with the terms 'synonym' and 'antonym'. Give some examples (happy: synonym is *glad*, antonym is *sad*). Elicit some examples from the pupils. Pupils suggest sentences for pairs of synonyms and antonyms, to be written onto the board; for example, happy = glad/sad. Ben was <u>glad</u> he had homework, but Krista was <u>sad</u>.

- Discuss the word reading activities on page 93, then allow pupils to complete the page independently.

Differentiated Individual/Paired/Group Work

- Provide pupils with words that have synonyms; for example, slow, sad, tired. Ask pupils to think of synonyms, and list them on the board.

- Less able pupils should be provided with a list of words from the text, and asked to write synonyms for them; for example, little, old, angry, wealthy, said.

- More able pupils should find their own words in the text, and then write synonyms for them.

Review

- As a class, compare the synonyms. Did pupils have different synonyms for the same word? For example, for the word 'angry', pupils might have thought of 'furious', 'annoyed', 'irate' or other words.

Assessment

C3	Ask the pupils to write three things they like and three things they dislike about the fairy tale. Would they recommend it to a friend to read?
C11	Write the following words onto the board. The pupils should write each word in a sentence, to demonstrate their understanding of the word in context: fortune, sweetheart, servant, stable, joiner, permission, bridge, manger
WR1	Write the following root words onto the board. Ask pupils to create two lists, one where the prefix 'un-' can be used to create a new word, and the other where the prefix 'dis-' can be used: belief, wrap, usual, appear, count, sure, steady, trust, respect, wanted

Answers

Comprehension

1. (c) imaginative
2. (a) assortment—a miscellaneous collection of things
   (b) wages—income earned from labour
   (c) manger—a long trough from which horses or cattle feed
   (d) restored—brought back; returned
3. Jack was angry that the girls only wanted to marry him because he was wealthy.
4. Answers will vary.
5. Answers may include that he was pretending to only consider the girls with a lot of money.
6. hard-working, constant, easily-tricked, innocent
7. Teacher check
8. Using the word 'sweetheart' shows that Jack loved the girl.

Word Reading

1. the girls who wanted to marry him
2. (a) un-, dis-, un-
   (b) un-, dis-, un-/dis-, dis-, un-/dis-, un-
3. travelling, travelled
4. (a) Unfortunately   (b) harshly
5. (a) ment, amaze   (b) ed, agree   (c) sion, permit
   (d) y, wealth
6. (a) seek   (b) attempting   (c) angry
   (d) wealthy   (e) eventually   (f) switched
7. (a) young   (b) harshly   (c) servant
   (d) night   (e) pulled   (f) open

The Ass, the Table and the Stick – 1

Read the fairy tale.

There was once a young man named Jack who left home to seek his fortune so he could marry his sweetheart.

After travelling a long way, Jack met a little old woman. After working as her servant for a year and a day, she gave Jack an ass. When the ass's ears were pulled, coins dropped from its open mouth. Pleased, Jack made his way home. On the way, he stopped at an inn and ordered food and a room. When the innkeeper demanded payment, Jack went to the stable, pulled the ass's ears and collected the coins. Unfortunately, the innkeeper followed Jack and saw what he had done. During the night, the innkeeper swapped Jack's ass with his own. The next morning, Jack rode home and asked for permission to marry. His father refused unless Jack had enough money to keep a wife. When Jack pulled the ears of the ass, no coins appeared. His angry father drove him out of the house.

Soon, Jack came to the shop of a joiner. After a year and a day, Jack received his wages—a fine wooden table. The magic words—'Table, be covered'—made fine food and drink appear. With the table on his back, Jack set off for home. On the way, he stopped at the same inn. When only ham and eggs were offered, Jack said the magic words. An assortment of fine food and drink appeared while the innkeeper watched in amazement. During the night, the innkeeper switched his own table for Jack's. The next day, Jack travelled home and again asked for permission to marry. His father refused unless Jack could look after a wife. When Jack said the magic words, nothing happened and Jack was driven from the house once more.

Eventually, Jack reached a river where a man was attempting to build a bridge. After helping the man, Jack was rewarded with a club fashioned from a tree branch. When the words 'Up stick and bang him' were spoken, the stick would knock down anyone who made Jack angry. On the way home, Jack stopped at the same inn. When the innkeeper appeared, Jack commanded the club to beat the innkeeper until he gave back the ass and table. With his property restored, Jack made his way home, only to discover that his father had died. Jack pulled the ears of the donkey and filled the manger with coins.

All the girls wanted to marry wealthy Jack. He invited them to his house and agreed to marry the one with the most riches in her apron. Jack's sweetheart was among them. Her apron contained all her money—two copper coins. Speaking harshly, Jack ordered her to go away. As she obeyed, tears fell into her apron, filling it with diamonds. Jack ordered his club to attack all the other maidens. Then he poured all the money from the manger into his sweetheart's apron, exclaiming that she was now the richest lass and he would marry only her.

And he did.

| My learning log | When I read this fairy tale, I could read: | ☐ all of it. | ☐ most of it. | ☐ parts of it. |

The Ass, the Table and the Stick – 2

1. Which word best describes this text?

(a) informative ☐   (b) persuasive ☐   (c) imaginative ☐

2. Use a dictionary to find the meanings of the words below.

(a) assortment _____

(b) wages _____

(c) manger _____

(d) restored _____

3. Why did Jack order his stick to beat the girls? Was he just being nasty?

_____

4. Paragraph 4 gives no information about how Jack helped the man build the bridge. Write a question that would give you more information.

_____

5. Why do you think Jack spoke harshly to his sweetheart?

_____

6. Circle the words that best describe Jack.

| hard-working   cruel   constant   easily-tricked   innocent |

7. Write one sentence to summarise what happened in each paragraph.

• Paragraph 2 _____

_____

• Paragraph 3 _____

_____

• Paragraph 4 _____

_____

8. Why is the word 'sweetheart' used to describe the girl Jack wanted to marry?

_____

My learning log	While doing these activities:		
	I found Q _____ easy.	I found Q _____ challenging.	I found Q _____ interesting.

92 · · · · · · · *Reading – Comprehension and Word Reading* ·Prim-Ed Publishing· · · · · · ·www.prim-ed.com

The Ass, the Table and the Stick – 3

1. In the sentence 'He invited them to his house and agreed to marry the one with the most riches in her apron.', the pronoun 'them' refers to …

_____ .

2. (a) Circle the prefixes in the following words.

   | unless | disappear | unfortunately |

   (b) These prefixes make words negative. Add prefixes to the following words to make them negative.

   _____invite _____obey _____cover _____agree _____appoint _____done

3. When a suffix starting with a vowel is added to a word of more than one syllable, ending in one vowel and one consonant, the final consonant letter is doubled before the suffix is added.

   Circle the two words below that follow this rule.

   | contained | travelling | attempting | speaking |
   | exclaiming | appeared | travelled | richest |

4. Underline the adverb in each sentence that tells that the action was not good.

   (a) Unfortunately, the innkeeper followed Jack and saw what he had done.

   (b) Speaking harshly, Jack ordered her to go away.

5. Underline the suffix in each word and write the root word.

   (a) amazement _____ (b) agreed _____

   (c) permission _____ (d) wealthy _____

6. Write the synonym in the text for each word.

   (a) search _____ (b) trying _____ (c) furious _____

   (d) rich _____ (e) finally _____ (f) swapped _____

7. Write the antonym in the text for each word.

   (a) old _____ (b) kindly _____ (c) master _____

   (d) day _____ (e) pushed _____ (f) close _____

My learning log	Colour:	I [can] / [can't] add prefixes to make words negative.
		I [know] / [don't know] about root words and suffixes.
		I [understand] / [need more practice on] synonyms and antonyms.

St Collen and the Fairy King

Curriculum Links

Activity	Code	Objective	Outcome
Text	C2	• Participate in discussion about both books that are read to them and those they can read for themselves	• Can identify legends and talk about their key features
	C3	• Listen to and discuss a wide range of fiction	
	C6	• Increase their familiarity with a wide range of books, including legends	
Comprehension	C9	• Discuss words and phrases that capture the reader's interest and imagination	• Can choose interesting phrases and sentences from a text
	C12	• Ask questions to improve their understanding of a text	• Can ask questions to better understand a character
	C13	• Draw inferences such as inferring characters' feelings, thoughts and motives from their actions, and justifying inferences with evidence	• Can infer feelings and actions of characters
	C16	• Identify how language, structure and presentation contribute to meaning	• Can explain why the author used direct speech
Word Reading	WR1	• Apply their growing knowledge of root words and suffixes	• Can recognise root words and the suffix '-ly'
	WR2	• Read further exception words, noting the unusual correspondences between spelling and sound	

Additional Teacher Information

Definition of Terms

Legend
Legends are told as though the events were actual historical events. Legends may or may not be based on an elaborated version of an historical event. Legends are usually about human beings, although gods may intervene in some way throughout the story.

Text
A book or other written or printed work, regarded in terms of its content rather than its physical form.

Direct speech
The actual words of a speaker; for example, 'I'll see you soon', she said.

Conclusion
The end or finish of an event, process or text.

Paragraph
A distinct section of a piece of writing, usually dealing with a single theme and indicated by a new line, indentation or numbering.

Links to other Curriculum Areas

• History—Britain's settlement by Anglo-Saxons and Scots
• Geography—Counties and cities of the United Kingdom; geographical regions and their identifying human and physical characteristics; key topographical features including mountains and hills

Terminology for Pupils

legend
text
direct speech
rhyming word
conclusion
phrase
paragraph
sentence
question
author
dictionary
Old English
noun
verb
adjective
adverb
suffix
root word
apostrophe
plural

Suggested Reading

• *Welsh Legends and Folk Tales* by **Dyfed Lloyd Evans** – Kindle™ edition (Teacher Resource)
• *The Essential Celtic Folklore Collection* by **Lady Gregory** (Teacher Resource)

Text

Teacher Information

- St Collen is recorded as having lived in the 7th century and died on 21 May. He was an abbot and travelling preacher. The site of this legend is believed to be Glastonbury Tor. St Collen is said to have fought bravely with a sword against a pagan leader named Bras and a flesh-eating giantess at Llangollen in north-east Wales. He was buried in his chapel known as the Old Church which was to the west of the current medieval church of St Collen in Llangollen.

Introduction

- The Otherworld (Annwn) mentioned in the legend and in Welsh mythology was a place filled with all manner of delightful things including eternal youth and abundant food. It was free of disease and sickness.

Development

- Read and discuss the text with the pupils, as a whole class or in groups. Assist pupils to decode new words if necessary. Discuss the meaning of any new or unfamiliar words and phrases such as 'Christian', 'saint', 'centuries', 'remote', 'cell', 'glorious', 'troops', 'minstrels' and 'graciously'. Question individual pupils to gauge their understanding of what they have listened to or read. Pupils should also ask questions about parts of the text they are unsure of, in order to improve their understanding.

Differentiated Individual/Paired/Group Work

- In mixed ability groups, pupils should reread the legend and verbally retell it in their own words.
- Working individually, pupils should rewrite the legend as a poem.
- Less able pupils could write six to eight lines and draw an illustration.
- More able pupils could write at least four stanzas and should try to include rhyme.

Review

- Pupils should share their poem in a small group.

Comprehension

Teacher Information

- Pupils should view Internet images of Glastonbury Tor, to better help them to answer questions 4 and 5.

Introduction

- Reread the legend. Ask pupils to focus on the sequence of events. Pupils take it in turns to retell the legend in their own words, sequencing the events correctly.

Development

- Discuss possible answers to questions 2 and 6 as they may vary. Pupils should justify their choice of phrase for question 2.
- Discuss the comprehension activities on page 98, then allow pupils to complete the page independently.

Differentiated Individual/Paired/Group Work

- In mixed ability groups, pupils should reread paragraph 8, which describes the 'glorious castle'. Pupils should make a list of all the things the wondrous castle had: troops; minstrels; horses; handsome young men; beautiful young women in fine clothes; delightful music; and a king on a golden chair.
- Working individually, pupils should draw the glorious castle. They should draw and label each of the things on their list.

Review

- Pupils should show the rest of their group their illustration, and tell about all the things from the list.

Word Reading

Teacher Information

- The activities on page 99 focus on dictionary usage, word origins, nouns and verbs, adjectives and adverbs, the suffix '-ly' and the possessive apostrophe.

Introduction

- Reread the text, but first explain to pupils that the focus will be on words. While reading, ask pupils to find and circle words with the suffix '-ly'.

Development

- Look at words with the suffix '-ly'. Tell pupils that this suffix is added to an adjective to form an adverb. Explain that usually the suffix is added straight onto the end of most root words; for example, sadly, finally. However, there are exceptions, which should also be explained to the pupils:

  (1) If the root word ends in '-y' with a consonant letter before it, the 'y' is changed to 'i', but only if the root word has more than one syllable; for example, happily.

  (2) If the root word ends with '-le', the '-le' is changed to '-ly'; for example, simply.

  (3) If the root word ends with '-ic', '-ally' is added rather than just '-ly'; for example, basically. An exception is 'publicly'.

  (4) The words truly, duly and wholly.

- Explain where the apostrophe is placed after plural forms of words. An additional '-s' is not added if the plural word already ends in 's', but it is added if the plural does not end in '-s' (i.e. is an irregular plural, like children's). Examples include, girls', boys', babies', children's, men's, mice's.

- Discuss the word reading activities on page 99, then allow pupils to complete the page independently.

Differentiated Individual/Paired/Group Work

- Pupils should be given a selection of root words; for example, cold, sprinkle, instant, vanish, knock.

- Less able pupils should see if the suffixes '-ed', '-ing' or '-ly' can be added to each root word to create a new word; e.g. knocked, knocking.

- More able pupils should also see if other suffixes can be added to the root words; e.g. knocker.

Review

- As a class, compare pupils' lists of words. Which of the root words can use the most suffixes?

	Assessment
C6	Ask the pupils to write a list of things that they think make a legend. (Refer to the 'Definition of Terms' section on page 94).
C12	Ask pupils to write a list of questions they would like to know the answers to, that they feel would better help them understand the legend.
	For example, Why did St Collen leave his church? Why did he go and live in a remote place?
WR1	Present the following list of words to the pupils and ask them to write the root words:
	peaceful, declared, angrily, talking, foolish, ignored, messenger, realising, glorious, beautiful

Answers

Comprehension

1. All should be ticked except 'rhyming words at the end of lines'.
2. Answers will vary.
3. Answers may include that he enjoyed living in a remote place because he would not be bothered by people.
4. a rocky shelter like a cell in a remote place
5. Answers will vary.
6. Answers will vary but may include that they went back to the Otherworld.
7. Answers will vary but may include that speech helped to show what happened clearly.

Word Reading

1. (a) a container for liquids
   (b) a medieval singer or musician
2. tongue
3. To move or sway to and fro or from side to side.
4. (a) wondrous   (b) graciously
5. (a) ly, gracious   (b) grace
6. (a) one: devil's clothes, fairy's wishes
       more than one: devils' clothes, fairies' wishes
   (b) The 'y' changes to 'i' before '-es' is added.

St Collen and the Fairy King

Read the legend.

Many centuries ago, a Christian saint named St Collen, left his church and made his home in a rock shelter in a remote place.

One day as he sat in his peaceful, rocky cell, he heard loud voices. The two men declared that Gwyn ab Nudd was the king of Annwn, the Otherworld, as well as king of the fairies.

St Collen poked his head out of his cell and said angrily to the men, 'Stop talking about those devils this instant!'

The men looked at him and replied sternly, 'Hold your tongue, foolish man, or the fairy king will come and scold you in person!' St Collen ignored the threat and quickly closed the door.

The following day, a messenger from Gwyn ab Nudd knocked on the cell door. 'The king of Annwn and the fairies commands you to come and speak to him on top of the hill at noon', he said.

St Collen, however, refused to go. The next day the same messenger knocked on his door again and ordered him to present himself to the king. Once more St Collen refused.

On the third day, the messenger repeated the order with the promise that if St Collen did not go, he would be very sorry. Feeling a little afraid, and realising he would have no peace until he agreed, St Collen decided to meet the king at the appointed time. He filled a flask with holy water and concealed it in his robes.

As St Collen approached the top of the hill, he saw the most glorious castle. It was a wondrous sight. There were troops, minstrels, horses and handsome young men and beautiful young women in the finest clothes. Delightful music filled the air. The king who sat in a golden chair welcomed St Collen graciously.

'Come and enjoy the finest food and drink!' he commanded. 'Anything you desire can be provided.' When St Collen refused, the king asked, 'Have you ever seen more beautiful clothing?' He pointed to the clothing of his young men.

'Their clothing only shows their true nature', replied the saint. 'Red is for the flames of hell and blue tells of the coldness of death.' Then St Collen withdrew the flask of holy water and sprinkled it on everything within reach. Instantly everything vanished, leaving St Collen alone on the hilltop.

St Collen retreated to his cell once more and was never bothered by fairies again.

| **My learning log** | When I read this legend, I could read: | ☐ all of it. | ☐ most of it. | ☐ parts of it. |

St Collen and the Fairy King – 2

1. Which language features are included in the text? Tick them.

   • time phrases ☐   • a hero ☐   • a magical place ☐

   • events in order ☐   • descriptions of people or places ☐

   • direct speech ☐   • rhyming words at the end of lines ☐

   • a problem to be solved ☐   • a conclusion ☐

2. (a)   Write an interesting phrase or sentence from the paragraph that describes the castle.

   _____

   _____

   (b)   Explain why you chose this phrase or sentence.

   _____

   _____

   _____

3. Why do you think St Collen was upset when his peace was disturbed?

   _____

   _____

4. Describe St Collen's house and its location.

   _____

5. The first and last paragraphs give a little information about why St Collen chose to live where he did. Write a question to give you a better understanding of St Collen.

   _____

6. Where do you think the castle and its inhabitants went?

   _____

7. Why do you think the author used direct speech in the text?

   _____

My learning log	While doing these activities:		
	I found Q _____ easy.	I found Q _____ challenging.	I found Q _____ interesting.

St Collen and the Fairy King – 3

1. Write the dictionary meaning of the following words.

   (a) flask _____

   (b) minstrel _____

2. Which word in paragraph 4 comes from the Old English word 'tunge' and means 'organ of speech, speech or a people's language'?

   _____

3. The word 'rock' is a noun that means 'solid mineral matter that forms part of the surface of the earth, on the surface or underneath the soil'. What does the verb 'rock' mean?

   _____

4. Underline an adjective or adverb in each sentence that tells that the noun or action is good.

   (a) It was a wondrous sight.

   (b) The king who sat in a golden chair welcomed St Collen graciously.

5. (a) Write the suffix and root word of 'graciously'.

   _____

   (b) What word do you think the word 'gracious' comes from?

   _____

6. (a) Add the possessive apostrophe in the correct place.

one	more than one
messenger's messages	messengers' messages
devils clothes	devils clothes
fairys wishes	fairies wishes

   (b) Explain why the spelling of 'fairy' changes to 'fairies' when plural.

   _____

My learning log	Colour:	I can / can't write definitions for words.
		I know / don't know about adjectives and adverbs.
		I understand / need more practice on possessive apostrophes.

A Day in the Indus Valley

Curriculum Links

Activity	Code	Objective	Outcome
Text	C2 C3 C6	• Participate in discussion about both books that are read to them and those they can read for themselves • Listen to and discuss a wide range of fiction • Increase their familiarity with a wide range of books	• Can identify diaries and talk about their key features
Comprehension	C5 C11 C12 C15	• Use dictionaries to check the meaning of words that they have read • Check that the text makes sense to them, discuss their understanding and explain the meaning of words in context • Ask questions to improve their understanding of a text • Identify main ideas drawn from more than one paragraph and summarise them	• Can explain the meanings of words • Can answer questions about the text • Can write a question to try and better understand a text • Can summarise historical information from several paragraphs
Word Reading	WR1 WR2	• Apply their growing knowledge of root words and prefixes • Read further exception words, noting the unusual correspondences between spelling and sound	• Can add 'un-' to words to make them opposite • Can read words with 'ei', 'eigh' and 'ey'

Additional Teacher Information

Definition of Terms

Text
A book or other written or printed work, regarded in terms of its content rather than its physical form.

Diary entry
A diary entry is a personal record of daily events, appointments and observations.

Paragraph
A distinct section of a piece of writing, usually dealing with a single theme and indicated by a new line, indentation or numbering.

Summary
A summary gives a brief statement of the main points of (a text).

Personal pronoun
A word such as I, me, you, him, her, she, we, they, or them that is used in place of a noun that has already been mentioned or that is already known.

Contraction
A shortened form of a word or group of words; e.g. 'they're' is a contraction of 'they are'.

Simile
A figure of speech involving the comparison of one thing with another thing of a different kind, used to make a description more emphatic or vivid (e.g. as brave as a lion).

Terminology for Pupils

diary
dictionary
phrase
writer
paragraph
summarise
question
personal pronoun
sentence
fact
opinion
simile
contraction
informal language
antonym
prefix

Suggested Reading

- <http://www.bbc.co.uk/schools/primaryhistory/indus_valley/>
- Indus Valley: Green Lessons from the Past (Smart Green Civilizations) by **Benita Sen**
- Life in the Ancient Indus River Valley (Peoples of the Ancient World) by **Hazel Richardson**

Links to other Curriculum Areas

- History—The achievements of the earliest civilisations – the Indus Valley

Text

Teacher Information

- The Indus Valley civilisation was located in an area of Pakistan and western India. Archaeologists discovered the site in 1861 and began excavation in the 1920s. Discoveries are on-going with important finds occurring, including over one thousand cities and settlements by 1999. Harappa is one of two major cities discovered. The other is Mohenjo-Daro.

- The diary entry is a method of imparting information that is unlike a report or straight-forward informational text. A diary entry aims to place the information into a more personal context.

Introduction

- Ask pupils if they have ever read a diary; for example, 'The Secret Diary of Adrian Mole', 'Diary of a Wimpy Kid' or 'The Diary of Anne Frank'.

- Show and read excerpts from these diaries, for pupils to discuss.

- Ask the pupils if anyone has ever kept a diary. Do they try and write in it every day, week or month? What kinds of things do they write about? Why do they think keeping a diary is a good idea?

Development

- Read and discuss the text with the pupils, as a whole class or in groups. Assist pupils to decode new words if necessary. Discuss the meanings of any new or unfamiliar words and phrases such as 'foreigners', 'diligent', 'drainage system', 'sewage', 'fragrant', 'civilisation', 'bullock', 'destination', 'inscribed', 'artisan', 'granaries', 'anticipating' and 'polluted'. The word 'seals' may need to be explained specifically. Question individual pupils to gauge their understanding of what they have listened to or read. Pupils should also ask questions about parts of the text they are unsure of, in order to improve their understanding.

Differentiated Individual/Paired/Group Work

- List the things that the child did during the day. Which things were chores and which things were for leisure?

- Pupils should write a diary entry to tell about one of their typical Saturdays or Sundays. They should include what they ate, any chores they did, whether they went anywhere, and what they did in their free time whilst at home.

- Less able pupils should write two or three paragraphs, whilst more able pupils should aim for at least eight paragraphs.

Review

- Pupils should share their work in a small group.

Comprehension

Teacher Information

- Pupils might need a dictionary to complete question 1.

Introduction

- Pupils take it in turns to retell the diary entry in their own words, sequencing the events correctly.

Development

- Discuss questions that may have varied answers, especially question 4. Pupils should tell why they chose that question.

- Discuss the comprehension activities on page 104, then allow pupils to complete the page independently.

Differentiated Individual/Paired/Group Work

- Pupils write a list of information the text gives about life in the Indus Valley; for example, Millions of people lived there, including foreigners; They ate barley cakes; They lived in houses constructed from mud bricks.

Review

- As a class, share their lists of information about the Indus Valley. What else would they like to know about life in the Indus Valley?

Word Reading

Teacher Information

- The activities on page 105 focus on word definitions, similes, contractions and antonyms.

Introduction

- Reread the text, but first explain to pupils that the focus will be on words. While reading, ask pupils to circle adjectives that describe life and objects in the Indus Valley.

Development

- Revise the term 'apostrophe'. Remind that this punctuation mark has two uses:

  ~ possession: to show that something belongs to somebody or something; for example, the child's home.

  ~ contraction: to show that two words have joined and letters have been omitted; for example, are not = aren't.

- Explain to pupils that the sound /eɪ/ can be spelt in three different ways: 'ei', 'eigh' and 'ey'. Practise saying words with these spellings with the pupils. Ask pupils to find words with these spellings in the text.

- Ensure pupils are familiar with the terms 'synonym' and 'antonym'. Give some examples (happy: synonym is glad, antonym is sad). Elicit some examples from the pupils. Pupils suggest sentences for pairs of synonyms and antonyms, to be written onto the board; for example, happy = glad/sad. Ben was <u>glad</u> he had homework, but Krista was <u>sad</u>.

- Discuss the word reading activities on page 105, then allow pupils to complete the page independently.

Differentiated Individual/Paired/Group Work

- Pupils should find and list words that can have the suffixes 'un-', 'dis-' or 'mis-' added to make them negative. They should add them to the table.

- More able pupils should produce a longer list of words than less able pupils.

un-	dis-	mis-
kind	cover	spell
safe	agree	behave
cover	obey	lead

Review

- As a class, compare pupils' lists of words. Can any of the words have more than one prefix? For example, 'uncover' and 'discover'.

Assessment

C2	Ask the pupils to list similarities and differences between their lives today and life in the Indus Valley over four thousand years ago.
C5	Present the following list of words to the pupils and ask them to write each in a sentence, using the correct context: foreigners, sewage, chores, artisan, dock, jewellery, platform, statues
WR1	Write the following words on the board and have pupils use a thesaurus to find at least two synonyms for each: fragrant, exquisite, civilised, quiet, proficient, careless, diligent, clean

Answers

Comprehension

1. (a) people from a country other than one's own – foreigners
   (b) being careful and hard-working – diligent
   (c) the place someone is going to – destination
   (d) a worker in a skilled trade like craft work – artisan
2. The writer of the diary entry was very excited/looking forward to go to Harappa.
3. Answers may be similar to the following:
   Paragraph 2: Food included barley; Water for homes came from wells; Mud brick homes; Bathing rooms in homes; Drainage systems complex/take sewage and waste water from homes out to streets; Covered drains in neighbourhoods.
   Paragraph 3: Bullock carts for transport; Wide, mud brick streets; Streets in straight lines and right angles; People made pottery and seals; Seals inscribed and used for stamping goods for sale; Bead and gold jewellery made; People in same neighbourhoods had similar trades; Parents passed on trades to children.
   Paragraph 5: Homes had courtyards and flat roofs; City raised on elevated ground or raised platforms to keep them safe from floods or sewage; Children played with clay figures.
4. Answers will vary.
5. These pronouns make the text more personal as though the writer actually lived in this place and time.
6. Answers will vary. Examples may include '... the drainage in our house carries all the sewage and waste water outside to covered drains.' (fact) OR 'I doubt if any civilisation is as advanced as ours.' (opinion)

Word Reading

1. fragrant—having a pleasant or sweet smell; civilisation—the society, culture, and way of life of a particular area; bullock—a male bovine animal; inscribed—written or carved on with words or symbols; granaries—a storehouse for threshed grain; anticipating—looking forward to; proficient— competent or skilled in doing something
2. (a) beautifully-inscribed, in great demand
   (b) clean and fragrant
   (c) extremely busy and noisy
3. like statues of gods
4. It's, I'm, I'll, I've, don't
5. ey = Teacher check, obey, ei = Teacher check, vein; eigh = Teacher check, weigh, neigh, eight
6. (b)
7. (a) unclean   (b) unlucky   (c) undone   (d) unsafe

A Day in the Indus Valley – 1

Read the diary entry.

Time: Around 2600 BC

Place: Indus Valley

It's trading day today in Harappa, and I'm hoping Mother and Father will allow me to accompany them this time. They worry that I'll get into trouble, with millions of people, especially foreigners, trading their goods.

I've been diligent getting my chores done so they have no cause to leave me behind. I ate my barley cakes without fuss and then fetched the water supplies from the well outside our mud brick house. The bathing area is now well-stocked. I don't really mind doing that job because I like how the drainage system in our house carries all the sewage and waste water outside to covered drains. It keeps the neighbourhood clean and fragrant. I doubt if any civilisation is as advanced as ours.

I'm brimming with excitement as we climb into the bullock cart and clatter over the wide, mud brick streets to the dock. It's lucky that Father is a good driver and the streets so wide, because some traders are impatient and careless! We reach our destination easily because the streets are laid out in straight lines and right angles. We help Father unload his pottery and Mother's beautifully-inscribed seals. They are in great demand for stamping goods for sale. Perhaps one day I'll be a fine artisan too. I enjoy making my bead necklaces but I'm not very proficient yet. The gold jewellery of the artisan next to us is exquisite. I will probably learn the craft of one of my parents like the others in our neighbourhood have done.

The market and dock area are extremely busy and noisy. The warehouses and granaries stand out like statues of gods. Traders are bargaining fiercely and weights and measures are never still or quiet.

It's very tiring trading. Luckily, it will be over for a long while until Mother and Father make more to sell. I'm anticipating returning to the tiny courtyard of our house and playing with my clay figures. The flat roof of our house is one of my favourite places. The city's houses are raised high above the land on elevated land or platforms so we are safe from floods and polluted water. You can almost see forever.

I would not want to live anywhere else. We live a very civilised life that is much better than any other in the known world. I'm sure in thousands of years people will still be able to see the greatness of our civilisation.

My learning log	When I read this diary entry, I could read:	☐ all of it.	☐ most of it.	☐ parts of it.

A Day in the Indus Valley – 2

1. Match the dictionary meanings to the correct words.

   (a) people from a country other than one's own •

   (b) being careful and hard-working   •

   (c) the place someone is going to   •

   (d) a worker in a skilled trade like craft work   •

   • artisan

   • destination

   • diligent

   • foreigners

2. What does the phrase 'I'm brimming with excitement ...' tell you about the feelings of the writer about going to Harappa?

   _____

3. For each paragraph, write ideas to summarise information about the Indus Valley civilisation.

   • Paragraph 2 _____

   _____

   _____

   • Paragraph 3 _____

   _____

   _____

   • Paragraph 5 _____

   _____

   _____

4. Was anything in the text difficult to understand? Write one question to find out information to help you understand the text better.

   _____

5. Why are so many personal pronouns like 'I' and 'we' used in the text?

   _____

6. Write one phrase or sentence from the text for each.

   • a fact   _____

   • an opinion _____

My learning log	While doing these activities:		
	I found Q _____ easy.	I found Q _____ challenging.	I found Q _____ interesting.

A Day in the Indus Valley – 3

1. Choose one of the following words and write the dictionary meaning: fragrant, civilisation, bullock, inscribed, granaries, anticipating, proficient.

   _____

2. Write descriptive words or phrases from the text for each thing.

   (a) the seals _____

   (b) the neighbourhood _____

   (c) the market and dock area _____

3. Underline the simile in the sentence below.

   The warehouses and granaries stand out like statues of gods.

4. Many contractions are used in the text to make the language informal (as though one person is speaking to a friend). Copy three different ones.

   _____

5. (a) Words with the /eɪ/ sound can be spelt in different ways. Research other words with these sounds and spellings.

   ey (e.g. they): _____

   ei (e.g. reign): _____

   eigh (e.g. neighbour): _____

   (b) Write a sentence using some of these words.

   _____

6. Circle the meaning of the word 'well', as it is used in the text.

   (a) in a good or satisfactory way

   (b) a shaft sunk into the ground to obtain water, oil or gas

7. Make antonyms of the words below by adding the prefix 'un-'.

   (a) clean _____   (b) lucky _____

   (c) done _____   (d) safe _____

My learning log	*Colour:*	I ⟨ can ⟩ / ⟨ can't ⟩ read and identify descriptive phrases.
		I ⟨ understand ⟩ / ⟨ need more practice on ⟩ similes.
		I ⟨ know ⟩ / ⟨ don't know ⟩ about apostrophes in contractions.

A Holiday Suggestion

Curriculum Links

Activity	Code	Objective	Outcome
Text	C2 C3	• Participate in discussion about both books that are read to them and those they can read for themselves • Listen to and discuss a wide range of non-fiction	• Can identify travel articles and talk about their key features
Comprehension	C1 C5 C9 C11	• Retrieve and record information from non-fiction • Use dictionaries to check the meaning of words that they have read • Discuss words and phrases that capture the reader's interest and imagination • Check that the text makes sense to them, discuss their understanding and explain the meaning of words in context	• Can answer questions about the text • Can explain the meanings of words • Can choose interesting words
Word Reading	WR1 WR2	• Apply their growing knowledge of root words and suffixes • Read further exception words, noting the unusual correspondences between spelling and sound	• Can recognise root words and a range of suffixes • Can recognise 'ou' words and homophones

Additional Teacher Information

Definition of Terms

Text
A book or other written or printed work, regarded in terms of its content rather than its physical form.

Travel article
A travel article, or feature, is a type of report that encourages readers to visit the place that is the subject of the article. Persuasive language is used as well as snippets of information about the location.

Paragraph
A distinct section of a piece of writing, usually dealing with a single theme and indicated by a new line, indentation or numbering.

Links to other Curriculum Areas

• Geography—Locational knowledge (North America— its environmental regions, key physical and human characteristics, countries and major cities)

Terminology for Pupils

travel article
paragraph
phrase
statement
dictionary
exaggeration
persuasion
sentence
compound word
suffix
homophone

Suggested Reading

• *North America* (New True Books: Geography) by **Libby Koponen**
• *North America* (Rookie Read-About Geography) by **Rebecca Hirsch**
• *North America* (The Seven Continents) by **Karen Bush Gibson**

Text

Teacher Information

- This text, while imparting information about the continent of North America, is also a persuasive text, encouraging readers to visit North America.
- Pupils will need to have some knowledge of different types of environmental regions to have a comprehensive understanding of paragraph 4 of this text. However, the main aims of comprehending the text and word reading can be achieved without this in-depth knowledge.

Introduction

- To help pupils understand the different types of environmental regions mentioned in paragraph 4, teachers should have the following images to show and discuss with the pupils: tundra; coniferous evergreen forests; plains; deserts; and tropical wet forests. Pupils could also discuss which of these places they would most like to visit and why.
- It may also be beneficial for pupils to view images of the fauna mentioned in the text: beaver; brown bear; moose; Arctic fox; and caribou.

Development

- Read and discuss the text with the pupils, as a whole class or in groups. Assist pupils to decode new words if necessary. Discuss the meaning of any new or unfamiliar words and phrases such as 'contemplating', 'entertainment', 'relaxation', 'catered for', 'aviation', 'buffs', 'bustling', 'captivate', 'urban dweller', 'Institute', 'unique', 'flora', 'fauna', 'coniferous' and 'majestic'. Question individual pupils to gauge their understanding of what they have listened to or read. Pupils should also ask questions about parts of the text they are unsure of, in order to improve their understanding.

Differentiated Individual/Paired/Group Work

- Pupils should choose one of the countries mentioned in the article: Canada; United States of America; Mexico; Bermuda; The Bahamas; or Jamaica.
- Pupils should write a fact file about their chosen country, to include: capital city; currency; population; area; languages; religions; climate; famous landmarks; and typical food. They should also include an illustration of the flag and a map.
- More able pupils should include other sections on their fact file.

Review

- Pupils should present their fact files neatly and display them in the classroom.

Comprehension

Teacher Information

- Pupils may need a dictionary to complete question 7.
- Question 5 reinforces the concept of images such as diagrams and maps to impart knowledge. Answers will depend on how familiar pupils are with maps of the various continents of the world.

Introduction

- Ask pupils to tell things that they learnt about North America as a result of reading this travel article.

Development

- Assist pupils to state the focus of each paragraph and summarise them.
- Remind pupils how to use a dictionary efficiently; i.e. alphabetical order and retrieval by 1st, 2nd and 3rd letters. Give each pupil, or pair of pupils, a dictionary. Write words from the text onto the board for pupils to find.
- Discuss the comprehension activities on page 110, then allow pupils to complete the page independently.

Differentiated Individual/Paired/Group Work

- Pupils should work in mixed-ability groups of four. Each group should be given a place in the local area to discuss; for example, a park, swimming pool, shopping centre, ice-skating rink. Pupils need to discuss the place and write a list of reasons why other pupils in the class should go there.

Review

- Each group should tell the rest of their class about their place in the local area, and why they think it is a good place to visit.
- Pupils could vote on which place they would most like to visit.

Word Reading

Teacher Information

- The activities on page 111 focus on word origins, word meanings, compound words, '-que', '-tion' and '-ous' suffixes, 'ou' words and homophones.

Introduction

- Reread the text, but first explain to pupils that the focus will be on words. While reading, ask pupils to underline words that are the names of continents, countries, cities and places. Explain that as these are names of places they should always start with a capital letter.

Development

- Remind pupils of the term 'compound word'. Give some examples (holidaymaker, sunset, evergreen). Elicit some examples from the pupils. Pupils should present the compound words as addition sums with illustrations; for example,

- Tell pupils that words ending in '-que' have a 'k' sound and are French in origin. Say some '-que' words aloud, and have pupils repeat them, to hear the sound. For example, technique, boutique, unique, antique.

- Discuss and list words which end with the suffix '-ion', specifically the spelling '-tion'. This spelling is used if the root word ends in 't' or 'te'; for example, invention, injection, action, hesitation, completion. Sort the words according to whether the root word ends in 't' or 'te'. There are some exceptions; for example, the words 'attend' and 'intend' both end in 'd', but add the '-tion' suffix to become 'attention' and 'intention'.

- Look at words with the suffix '-ous'. Discuss that sometimes there is not an obvious root word; for example, 'poisonous' has the root word 'poison', but there is no root word for 'jealous'. Explain that whilst '-ous' can be added to many root words, '-our' is changed to '-or' before '-ous' is added; for example, humorous, glamorous.

- The 'ou' words in question 6 should be spoken out loud, so pupils can hear the specific phonemes focused upon.

- Ensure pupils are familiar with the term 'homophone'. Give some examples (berry/bury, scene/seen, plain/plane). Elicit some examples from the pupils. Pupils suggest sentences for pairs of homophones, to be written onto the board; for example, main/mane = He is walking down the <u>main</u> road./That horse has a beautiful <u>mane</u>.

- Discuss the word reading activities on page 111, then allow pupils to complete the page independently.

Differentiated Individual/Paired/Group Work

- Pupils should write pairs of sentences using the homophones in question 7.

- More able pupils should write sentences using the homophones heel/heal/he'll and rain/rein/reign.

Review

- In groups, pupils should share their sentences.

Assessment

C1	Ask the pupils to write a list of factual information that this travel article gives about North America; for example, the countries and their capital cities, places to visit and environmental regions.
C5	Present the following list of words to the pupils and ask them to write a definition for each: extensive, aviation, urban, flora, fauna, caribou, magnificent, majestic
WR2	Say the following words. Ask pupils to write them down, using the correct spelling of the 'k' sound: antique, boutique, brick, plaque, cheque, unique, magic, stick

Answers

Comprehension

1. To persuade people to visit North America./To give information about North America.
2. (a) Paragraph 2   (b) Paragraph 3   (c) Paragraph 5
   (d) Paragraph 4
3. Answers will vary but may include examples such as '... vast and varied continent ...', '... many wondrous places ...', '... untold entertainment and relaxation ...'.
4. Answers should indicate that the reader will be so interested they may want to find out more about North America.
5. Answers will vary.
6. The writer thinks North America is a worthwhile place to visit.
7. (a) contemplating—thinking about
   (b) aviation—the flying or operating of aircraft
   (c) institute—an organisation with a particular purpose such as science, education or a specific profession
8. Answers will vary but may include '... will captivate any urban dweller.', '... wondrous fauna ...', '... nothing more stunning ...'.

Word Reading

1. aviation
2. city
3. holidaymaker, evergreen, sunset
4. (a) unique   (b) Teacher check; antique, boutique
5. (a) -tion: relaxation, aviation; -ous: coniferous, wondrous
   (b) Teacher check
6. touches, country
7. (a) plains   (b) great   (c) see
   (d) raise   (e) bear   (f) course

A Holiday Suggestion – 1

Read the travel article.

If you are contemplating an extensive holiday soon, consider visiting North America. This vast and varied continent offers something for everyone!

Comprising the countries Canada, the United States, Mexico and smaller states in the Central American and Caribbean regions, North America is the third largest continent. Each country has much to offer the holidaymaker. The only problem will be trying to choose from the many wonderful places on offer!

The capitals of each country—Washington D. C. (United States of America), Ottawa (Canada), Mexico City (Mexico), Hamilton (Bermuda), Nassau (the Bahamas), Kingston (Jamaica) and many others provide untold entertainment and relaxation choices for everyone. From snow-topped mountains and skiing in Canada to the warm, sandy beaches of the Bahamas, every holidaymaker is catered for. History and aviation buffs will thrill to see the National Air and Space Museum at the Smithsonian Institute or visit the White House, Lincoln's statue or the Capitol building in Washington D.C. These bustling cities will captivate any urban dweller.

Nature lovers have a wide variety of environmental regions to discover—each with its own unique flora and fauna. From the high, dry tundra of Canada and Alaska to the taiga regions with its coniferous, evergreen forests, there is almost too much to consider. Who would not wish to wander through the forests, drive through sprawling plains, slip their feet into a crystal clear lake or river or climb a grassy mountain to see

a spectacular view? There is nothing more stunning than the sunset in a desert or the coolness of a tropical wet forest!

One cannot think about North America without mentioning the wondrous fauna found there. Visitors can view the clever beaver, the frightening brown bear, the majestic moose, the stunning white Arctic fox and the caribou.

This article only touches on some of the magnificent features of the great continent of North America. It does, however, raise many questions. Which part of the continent to visit first? How long to stay? When to return for another trip? And, of course, which parts are the best? Surely, the answer will be all!

| My learning log | When I read this travel article, I could read: | ☐ all of it. | ☐ most of it. | ☐ parts of it. |

A Holiday Suggestion – 2

1. What are the two main purposes of the travel article?

   • _____

   • _____

2. Which paragraph contains information about:

   (a) the countries that make up North America?   _____

   (b) the capitals of the countries of North America?   _____

   (c) some of the fauna of North America?   _____

   (d) different environmental regions of North America? _____

3. Copy two phrases from the text that you think try to grab the reader's interest or imagination.

   • _____

   • _____

4. The writer says, 'This article only touches on some of the features of the great continent of North America.' What do you think the writer is hoping this statement will do?

   _____

5. Does the map help you understand parts of the text? [Yes] [No] Explain.

   _____

6. How do you think the writer feels about North America?

   _____

7. Use a dictionary to write the meanings of the following words.

   (a) contemplating _____

   (b) aviation _____

   (c) institute _____

8. This text uses exaggeration and persuasive phrases and sentences. Write one. _____

My learning log	While doing these activities:		
	I found Q _____ easy.	I found Q _____ challenging.	I found Q _____ interesting.

A Holiday Suggestion – 3

1. Which word comes from the Latin word 'avis' meaning 'bird'?

   _____

2. Circle the word from the list that could replace 'urban' in the sentence below.

   These bustling cities will captivate any urban dweller.

continent	city	capital	country	captivate

3. Draw lines to match the first and second words in these compound words.

   (a) holiday •   • green

   (b) ever   •   • set

   (c) sun   •   • maker

4. (a) Look for a word in the text that ends in '-que'. _____

   (b) Words ending in '-que' are of French origin.
       Research another word with this ending.   _____

5. (a) Find words in the text with the following suffixes.

   -tion: _____   _____

   -ous: _____   _____

   (b) Write a sentence containing two of these words.

   _____

6. The text has many 'ou' words. Circle the words with the /ʌ/ sound; for example, young, trouble.

mountains	touches	caribou	without	country

7. Find a homophone for each word in the text.

   (a) planes _____   (b) grate   _____

   (c) sea   _____   (d) rays   _____

   (e) bare   _____   (f) coarse _____

My learning log	*Colour:*	I [can] / [can't] join words to make compound words.
		I [can] / [can't] identify a range of suffixes.
		I [understand] / [need more practice on] homophones.

The Cycle of Water

Curriculum Links

Activity	Code	Objective	Outcome
Text	C2 C3 C6	• Participate in discussion about both books that are read to them and those they can read for themselves • Listen to and discuss a wide range of poetry • Increase their familiarity with a wide range of books	• Can identify poems and talk about their key features
Comprehension	C5 C10 C11 C15	• Use dictionaries to check the meaning of words that they have read • Recognise some different forms of poetry • Check that the text makes sense to them, discuss their understanding and explain the meaning of words in context • Identify main ideas drawn from more than one paragraph and summarise them	• Can explain the meanings of words • Can recognise rhyme in poems • Can answer questions about the text • Can summarise the water cycle in a diagram
Word Reading	WR1 WR2	• Apply their growing knowledge of root words, prefixes and suffixes • Read further exception words, noting the unusual correspondences between spelling and sound	• Can recognise root words, the prefix 're-' and a range of suffixes

Additional Teacher Information

Definition of Terms

Text
A book or other written or printed work, regarded in terms of its content rather than its physical form.

Poem
A piece of writing in which the expression of feelings and ideas is given intensity by particular attention to diction (sometimes involving rhyme), rhythm and imagery.

Diagram
A simplified drawing showing the appearance, structure or workings of something; a schematic representation.

Report
A report is a written document describing the findings of an individual or group. A report may take the form of a newspaper report, sports or police report, or a report about an animal, person or object.

Non-fiction
Prose writing that is informative or factual rather than fictional.

Verse
A group of lines that form a unit in a poem or song; a stanza.

Links to other Curriculum Areas

• Science—Identifying the part played by evaporation and condensation in the water cycle

Terminology for Pupils

poem
phrase
diagram
writer
report
non-fiction
verse
prefix
suffix
consonant
verb
noun
compound word

Suggested Reading

• *The Water Cycle* (Nature's Changes) by **Bobbie Kalman** and **Rebecca Sjonger**
• *The Water Cycle* (Water all Around) by **Rebecca Olien**
• *Water Dance* by **Thomas Locker** (an imaginative look at types of precipitation in poetry form)
• *The Water Cycle: Evaporation, Condensation and Erosion* (Earth's Processes) by **Rebecca Harman**

Text

Teacher Information

- The poem also functions as a non-fiction text, as it relates information about the water cycle.
- Transpiration (water lost from plants) can also be included with the section of the water cycle on evaporation.

Introduction

- Look at a diagram of the water cycle. Discuss the diagram with pupils and explain how it works. As the poem is reread to the class, point to the relevant parts of the diagram.

Development

- Read and discuss the text with the pupils, as a whole class or in groups. Assist pupils to decode new words if necessary. Discuss the meaning of any new or unfamiliar words and phrases such as 'tending', 'reveals', 'continuous', 'relative', 'evaporates', 'vapour', 'condenses', 'precipitation', 'groundwater', 'evaporation' and 'condensation'. Question individual pupils to gauge their understanding of what they have listened to or read. Pupils should also ask questions about parts of the text they are unsure of, in order to improve their understanding.

Differentiated Individual/Paired/Group Work

- As a class, look at a diagram of the water cycle, and discuss how it works.
- Pupils should write an explanation of the water cycle. More able pupils should also include an explanation on transpiration.

Review

- Pupils should share their work in a small group.

Comprehension

Teacher Information

- Pupils may need a dictionary to complete questions 1 and 2.

Introduction

- Discuss the meaning of some of the trickier vocabulary to be found in the text: tending, cycle, continuous, evaporates, vapour, condenses, droplets, precipitation, fog, sleet, groundwater, hastens, commences, constant.
- Pupils take it in turns to summarise each stanza of the poem in their own words.

Development

- Remind pupils how to use a dictionary efficiently; i.e. alphabetical order and retrieval by 1st, 2nd and 3rd letters. Give each pupil, or pair of pupils, a dictionary. Write words from the text onto the board for pupils to find.
- Discuss the comprehension activities on page 116, then allow pupils to complete the page independently.

Differentiated Individual/Paired/Group Work

- Pupils create a glossary for some of the more technical vocabulary in the procedure; for example, earth, cycle, land, sky, sun, ocean, evaporation, vapour, condensation, droplets, clouds, precipitation, fog, sleet, snow, rain, thunderstorm, ground, groundwater, downhill.
- Less able pupils could create a glossary for eight words, more able pupils for all 20 words.

Review

- As a class, compare pupils' definitions of the words. Which words were the hardest and easiest to define?

Word Reading

Teacher Information

- The activities on page 117 focus on root words; the prefix 're-', a variety of suffixes and compound words.

Introduction

- Reread the text, but first explain to pupils that the focus will be on words. While reading, ask pupils to circle scientific or technical vocabulary associated with the water cycle.

Development

- Tell pupils that when a suffix is added to a word with more than one syllable, and the last syllable is stressed and ends in one vowel and one consonant, the consonant is doubled before adding the suffix; for example, controlled, beginner, forgetting.

- Tell pupils that the suffix '-ation' is added to verbs to form nouns. An example from the text is inform/information. Rules that have already been learnt for adding suffixes also apply to this suffix.

- Discuss the word reading activities on page 117, then allow pupils to complete the page independently.

Differentiated Individual/Paired/Group Work

- Remind pupils of the term 'compound word'. Give some examples (thunderstorm, downhill, groundwater). Elicit some examples from the pupils. Pupils should present the compound words as addition sums with illustrations; for example,

sun + glasses = sunglasses

Review

- As a class, compare pupils' compound word sums.

Assessment

C3	Ask the pupils to write about the poem's use of stanzas and rhyme. They should explain how the stanzas are organised and discuss the poem's rhyme.
C15	Ask pupils to write a summary of the poem (and therefore the water cycle). They may choose to write this using paragraphs or in the form of a diagram.
WR1	Present the following list of words to the pupils and ask them to write the root words: stopping, collection, carefully, continuous, connection, evaporation, controlling, condensation

Answers

Comprehension

1. 'fog, sleet, snow or rain for a thunderstorm'
2. Evaporation and precipitation are opposite processes. Evaporation is the process that occurs when heat from the sun picks up water and takes it into the clouds as water vapour. In short—Evaporation is the process of turning liquid water into water vapour (a gas). Precipitation is the process of water vapour (a gas) being turned into a liquid. Precipitation appears as rain, snow, hail, sleet and fog.
3. Water vapour condenses in the clouds.
4. Answers may include: the amount and type of precipitation that falls; how lightly or heavily it falls; how hard or soft the ground is, and so on.
5. Teacher check
6. Answers may be similar to: The water cycle is continuous; it does not stop; one phase connects to the next to make it work.
7. Answers may include: to impart information about the water cycle in a more interesting manner than a straight-forward report or non-fiction text.

Word Reading

1. (a) evaporate   (b) condense   (c) connect
   (d) precipitate
2. (a) goes back   (b) back/again
3. (a) evaporate<u>s</u>, evapora<u>tion</u>, condense<u>s</u>, condensa<u>tion</u>, drop<u>let</u>s, care<u>full</u>y, tend<u>ing</u>, stopp<u>ing</u>, end<u>ing</u>, form<u>ing</u>, soak<u>ing</u>, reveal<u>s</u>, connec<u>tion</u>, controll<u>ing</u>, commence<u>s</u>, giv<u>ing</u>
   (b) stopping, controlling
   (c) evaporation, condensation, giving
4. precipitation, evaporation, condensation
5. downhill, thunderstorm, groundwater

The Cycle of Water – 1

Read the poem.

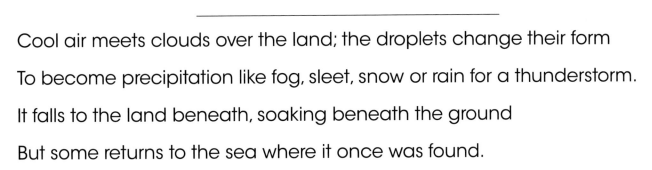

Round and round it goes, never stopping, never ending

Giving earth its life and health, carefully tending.

A cycle reveals the continuous journey of water

From land to the sky and back again. It never alters.

_____

The sun heats the water in oceans and seas,

Controlling the water cycle with relative ease.

This water evaporates as vapour into the air.

Water vapour condenses forming droplets in the clouds up there.

_____

Cool air meets clouds over the land; the droplets change their form

To become precipitation like fog, sleet, snow or rain for a thunderstorm.

It falls to the land beneath, soaking beneath the ground

But some returns to the sea where it once was found.

_____

Some water soaks into the earth to become groundwater.

Some flows downhill and hastens back to the sea. That fact never alters.

And so the cycle commences again. It's a constant connection,

Evaporation, condensation, precipitation and collection.

_____

Round and round it goes, never stopping, never ending

Giving earth its life and health, carefully tending.

| My learning log | When I read this poem, I could read: | ☐ all of it. | ☐ most of it. | ☐ parts of it. |

The Cycle of Water – 2

1. Which phrase from the text explains the meaning of the word 'precipitation'?

   _____

2. What is the difference between evaporation and precipitation?

   _____

   _____

   _____

3. What causes water droplets to form in the clouds?

   _____

4. What things could affect how much water soaks into the ground and becomes groundwater?

   _____

   _____

5. Use the box below to draw a diagram to show your understanding of the water cycle.

6. Why is the phrase 'constant connection' used to talk about the water cycle?

   _____

7. Why do you think the writer put the information in a poem instead of a report or other type of non-fiction text?

   _____

My learning log	While doing these activities:		
	I found Q _____ easy.	I found Q _____ challenging.	I found Q _____ interesting.

The Cycle of Water – 3

1. Which word does each word (or pair of words) below come from?

(a) evaporates, evaporation _____

(b) condenses, condensation _____

(c) connection _____ (d) precipitation _____

2. (a) Write the meaning of the word 'returns' in verse 3.

_____

(b) What do you think the prefix 're-' in the word means?

_____

3. (a) Underline the suffix in each word below. Use a circle as well if a word has two different suffixes.

evaporates	evaporation	condenses	condensation
droplets	carefully	tending	stopping
ending	forming	soaking	reveals
connection	controlling	commences	giving

(b) Write the two words above that double their final consonant before adding their suffix.

_____   _____

(c) Write the three words above that drop their final 'e' before adding their suffix.

_____   _____   _____

4. Write three words from the text with the suffix '-ation'. This suffix is added to change verbs into nouns.

_____   _____   _____

5. Make compound words by joining two words together.

(a) down   *   *   storm

(b) thunder   *   *   water

(c) ground   *   *   hill

My learning log	Colour:	I can / can't recognise root words.
		I understand / need more practice on suffixes.
		I know / don't know about compound words.

Animal Camouflage

Read the report.

Camouflage is a type of disguise that makes it hard to see something against its surroundings. Many animals are camouflaged by the colours and patterns of their skin, scales, fur or feathers. Camouflage helps them to survive.

Both hunting and hunted animals use camouflage. Predators that catch other creatures are camouflaged so they can creep up on their prey. A lioness has a tawny, brown-coloured coat to mix in with the soil and grasslands of Africa. She can slowly sneak up on her prey without being seen. Many animals that are hunted also use the colour of their coat to blend in with their surroundings. A rabbit's fur blends in with the earth and grass and can make it almost invisible—unless it moves!

Many animals have spots, stripes or patches of colour on their coats which are difficult to see against the background. A zebra's stripes make it hard to see in the dim light of dawn and dusk. During the day, it is difficult for a predator to pick out a single zebra because the whole herd has similar stripes.

A chameleon is a lizard with an amazing ability—it can change colour! Its eyes pick up the colours of its surroundings. The brain sends signals along nerves to the pigment or colour cells in its skin. Its colour changes in seconds.

Some animals have warning colouration. The female redback spider has a poisonous bite. Her red back warns or reminds other animals that they should choose another meal! Harmless creatures such as the wasp fly do this too. The wasp fly is coloured like a wasp but does not have the harmful sting.

Other animals pretend to be part of a plant, such as a flower, leaf or twig. A stick insect can remain motionless for hours, pretending to be part of a twig. A tree frog is perfectly coloured to look like part of the leaf in its tree home. It can hide from enemies or, if an insect comes too close, it can flick out its tongue and catch it.

Animal Camouflage

1. Predators are animals that:

1 mark

(a) are hunted. ⬜   (b) hunt others. ⬜   (c) are camouflaged. ⬜

2. The word 'them' in paragraph 1 is used instead of:

1 mark

(a) feathers. ⬜   (b) patterns. ⬜   (c) animals. ⬜

3. True or **False**?

2 marks

(a) All lizards can change colour. _____

(b) Only hunted animals use camouflage. _____

(c) A stick insect hides on rocks. _____

(d) A tree frog can look like part of a leaf. _____

4. Tick the best answer. This text was written for the reader to learn about:

1 mark

(a) different animals. ⬜   (b) animal disguises. ⬜

(c) dangerous animals. ⬜

5. A lioness would be more likely to catch a zebra if the zebra was:

1 mark

(a) on its own. ⬜   (b) in a herd. ⬜   (c) out at dawn. ⬜

6. Which animals use warning colouration?

1 mark

_____

7. How are stick insects and tree frogs similar?

2 marks

_____

_____

8. A fox could more easily catch a rabbit if the rabbit:

1 mark

(a) didn't move. ⬜   (b) was eating grass. ⬜

(c) stayed still. ⬜

Total for this page	/10

Animal Camouflage

1. The word 'invisible' has the prefix 'in-', to give it an opposite meaning. Write a sentence using the words 'visible' and 'invisible'. ☐ 2 marks

_____

2. These words are in the top two paragraphs that have a box around them. Write the antonym of each word that is in the same paragraph. ☐ 1 mark

   (a) predator _____   (b) dawn _____

3. Circle the suffix and write the root word for each of these words. ☐ 1 mark

   (a) colouration _____

   (b) poisonous _____

4. Which word in the last paragraph comes from the Old English word 'tunge' meaning 'an organ of speech' (in humans). ☐ 1 mark

_____

5. Draw lines to match the beginnings and endings of the compound words. ☐ 1 mark

   (a) grass   *   *   back

   (b) back   *   *   lands

   (c) red   *   *   ground

6. (a) Who does the fur belong to in 'the rabbit's fur'? _____ ☐ 1 mark

   (b) Who do the stripes belong to in 'the zebra's stripes'? _____

7. (a) In the report, what does the word 'whole' mean? ☐ 2 marks

_____

   (b) Write the homophone for 'whole' and its meaning.

_____

8. Which word in the report means 'orange-brown' or 'yellowish-brown'? ☐ 1 mark

_____

Total for this page	/10	Total for this assessment	/20

Animal Camouflage

Genre: Report

Breakdown of question type/content and mark allocation

Comprehension		Word Reading	
Q 1. Finding information	1 mark	Q 1. Prefix 'in-'	2 marks
Q 2. Finding pronouns	1 mark	Q 2. Antonyms	1 mark
Q 3. Identifying true and false statements	2 marks	Q 3. Root words and suffixes	1 mark
Q 4. Choosing best answer	1 mark	Q 4. Word origins	1 mark
Q 5. Finding information	1 mark	Q 5. Compound words	1 mark
Q 6. Finding information	1 mark	Q 6. Possessive apostrophes	1 mark
Q 7. Identifying main idea	2 marks	Q 7. Homophones	2 marks
Q 8. Inferring	1 mark	Q 8 Word meanings	1 mark
Sub-total		Sub-total	
		Record the pupil's total result for this assessment.	

Assessment Answers

Assessment – Animal Camouflage

Comprehension ....*Page 119*

1. (b) hunt others
2. (c) animals
3. (a) False   (b) False
   (c) False   (d) True
4. (b) animal disguises
5. (a) on its own
6. female redback spider and wasp fly
7. They both pretend to be part of a plant.
8. (b) was eating grass

Word Reading..*Page 120*

1. Teacher check
2. (a) prey   (b) dusk
3. (a) -ation, colour
   (b) -ous, poison
4. tongue
5. (a) grasslands   (b) background   (c) redback
6. (a) rabbit   (b) zebra
7. (a) entire; making up the full quantity/number of things
   (b) hole – a hollow place or cavity in a surface
8. tawny